# WELFARE AND WELFARE REFORM

# LIBRARY IN A BOOK

# WELFARE AND WELFARE REFORM

*Tom Streissguth*

Facts On File
*An imprint of Infobase Publishing*

**WELFARE AND WELFARE REFORM**

Facts On File, Inc.
An imprint of Infobase Publishing
132 West 31st Street
New York NY 10001

**Library of Congress Cataloging-in-Publication Data**
Streissguth, Thomas, 1958-
  Welfare and welfare reform / Tom Streissguth.
    p. cm. — (Library in a book)
  Includes bibliographical references and index.
  ISBN-13: 978-0-8160-7114-2 (hardcover : alk. paper)
  ISBN-10: 0-8160-7114-4 (hardcover : alk. paper)
  1. Public welfare. 2. Welfare reform. I. Title.
  HV51.S87 2009
  361.60973—dc22                    2008016231

Facts On File books are available at special discounts when purchased in bulk quantities for businesses, associations, institutions, or sales promotions. Please call our Special Sales Department in New York at (212) 967-8800 or (800) 322-8755.

You can find Facts On File on the World Wide Web at http://www.factsonfile.com.

Text design by Ron Monteleone
Graphs by Dale Williams

Printed in the United States of America

Bang Hermitage 10 9 8 7 6 5 4 3 2 1

This book is printed on acid-free paper.

# CONTENTS

# PART III
## APPENDICES

# PART I

## OVERVIEW OF THE TOPIC

# CHAPTER 1

## INTRODUCTION TO WELFARE AND WELFARE REFORM

Public welfare in the United States has roots in the Christian doctrines of the European societies that colonized North America beginning in the 16th century. The traditional seven works of mercy of the Christian Church, to be performed by the faithful individual, were set out in the New Testament Book of Matthew: feeding the hungry, giving drink to the thirsty, welcoming the stranger, caring for the sick, clothing the naked, visiting the prisoner, and burying the dead. Charity was an ennobling work of piety, as well as a means of displaying one's personal wealth. Rich nobles kept open tables, to which any hungry man might come for a meal; gifts of food and drink were passed out to the poor on the occasion of weddings or other public celebrations; monasteries offered alms at their gates; and churches donated a large part of their wealth and earnings to charity.

The Protestant Reformation, however, disrupted the traditional Catholic teachings in those countries that rebelled against the pope. A man's true worth in the eyes of God was measured by his faith, and not his works; this central doctrine of Martin Luther's philosophy forever changed the nature of charity in the Protestant nations that adopted Lutheran doctrine. Charity was brought out of the private realm and charged to the public authorities, becoming a task of the state. The debate over the proper balance between public and private welfare continues in the 21st century.

While the medieval world of Europe lived by the biblical doctrine that "the poor shall be with you always," in Tudor England, poverty became a social problem to be faced and solved. Among the reasons, as described by Dorothy Marshall in her classic work *The English Poor in the Eighteenth Century*, were "the decay of serfdom, which meant that men were free, but also free to starve; the breakdown of the self-sufficiency of the manor; [and] the increase of sheep farming; the end of civil war and the abandonment of large bodies of retainers; the dissolution of the monasteries. . . . What people, and especially the governing classes, chiefly desired, was not an opportunity for indiscriminate alms-giving, but a method for the prevention of poverty. For poverty was regarded as a potential danger to the State, and was, therefore, a peril to the King."[1]

The earliest efforts in England to identify and classify the poor began in the middle of the 16th century. Parish registers of the poor were drawn up in 1552; in 1563 the justices of the peace were empowered to levy taxes for poor relief. Those who could not find work were to be given food and water, or a job in return for a wage. The idle poor—those who could work but would not—were to be publicly whipped, imprisoned, exiled, or put to death. For those too old, sick, or infirm to work, almshouses were set up to provide food and shelter. Their children were given apprenticeships in a useful trade.

England passed a comprehensive Poor Law in 1601. This law classified the poor and provided assistance to them through the parishes, which to support the program levied a poor tax on their members. The parishes elected two overseers of relief every Easter. The overseers set and collected the poor tax; managed the poorhouse; and arranged food, money, and work for the needy. The English made a distinction between "outdoor relief," which was food or money distributed to the poor in their homes, and "indoor relief" provided by hospitals, poorhouses, orphanages, and workhouses.

# EARLY POOR LAW IN AMERICA

The British colonies adopted the customs of their homeland. Public almshouses and orphanages in North America sheltered the indigent. Local town councils provided poorly paid tasks for the unemployed. Churches raised money for the needy. Fraternal and benevolent societies collected dues from members, then paid out money for food and shelter when needed. These groups, such as the Scots Charitable Society of Boston (founded 1657), represent an early system of private health and disability insurance.

Through the first half of the 18th century, the number of indigent on relief grew, as did town expenditures on them. War refugees and injured veterans, widows and orphans of lost sailors and soldiers, poor outcasts such as the Acadians of Nova Scotia, economic downtrends, and growing illegitimacy contributed to the problem. Poor relief was most acute in the major cities—Boston, Philadelphia, and New York—where a growing number of people were hard pressed to survive. Poverty, homelessness, and dislocation caused disillusionment with British management of the colonies, as did the mercantilist system that treated the colonies as factories for the benefit of British trade. The social turmoil the poor caused was a key ingredient in the revolutionary movement that gathered steam in the 1760s.

## PROVIDING FOR THE GENERAL WELFARE

The humanitarian ideals of the Enlightenment were enshrined in the Declaration of Independence (1776) and the Constitution (1787), the founding documents of the newly independent United States of America. Improving the lot of the ordinary man, the free citizen of the republic, was implied in the concepts of natural rights and democratic equality. The spending and taxing powers of the federal government, however, were a subject of ongoing debate. The language of the Constitution, which empowers Congress to "provide for the general welfare," was interpreted differently by Alexander Hamilton and James Madison. While Hamilton believed the provision allowed new spending programs as they became needed, Madison maintained that Congress was allowed to spend only for purposes specifically given in the Constitution—the "strict constructionist" view also held by Thomas Jefferson. The Hamiltonian/Madisonian debate played a prominent role at the origins of the modern welfare system and continues to the present day.

After the United States achieved independence, its town and county governments provided food, fuel, and small cash payments to the truly needy, such as widows, the disabled, and those unable to work and support themselves. People who accepted this public charity were often required to work at road building or some other task useful to the general public. Some communites had a public welfare system in place for the elderly; their eligibility was decided by local officials.

Benevolent societies multiplied after the Revolution, but private charities were inadequate to help the war's many refugees and broken families. Americans raised the first calls for a public system of social welfare at this time. In some states, local treasuries were reimbursed by the state for relief of the poor. In New York, for example, agencies were set up under state management for sheltering the poor and the mentally ill. The states also dealt with the poor by holding auctions for them. The indigent were sold to the highest bidder, who agreed to take care of them as a form of charitable work. In many cases, however, the purchased individual was used as a cheap or free laborer, in effect an indentured servant for an indefinite time. The auctioning of the poor became the subject of unfavorable reports, and the practice eventually died out.

In 1824, New York secretary of state John Yates wrote the Yates Report criticizing the chaotic situation in poor relief, in which costly systems of private charity and public agencies competed with and overlapped each other yet did not address society's basic needs. The report claimed: "Our poor laws are manifestly defective in principle and mischievous in practice. Under the imposing and charitable aspect of affording relief exclusively to the poor and infirm, they frequently invite the able-bodied vagrant to partake of the same bounty."[2]

5

The solution proposed by Yates was to replace "outdoor relief" with the public institution, a refuge for the very young and the elderly. Public relief would be denied to able-bodied persons between 18 and 50 years of age, and the county, rather than the town, would administer the system. The state legislature of New York responded with the County Poorhouse Act, which called for each county to establish at least one almshouse. This system of "indoor relief" would be managed by county supervisors and paid for out of country tax revenues.

In Boston, the upper crust of "Brahmins" took upon themselves the newly worthy cause of ministering to the needs of the poor, as recorded by author Frederic Cople Jaher in *The Urban Establishment: Strata in Boston, New York, Charleston, Chicago, and Los Angeles:*

> . . . the establishment discovered the existence of large numbers of poor and began to doubt the adequacy of traditional benevolence. Destitution, argued contemporary observers, led to delinquency, and enflamed by Jacksonian democracy, the immigrant influx, local riots, and rising rates of drunkenness, pauperism and arrests for assault and battery, could kindle a social conflagration that might consume the propertied. Fears of class conflict mixed with the higher morality of human sympathy and noblesse oblige stimulated public and private efforts to reform the poor and improve the quality of relief.[3]

As in the time of England's Tudor dynasty, the poor were seen as a threat to civil order, and those in a position of authority sought an effective way of relieving (and calming) them.

## LOCAL POOR RELIEF

As the country expanded westward, settlers implemented the colonial-era system of local poor relief in the new states and territories. They elected administrators to oversee the collection and payment of benefits. Gradually, following the model of New York State, administration passed from the towns to the counties. Although church charity continued, the parish relief system gradually disappeared. The rapid westward expansion left many localities without an organized church, and the separation clause of the Constitution discouraged church involvement in government affairs. Poor relief was administered by local jurisdictions: counties and municipalities governed by state law.

Through the 19th century, state governments became increasingly involved in the practice of poor relief, but the federal government played no role. When congress passed a bill in 1854 granting land to the states to allow them to build homes for the insane, President Franklin Pierce unhesitatingly vetoed it, commenting, "I cannot find any authority in the

Constitution for making the Federal Government the great almoner of public charity throughout the United States. To do so would . . . be contrary to the letter and the spirit of the Constitution and subversive of the whole theory upon which the Union of the States is founded."[4] The public welfare system would not be truly nationalized until the 20th century.

President Pierce's view on this matter was representative of the view of many citizens. Americans favored the individual over the state and believed in self-reliance. The statist nations of Europe were out of vogue; Americans regarded top-down European social systems as legacies of the monarchy and tyranny that the American Revolution had meant to overturn. Popular attitudes maintained a distinction between the "poor" and "paupers." This distinction is recorded in an 1834 sermon by the Reverend Charles Burroughs. In *A Discourse Delivered in the Chapel of the New Alms-House in Portsmouth, N.H.*, Burroughs explained that to be poor "is an unavoidable evil, to which many are brought from necessity, and in the wise and gracious Providence of God. It is the result, not of our faults, but of our misfortunes. Pauperism is the consequence of willful error, of shameful indolence, of vicious habit."[5] Americans of this period labeled specific categories of the poor as "paupers": the lazy, the freeloaders, and those superfluous members of society who simply would not seek or accept gainful employment.

The system of local relief came under ever greater strain while waves of immigrants arrived in the 1830s. Their condition upon arrival was often poor, but their numbers were so great that public relief could not possibly hope to cope with their pressing needs for food, shelter, and employment. Benevolent societies among the Irish and other immigrant groups sprouted in every city. Among those whose families were long established, charitable works became a sign of high social status. Industrialists, financiers, and other financially successful Americans set up foundations in their family names, and underwrote hospitals, schools, orphanages, and institutions for the disabled and the mentally ill.

# PUBLIC WELFARE IN AN INDUSTRIAL SOCIETY

The Civil War created another wave of poverty and dislocation. The war did settle the question of states' rights and establish the indivisible Union; as such, it strengthened the powers and expanded the role of the federal government. One of the tasks that this more powerful federal government faced was to provide pensions and benefits to disabled veterans of the war. Another major problem addressed by Washington was the condition of freed slaves, millions of whom were facing racial discrimination in jobs and housing, as well as barriers to their education and training. Congress responded by establishing the Bureau of Refugees, Freedmen, and Abandoned Lands, also known as the Freedmen's Bureau, in March 1865 under the direction of General Oliver Howard.

Initially the Freedmen's Bureau was strongly opposed by Democrats and by President Andrew Johnson, who saw no provision in the Constitution for any kind of federal social welfare system. But the Congress, dominated by Republicans in favor of federal Reconstruction policy, overrode Johnson's attempts to eliminate it. The Freedmen's Bureau distributed food rations, helped former slaves to find work, settled black farmers on small plots of cultivable land, underwrote schools and hospitals, and set up courts to deal with civil and criminal cases involving former slaves. Although the Bureau was effective in relieving desperate conditions for millions of African Americans, it did little to solve discrimination in public social welfare institutions, particularly in the South, and its mandate came to an end in 1872.

After the Civil War, immigrants from Britain, Ireland, Germany, Scandinavia, and Italy arrived at the eastern ports and in California, while the rural poor migrated to the cities in search of better-paid employment. The poorhouses of northeastern cities were burdened with a rising number of homeless, disabled, mentally ill, and unemployable people who otherwise would have been forced to roam the streets. The state of county poorhouses became a source of public scandal, with many of them forced to close their doors due to dangerous and unsanitary conditions.

## STATE-RUN POOR RELIEF

In the late 19th century, public welfare became a business of the states. Public boards were set up in the state capitals to supervise poorhouses and other institutions. They controlled state budgets for poor relief, and some also had the authority to supervise private charities. State charity boards set down standards of care for public institutions, sent inspectors around to ensure the standards were being met, and investigated complaints of poor treatment.

These bodies, like many other government systems, were subject to corruption and incompetence. This undermined support for public welfare of any kind, particularly in an era when the free market was enshrined and poverty was still seen as a result of moral failure. (Natural disasters, however, took no measure of an individual's morality or willingness to work. The national government freely granted relief to victims of floods, drought, and locust plagues in the late 19th century, setting the precedent for modern federal disaster aid.)

The severe economic depression of 1877 brought the situation to a head. Thrown out of work, millions of laborers found themselves without recourse to public welfare of any kind. In some cities, the situation sparked rioting. In St. Louis, a general strike shut down an entire city. The St. Louis "Commune" was reminiscent of the Paris uprising of 1871 and downright frightening to business and political leaders all over the country. State governments responded by calling out their militias and rewriting their laws. In many towns and counties, homelessness now became a crime, and vagrancy laws put people without a permanent abode into a temporary one—the local jail. The major cities had almost completely abandoned outdoor relief by the end of the 19th century.

## SCIENTIFIC CHARITY AND THE SETTLEMENT HOUSE

In the meantime, in an industrial age, a scientific approach took precedence. In the view of many, the proliferation of private charities and the ineffectiveness of public relief systems called for a more rational, efficient method of getting benefits to the needy. A pioneer of this movement was Reverend Stephen Humphreys Gurteen. An English immigrant, Gurteen brought a new idea—the charity organization society—from his former home.

In 1877, Gurteen founded the first American charity organization society in Buffalo, New York. The charity organization society operated in the tradition of outdoor charity. It kept public records of the poor, directed services of private charities to the needy, served as an employment agency for the jobless, and attempted to guide the poor into some useful work, in order to get them off of relief altogether. The idea spread rapidly, and by the end of the 19th century, more than 100 cities had followed Buffalo's example.

As public opinion generally turned against state institutions—widely seen as costly failures—the poorhouse was gradually replaced by specialized institutions for the disabled, the insane, and the elderly. At the same time, cities were growing more crowded and more chaotic, with a tide of immigrants moving into tenements and putting a greater strain on public services and the social fabric. Simply dispensing food or pittances to the poor and moving the neediest into poorhouses and orphanages were methods going out of favor. One answer to these urban problems was the settlement house, another tradition that started in England and arrived almost simultaneously with the charity organization society.

The settlement house was a 19th-century precursor to the 20th-century shelter. It was more ambitious, however, as it was founded on the ideal of creating a more cohesive urban community. It saw the causes of poverty in environmental conditions and not moral turpitude. In contrast to the charity organization society, the settlement house reached no judgment about who did or did not deserve charity. Although some settlement houses were run by religious institutions, for the most part the concept was a secular answer to the longstanding tradition of private church charities, which emphasized moral improvement above all.

Settlement houses were run by volunteers who provided a temporary home, a soup kitchen, classrooms for teaching basic skills and/or English, and referrals for employment and health services. The larger settlements offered libraries, gymnasiums, savings banks, theaters, and pharmacies. The settlement house movement also advocated legal and social reform: better sanitation, the regulation of tenements, racial equality, and the improvement of working conditions.

In many ways, the concept of the settlement house was at odds with the methods of the charity organization society, whose advocates saw their work as rational, scientific, and practical. Proponents of the charity organization society were not interested in social betterment or moral reform. They simply wanted to make the system of private and public charity more useful and effective.

For Jane Addams, a prominent leader of the movement, the settlement house was an effort to make society more cooperative and mutually supportive. Addams considered the settlement house as much a benefit to the volunteers as to those they served. It was a necessary safety valve for the restless ambitions of idealistic youth:

> *It is easy to see why the Settlement movement originated in England, where the years of education are more constrained and definite than they are here, where class distinctions are more rigid. The necessity of it was greater there, but we are fast feeling the pressure of the need and meeting the necessity for Settlements in America. Our young people feel nervously the need of putting theory into action, and respond quickly to the Settlement form of activity.[6]*

The first settlement house in the United States was Neighborhood House, founded in New York by Stanton Coit in 1886. Other well known settlement houses were Hull-House in Chicago, founded by Jane Addams; Chicago Commons, established by Graham Taylor; and the Henry Street Settlement, founded by Lillian Wald. By the turn of the century, more than 100 settlement houses had opened for business.

# THE PROGRESSIVE ERA

At the turn of the century, social welfare in the United States was fragmented and divided. Two basic systems were at work: private and public. The settlement house and the charity organization society represented two opposing approaches to private charity, while public welfare and the state institution came under fire from the general public and political leaders.

Journalists and book authors took up a new literary genre: an unblinking account of the harsh reality of urban poverty and hopelessness. The slums of big eastern cities provided a favorite backdrop for sensational accounts of hunger, misery, and degradation in the midst of a prospering nation. The prolific journalist Lafcadio Hearn set the tone with his florid accounts of city tenements: ". . . the same rickety room, the same cracked stove, the same dingy walls bearing fantastic tapestry of faded rags and grotesque shadow-silhouettes . . . the same pile of city coal in one corner, the same ghastly candle stuck in the same mineral water bottle . . . the same heavily warm atmosphere and oppressive smell . . . Shadowy tenement houses and dilapidated cottages, and blind, foul alleys with quaint names suggestive of deformity and darkness."[7]

While muckraking journalists revealed the grimness of industrial-age poverty, the nations of Europe were setting a new standard in public welfare policy. The emergence of constitutional monarchies and the rise of socialism were beginning to change the general American view of the old continent. Germany was the first nation to create a system of national social insurance in 1884, when the German government began funding a system of workers' compensation, which compensated industrial workers for injuries suffered at their jobs. In 1889, the program added disability and death benefits, as well as old-age pensions. By the end of the 19th century, Germany was spending more than half of its national budget on its social programs.[8] Otto von Bismarck, the German chancellor who installed these provisions, was motivated not by altruism or sympathy for the working class but by the need for a docile and productive labor force. Bismarck's intention was to head off the rising tide of socialism, a movement for public ownership of industry that found strong advocates in the German authors Karl Marx and Friedrich Engels.

According to author Michael Kronenwetter, the result was a rising economic and military power:

> By 1910, Germany was the leading power in western Europe. Its workforce was the envy of its neighbors. What's more, even though it spent most of its budget on social programs, its army was second to none. One reason was the fact that German soldiers, most of whom came from the working class, were in better physical condition than any others in Europe, thanks largely to Bismarck's welfare measures.[9]

Germany's new policies were soon imitated in other European nations. Most of the western European countries adopted old-age insurance, health insurance, and unemployment insurance. The United Kingdom established the most comprehensive and generous social benefits, including old-age pensions, a minimum wage, and unemployment and health insurance. The European "welfare state" had come into being, its benefits to serve as a model—and its expenses a precaution—to the United States through the 20th century.

While European states were following Germany's lead, in the United States conditions among the urban poor were scandalizing the public through lurid exposés in the press. Child labor, government corruption, and dangerous working conditions became fodder for a reformist "muckraking" press, whose leading lights became celebrities for exposing fraud, corruption, and exploitation among the once-revered captains of industry. Legislation to address these issues was forthcoming. Many states passed new laws regulating wages and hours, set up workers' compensation systems to assist those injured on the job, and passed a minimum working age. Public education and health were more closely regulated; many cities passed new laws concerning the height, density, and design of tenement blocks. In 1912, Congress established the Children's Bureau, the first federal-level social welfare agency. The bureau received a budget of $25,640 and a mandate to study child welfare, juvenile courts, orphanages, and infant mortality.

At the state level, the first mothers' pensions were established in 1911 in Illinois. The mothers' pension was financial aid for children living with their single mothers. The intention was to allow mothers to avoid the necessity of full-time work. Relieved from the burden of working, single mothers would thus be better able to care for and supervise their children, who in turn would avoid a life of juvenile delinquency and adult criminality. The program was often denied to those who were divorced, however, and to minorities. Administered by juvenile courts, the mothers' pensions were in effect in all but two states by 1934.

World War I, which the United States entered in 1917, wrought important changes in economic conditions. Factories were put to work making munitions and war matériel, temporarily solving the unemployment problem. The war closed borders and cut immigration from Europe, and it claimed the services of young men through a military draft. Around this time, the settlement house movement lost steam, with many of its leaders branching out into politics or reform movements that took them out of the business of dispensing food and aid to the poor.

The Red Scare that followed the war cast suspicion on radicals, anarchists, Communists, and any sympathizers that might have a bent toward socialist ideals. This included settlement house leaders, whose urban communes were seen as dangerously reminiscent of Soviet methods. At the same time, the need for their services was becoming less acute. The 1920s brought a growing economy and general prosperity as the private sector succeeded in raising the general welfare. Incomes grew, working conditions improved, and much of the grinding poverty of the cities faded into an unpleasant memory.

The urban industrial economy had its shortcomings, however. Manufacturing companies were vulnerable to swings in the national economy, and in times of economic stagnation, a rising number of jobless workers were left with unmarketable skills, if they had any skills at all. As workers aged, their usefulness in factories and assembly plants declined. No laws prohibited age discrimination in employment, so a growing number of the elderly had few job prospects and no means of supporting themselves.

The federal government made some response to these problems in the form of the Sheppard-Towner Maternity and Infancy Act of 1921. This legislation provided matching funds to the states to establish health centers for prenatal care of expectant mothers and health care for their infants. The program was closed down in 1929.

# THE GREAT DEPRESSION

The prosperity of 1920s came to an abrupt end with the stock market crash of October 1929. The Great Depression that followed threw millions of people out of work. Breadlines and soup kitchens fed the hungry in the cities. People begged on the streets or sold their household goods and clothing to survive. Their homes lost to foreclosure, or their rent unpaid, many people lived in the open in public parks or in shantytowns, called "Hoovervilles" in criticism of President Hoover, built on city outskirts, railroad yards, and vacant lots. In 1932, the national unemployment rate reached 25.2 percent; unemployment among the nonfarm workforce reached 38 percent.

The economic slowdown that followed the crash shuttered factories, retail businesses, and banks, many of them for good. About one of every four workers lost his or her job. There was no economic safety net. Personal savings accounts, retirement pensions, and the like were largely unknown even for those with regular employment. Many of those with money saved had it invested in the stock market, where it had evaporated in the 1929 crash.

The depression spread around the world. Trade fell, and the economic growth of the 1920s reversed into annual declines. In Europe, a continent still recovering from the damages of World War I, unemployment rose steeply. Many people viewed the capitalist industrial economy as a failure—a now-obsolete stage in the historical movement toward a planned and more efficient socialist system. Nations in Europe, Asia, and South America had already followed Germany's lead in providing national social insurance. The United States had not, although 24 states were providing old-age pensions, 46 were paying widows' pensions, and 44 offered workers' compensation benefits.[10]

State and local governments and charities struggled to cope with the massive poverty, hunger, and homelessness. Property tax receipts fell and in some locales went largely uncollected, making it harder for state and local governments to run social welfare programs of any kind. Even schools closed down in many areas for lack of money to operate. Idle children roamed the streets, begging from passersby or fighting in gangs. Private charities were also overwhelmed. Donations fell sharply, and these agencies were unable to cope with hunger and homelessness on a massive scale.

The depression tore at the social fabric of the nation. Joblessness broke up millions of families and forced many out of their homes. The rate of new marriages fell, as did the birthrate. Among the unemployed, in particular, the hard times inspired murmurs of outright revolt and defiance. In 1932, a "Bonus Army" of veterans marched on Washington, demanding some form of federal compensation for their military service. The Republican Party, long considered the guardians of economic prosperity, fell into widespread disrepute.

Political leaders began to call for some kind of income redistribution, to eliminate poverty and to make the system more just. For instance, Senator Huey Long of Louisiana proposed a "Share Our Wealth Society" that would make every man "a king":

> *There is an average of $15,000 in wealth to every family in America. That is right here today. We do not propose to divide it up equally. We do not propose a division of wealth, but we propose to limit poverty that we will allow to be inflicted upon any man's family. . . . One third of the average is low enough for any one family to hold, that there should be a guaranty of a family wealth of around $5,000; enough for a home, an automobile, a radio, and the ordinary conveniences, and the opportunity to educate their children; a fair share of the income of this land thereafter to that family so there will be no such thing as merely the select to have those things, and so there will be no such thing as a family living in poverty and distress.[11]*

The apparent ties between poverty and economic—not personal—shortcomings ended (temporarily) the debate over the moral dimension of welfare. It was apparent that millions of hardworking, middle-class people needed help and that government had some obligation to provide it. The first public relief program to address unemployment was initiated in New York State in 1931, under Governor Franklin Roosevelt. In August of that year, Roosevelt called a special session of the state legislature to address the unemployment emergency. The governor announced that the state had an obligation to help the jobless—who had, when employed, already contributed payroll taxes to the New York treasury. The lawmakers responded with the State Unemployment Relief Act, enacted on September 23, 1931, and better known as the Wicks Act. The law set up a new state agency, the Temporary Emergency Relief Administration, to match local spending on unemployment benefits and home relief. The first director of this agency was Harry Hopkins. Similar laws were enacted in 24 states by the end of 1931.

Demands went out for federal relief as well. In the Senate, a committee led by Robert LaFollette, Jr. of Wisconsin and Thomas P. Costigan of Colorado held hearings on the matter of unemployment benefits. President Herbert Hoover, while head of the federal Department of Commerce, had already shown energy and ability in applying bureaucratic methods to social problems. He had ably administered food shipments in Europe in the aftermath of World War I, and in 1927 he had organized a massive federal effort to alleviate the problems caused by a flood of the Mississippi River. But as president, he resisted the committee's recommendation that the federal government now step in. He opposed the creation of a new federal bureaucracy, seeing federal welfare programs as an infringement of the rights of the states to run their own affairs. Faith in the American virtues of individualism and self-help, and confidence that the economy would soon turn around, convinced Hoover that federal relief programs were an unnecessary, unwise expansion of federal authority over the states. In 1931, when Congress passed a $2.6 billion federal works program, Hoover vetoed the measure.

In the summer of 1932, as the situation worsened and many locales were already in bankruptcy, Hoover signed the Emergency Relief and Construction Act. This program set up the Emergency Relief Administration (ERA), which offered loans to the states for unemployment relief. As loans, however, these funds would have to be repaid, and in the economic emergency many states refused to contract further debts. The federal treasury loaned only $30 million of the $300 million appropriated for the program. Hoover suffered landslide defeat in the fall of 1932, and his statements and inaction on the subject of federal relief programs played a major role in his ouster.

## FEDERAL POOR RELIEF

In his successful presidential campaign of 1932, Franklin Roosevelt promised a New Deal to address the problem of unemployment. He contended that the national economic depression made unemployment a national issue, one that could only be solved by the federal government. Congress convened in early 1933, and in what became known as the Hundred Days Congress, it passed a flurry of new federal measures to address the issue of the jobless. The legislation proceeded with little opposition, and Roosevelt signed the Federal Emergency Relief Act in May 1933.

The act, modeled on New York's Wicks Act, raised the curtain on the modern era of federal welfare programs. The government set up the Federal Emergency Relief Administration (FERA), with Harry Hopkins as its head, and appropriated $500 million to the states as "grants-in-aid." These were funds that did not have to be paid back. The amount of the money sent to each state was determined by the federal agency, while the states had discretion on how to use it for unemployment relief, which took the form of cash payments as well as a program that distributed surplus food to the needy. Individuals seeking the aid had to appear at an unemployment office and certify that they were in need; they also had to pass a means test, which screened out those with sufficient assets or savings to look after themselves.

Once a business of the state and county governments, unemployment relief became a federal responsibility. Hopkins and Roosevelt were adamant about uniformity and efficiency. In view of the problems surrounding private relief efforts in the past they prohibited local governments from turning the money over to private charities.

Federal measures to combat unemployment expanded from there. The Civil Works Administration (CWA) was created in November 1933 by a presidential order. Instead of relief, the jobless were to be given jobs. There was no screening procedure or means testing for those who took part. The pay was a market wage, substantially higher than the rate of relief available under FERA. Although the CWA was well received, it was terminated in March 1934, abruptly ending the employment of 4 million people. FERA in turn was closed down in December 1935 (shortly after passage of the Social Security Act).

In the meantime, the federal National Recovery Administration (NRA) was organized to run a variety of other federal relief programs. The Civilian Conservation Corps (CCC) employed the jobless in forestry and flood-control projects on federal lands. A Public Works Administration (PWA) set up work programs in depressed industries. Students found work through the National Youth Administration (NYA) and the Works Progress Administration (WPA), which were established in 1935; the WPA was the largest federal job agency, employing millions. Under the direction of Harry Hopkins, the WPA paid the prevailing local wage while building roads, monuments, and public buildings.

To cope with household poverty, economists and public officials proposed ways to create a system of federally guaranteed minimum income. One proposal from February 1935, the Workers' Unemployment, Old Age, and Social Insurance Bill, called for simply paying the unemployed a stipend based on prevailing wages; it was to be financed through taxes on the wealthy, whose investment dollars were to be dedicated, partially, toward stimulating the demand for goods. "The taxation of the well-off would keep funds from being invested in useless capital," noted historians Sylvester Schieber and John B. Shoven in *The Real Deal*. "The distribution of money to those who would spend it on consumption of goods and services would stimulate the demand for these and revive production. The result of expanding production, of course, would be that the unemployed would be called back to jobs."[12]

Another notable proposal was advanced by Francis Townsend, a retired California doctor. Townsend suggested that a monthly $200 stipend be paid out of the federal treasury to all those over the age of 60 and unemployed—who would then be obligated to spend the money within 30 days. By 1935, petitions in support of the Townsend Plan had accumulated more than 25 million signatures. That same year Huey Long, the populist U.S. senator from Louisiana, was also riding a groundswell of support for his proposal to tax the rich in order to fund free college education, bonuses for veterans, and homesteads for working families. The plans advanced by Townsend and Long posed a serious political challenge to Roosevelt, who found himself on the defensive as the depression continued. Unemployment remained stubbornly high, and the election of 1936 loomed on the near horizon.

## THE SOCIAL SECURITY ACT

The public demanded a response and a plan. In his State of the Union address in 1935, Roosevelt called for a new, national system of welfare relief, federal unemployment insurance, and a retirement pension program. He also proposed relief for poor single mothers and their dependents. FDR believed these measures would alleviate the necessity for work programs, as he explained in this speech:

> *Closely related to the broad problem of livelihood is that of security against the major hazards of life. . . . The time has come for action by the national Government. I shall send to you, in a few days, definite recommendations based on these studies. These recommendations will cover the broad subjects of unemployment insurance and old age insurance, of benefits for children, for others, for the handicapped, for maternity care and for other aspects of dependency and illness where a beginning can now be made.[13]*

Roosevelt maintained that such relief programs should be temporary. He did not want the federal government to be permanently involved in the business of relieving poverty:

> *The lessons of history, confirmed by the evidence immediately before me, show conclusively that continued dependence upon relief induces a spiritual and*

17

*moral disintegration fundamentally destructive to the national fiber. To dole out relief in this way is to administer a narcotic, a subtle destroyer of the human spirit.*[14]

Roosevelt believed that some new mechanism was needed for preventing the dependence of the unemployed and the elderly on public relief funds. At the same time, he did not want to create lasting and burdensome obligations for the federal treasury. "I am not willing that the vitality of our people be further sapped by the giving of cash, of market baskets, of a few hours of weekly work cutting grass, taking leaves, or picking up papers in public parks."[15] The new pension system was to be financed by the workers who would ultimately benefit from it. The welfare benefits would be paid out by the states, with contributions from the federal treasury. Unemployment insurance would be financed by employers, who would pay a percentage of their payroll into a financial pool operated by the states.

To work out a plan, the president had already issued an executive order on June 29, 1934, creating a Committee on Economic Security, chaired by Secretary of Labor Frances Perkins. The CES hired Edwin E. Witte, an economist from the University of Wisconsin, to serve as its executive director. The committee deliberated over various proposals, heard witnesses, and considered the spending constraints of the U.S. Constitution and the use of the federal treasury. Its proposals were then written into a bill sponsored by Senator Robert Wagner of New York and Representative David Lewis of Maryland in 1935.

The Economic Security Act passed the House by 371 to 33 and the Senate by 77 to 6. Roosevelt signed the legislation, more commonly known as the Social Security Act, on August 18, 1935. The new law set up a national system of unemployment insurance and a national pension system for workers over the age of 65. (Initially, this pension was known as Old Age Insurance or Old Age Assistance.) The states would administer the program, and the federal government would fund it. A tax on payrolls would levy equal contributions from employers and employees. Employers would pay fully for unemployment insurance. The program did not cover agricultural or domestic workers.

A third major component of the law was Title IV, Aid to Dependent Children (ADC). (The program would be renamed Aid to Families with Dependent Children, or AFDC, during the Kennedy administration, reflecting the payment of benefits to parents as well as children.) This program, explained in just three pages of new law, was initially designed to assist dependent children under the age of 16. Participation by the states, however, was voluntary, and the state plans would set the eligibility rules as well as the benefit levels. To qualify for ADC benefits, a child had to be deprived of the care of one or both parents by reason of death, absence, or incapacity (notably, not by reason of unemployment). The beneficiary also had to live with a father, mother, grandparent, brother, sister, stepparent, stepsister, stepbrother, uncle, or aunt, and in the home of the relative.

The federal government granted one third of the total amount spent through this program by the states, appropriating $24,750,000 to fund the first year of ADC (with no ceiling on later expenditures). For a one-child family, the federal payments amounted to a maximum of $6 per month; for second and remaining children, $4 each per month. The government also set down guidelines the states had to meet in order to be paid. A state ADC plan had to be mandatory in all political subdivisions, and local governments could not set varying eligibility rules. It had to be administered and/ or supervised by a single agency. It had to provide a fair hearing for anyone denied benefits. In addition, there could be no residency requirement for any child living in the state for at least one year, or children born in the state within one year of the application, if the mother held residency for at least one year (residency requirements would later be brought to the Supreme Court). The ADC law was written by Grace Abbott and Katherine Lenroot, both of whom served as directors of the Children's Bureau, a part of the Department of Labor.

In the meantime, each state had to pass its own legislation in order to set up agencies to collect and distribute unemployment and ADC benefits, a process that took two years. The first 32.9 million workers were enrolled in the Social Security program in 1937. By June 1937, $45 million in unemployment benefits and $20 million in retirement benefits had been paid out.[16]

## OPPOSITION TO THE SOCIAL SECURITY ACT

The New Deal and the Social Security Act were not universally popular. In his 1950 book *Roosevelt in Retrospect*, John Gunther described the main opposition as follows:

> *The New Deal alienated a large segment of the business community of the country, most of the propertied class, roughly 80 percent of the newspapers, and most of the rich, the archaic, and the privileged. Two main reasons account for this. First, fear that Roosevelt's "deficit spending" would result in a permanently unbalanced budget and wreck the finances of the country. Second, indignation at soaring taxes. "Tax the wealth" was, quite frankly, FDR's keynote.[17]*

Yet the ADC program—the future focal point of the debate over welfare—came in for little comment. State treasuries were stretched thin by the depression, and most state governments had no trouble passing a law that would bring federal dollars to assist their public charities. Instead, opposition to Roosevelt's program was based on financial and philosophical grounds, on the need for careful budgeting, and on the tradition of limited government in which the constitutional meaning of "providing for the public welfare" was variously interpreted by Madisonians and Hamiltonians.

This opposition grew through the 1930s. Conservatives saw the Social Security program as an unconstitutional intrusion of the federal government into the business of the states, and into economic matters that were none of its business. Critics charged that the program violated the Tenth Amendment to the U.S. Constitution, which states, "The powers not delegated to the United States by the Constitution, nor prohibited by it to the States, are reserved to the States respectively, or to the people." Supporters responded with Article I, Section 8, which empowers Congress to impose taxes and to "provide for . . . the general Welfare of the United States."

The Supreme Court seemed to concur with opponents by its opinion invalidating the Railroad Retirement Act, a precursor to the Social Security system that provided for railroad employees' pensions. Through early 1936, the Court also struck down the National Industrial Recovery Act; the Frazier-Lemke Farm Bankruptcy Act; and finally the Agricultural Adjustment Act (AAA), which levied a tax on food processing in order to fund agricultural price supports. The Court's decision (*United States v. Butler*) on the AAA stated, in the vein of James Madison, that "a statutory plan to regulate and control agricultural production [is] a matter beyond the powers delegated to the federal government." But it went on, in the more generous Hamiltonian view, to say, "the power of Congress to authorize expenditure of public monies for public purposes is not limited by the direct grants of legislative power found in the Constitution."[18]

Lawmakers had carefully crafted the Social Security Act in order to give it the best chance of survival in the courts, where it was certain to be challenged on constitutional grounds. The taxation (Title VII) and spending (Title II) provisions of the Act were contained within separate titles, so its defenders could claim that the federal government was not deliberately engineering social policy through an unconstitutional exercise of its taxing power.[19]

The new Social Security law eventually did survive two major challenges in the United States Supreme Court. In spring 1937, the Court heard the case of *Steward Machine Company v. Davis*, which challenged the constitutionality of the payroll tax. The case began with the suit of an Alabama company seeking to recover $46.14 paid to the Internal Revenue Service for unemployment compensation benefits. The company challenged the tax as both an unconstitutional excise on the right of employment and a usurpation of powers reserved to the states. The Supreme Court upheld the constitutionality of the new Social Security system, stating in the majority opinion: "The Social Security Act is an attempt to find a method by which . . . public agencies may work together to a common end."[20]

To save Social Security and what remained of the New Deal, Roosevelt counterattacked by attempting to deliberately engineer some early retirements. In February 1937, he asked Congress for the authority to appoint new justices when those sitting on the Court reached the age of 70, and thus allow him the authority to expand the Court by up to six justices. He intended to appoint new justices whose judicial philosophies were more in line with his own.

Faced with this prospect, the Supreme Court began retreating on its opposition to the New Deal. The Court heard the case of *Helvering v. Davis*, which tested the legality of the Social Security system, at this crisis moment in its history. The case was brought by George Davis, who alleged that the tax collected for Social Security was unconstitutional and who sought to prevent the Edison Electric Illuminating Company, of which he was a shareholder, from paying it. In its brief supporting Social Security and the ADC program, the administration described Social Security taxes as valid general revenue taxes, and not a scheme of compulsory public insurance. The Court agreed by a vote of seven to two.

In the meantime, the political debate over the New Deal brought about a labeling that went beyond "Democrat" and "Republican." Those who supported these programs and the expansion of the federal government into work relief programs were labeled "liberals," while those opposing became "conservatives." Roosevelt's liberal support came from labor unions, farmers, African Americans, Jews, Catholics, and big-city political machines. The conservative camp came to include eastern financial and business interests, small-town Republican voters from the Midwest, and southern Democrats opposed to any federal infringement of states' rights.

# WELFARE LAW IN THE MID-20TH CENTURY

Social Security law went through frequent amendments as lawmakers adjusted the law to account for changes in public opinion. The lawmakers expressed in new statutes the public's view of who did and who did not deserve benefits. The amendments were also meant to guide the behavior of beneficiaries. In 1940, for example, ADC eligibility was extended to children age 17, as long as they regularly attended school. The ADC program was enrolling an increasing number of families as well. As early as 1938 there were 243,000 families and more than 600,000 children on the ADC rolls; the total cost of the program had reached $103 million, of which $34 million was being paid by the federal government.[21]

At the same time, federal lawmakers were manipulating the system by paying out or withholding matching funds from the federal treasury to the state ADC programs. In 1950, federal funds were extended to include coverage of a single needy relative living with the beneficiary—thus, single mothers (and fathers) became eligible along with their children. In 1956, "needy relatives" with whom the beneficiary could live came to include first cousins, nieces, and nephews. In 1957, the federal government stopped withholding funds to a state paying benefits to children aged 16 or 17 who were not attending school.

The New Deal was passing into history, having in the general view saved the country from the depression and incidentally expanded the powers of Congress to steer social policy. By the National Mental Health Act of 1946, for example, the government provided grants to the states to pay for existing or new outpatient facilities that treated the mentally ill. The National School Lunch Program, launched in 1946, made a temporary program permanent and provided aid to the states to support it. The legislation had an educational as well as a nutritional role, according to the House Committee on Agriculture report: "The educational features of a properly chosen diet served at school should not be under-emphasized. Not only is the child taught what a good diet consists of, but his parents and family likewise are indirectly instructed."[22]

## THE FOOD STAMP PROGRAM

At the same time that the ADC caseload was increasing dramatically, so was the provision of food stamps, the second major program that was now being categorized under the heading of "welfare." Food stamps originally had a mundane, utilitarian economic purpose. Farmers had borne the brunt of the collapse in prices and living standards during the depression. In the interest of supporting agriculture, the federal government had initiated a program to purchase agricultural surpluses during the 1930s and in this way keep market prices from falling even further. The scheme was expanded in 1939, at the outbreak of World War II, into a social welfare program. All those on public relief rolls bought orange stamps; in addition, they received half the value of orange stamps in the form of free blue stamps. Orange stamps could be freely used as vouchers in stores enrolled in the program, while blue stamps were used to buy commodity foods designated by the Department of Agriculture.

As war industries provided a powerful stimulus to production and employment, the problem of agricultural surpluses ended. But the idea of a national program to combat hunger survived, and the ADC program began to expand in the 1950s, when the government extended aid to caretaker relatives.

In 1959, Congress passed a measure to authorize the Department of Agriculture to revive the Food Stamp Program. A food stamp "pilot program" went into effect in 1962 as one of the first measures taken by the Kennedy administration. The program eliminated the government-subsidized purchase of surplus foods and again provided for the use of food stamps for ordinary purchases. In 1964, Congress passed a law establishing a permanent food stamp program, with a complex set of rules and guidelines. The program involved state certification and issuance of food stamps to beneficiaries, and federal responsibility for funding and for authorization of retailers to participate. As the program was developed in new geographical areas, the number of participants expanded rapidly, from 500,000 in the first year of the program to 15 million by 1975.

The ADC and Food Stamp programs were one side of an important distinction in federal benefit programs. Social Security and Medicare (introduced in 1965) were funded by workers' contributions and were not considered "welfare," while ADC (renamed AFDC in 1962) was increasingly associated with the idle poor and African Americans. An increasing percentage of the African-American population was becoming dependent on the welfare system, which in the opinion of many Americans was now encouraging illegitimate births and broken, one-parent families. The proportion of African Americans receiving AFDC benefits increased to 40 percent by 1961. The number of illegitimate children on AFDC rolls also increased, as did the overall caseload, which rose 333 percent between 1950 and 1970. By 1971, the number of eligible recipients who were actually receiving benefits increased to 90 percent.[23] These statistics prepared the ground for the modern welfare debate, which hinged on the nature of AFDC as direct charity dispensed by the federal government.

## WELFARE AND THE "GREAT SOCIETY"

Welfare benefits were further expanded in the 1960s. Effective May 1, 1961, the "unemployed parent" amendment allowed children eligibility for "ADC-Unemployed Parent" if a parent lost his or her job. In the next year, the law allowed states to add a spouse to the AFDC rolls for matching funds from the federal government. Later, in 1968, the "essential person" option was passed, allowing federal reimbursement for state payments to any individual deemed to be essential to the child. States could add or subtract these provisions as they saw fit. The result was a patchwork-quilt welfare system, with varying benefits and eligibility, which became an important target of reform in the 1990s.

In the meantime, the assassination of President John F. Kennedy in November 1963 brought Vice President Lyndon Johnson to the office of president. Johnson was a Democrat from Texas and a believer in vigorous government action. He began using the phrase "Great Society" at speeches and dinners in early 1964. In May 1964, Johnson delivered a key speech at the University of Michigan in which he outlined the philosophical basis for a "Great Society":

> *Your imagination, your initiative, and your indignation will determine whether we build a society where progress is the servant of our needs, or a society where old values and new visions are buried under unbridled growth. For in your time we have the opportunity to move not only toward the rich society and the powerful society, but upward to the Great Society.*
>
> *The Great Society rests on abundance and liberty for all. It demands an end to poverty and racial injustice, to which we are totally committed in our time. But that is just the beginning.*
>
> *The Great Society is a place where every child can find knowledge to enrich his mind and to enlarge his talents. It is a place where leisure is a welcome chance to build and reflect, not a feared cause of boredom and restlessness. It is a place where the city of man serves not only the needs of the body and the demands of commerce but the desire for beauty and the hunger for community. . . .*
>
> *Aristotle said: "Men come together in cities in order to live, but they remain together in order to live the good life." It is harder and harder to live the good life in American cities today. The catalog of ills is long: there is the decay of the centers and the despoiling of the suburbs. There is not enough housing for our people or transportation for our traffic. Open land is vanishing and old landmarks are violated. . . . Our society will never be great until our cities are great. Today the frontier of imagination and innovation is inside those cities and not beyond their borders.*[24]

"The Great Society" became a popular label for Johnson's many legislative initiatives on civil rights and poverty. Among these were the Food Stamp Program, reestablished in 1964; Medicare, a low-premium medical insurance for the elderly; and Medicaid, a health program for the poor. Both Medicare and Medicaid were created by the Social Security Act of 1965. The Great Society initiatives that concerned the poor were collectively known as the "War on Poverty." Most of the War on Poverty initiatives were administered by the new Office of Economic Opportunity, established by the Economic Opportunity Act of 1964.

The idea of a government affording individuals a method of escaping destitution had evolved, in the opinion of some, into an individual right. The argument was made most cogently in a famous 1964 *Yale Law Review* article, "The New Property," by Charles Reich. A countercurrent to the Great Society was developing as well. Ronald Reagan, running for governor of California in 1964, questioned its cost and efficiency:

*Federal welfare spending is today ten times greater than it was in the dark depths of the Depression. Federal, state, and local welfare combined spend 45 billion dollars a year. Now the government has announced that 20 percent, some 9.3 million families, are poverty-stricken on the basis that they have less than a $3,000 a year income. If this present welfare spending was prorated equally among these poverty-stricken families, we could give each family more than $4,500 a year. Actually, direct aid to the poor averages less than $600 per family. There must be some administrative overhead somewhere.[25]*

## THE WELFARE RIGHTS MOVEMENT

Despite the enactment of Great Society laws and programs and a general improvement in economic conditions, social turmoil ran strong in the late 1960s, occasionally erupting in violent demonstrations and urban rioting. Welfare rights demonstrations began in 1966, with a large "Walk for Adequate Welfare" protest taking place in May in Washington, D.C., and welfare protests soon following in several major cities. In the same year, welfare beneficiaries began to organize themselves, forming the National Coordinating Committee of Welfare Rights Groups in Chicago. The goals of this and other welfare rights groups were a guaranteed minimum income level, an end to invasive investigations of welfare abuse, allowances for clothing and medical care, and an end to residency requirements by the states.

In May 1966, the National Welfare Rights Organization (NWRO) came into being, founded by a former Syracuse University chemistry professor, George Wiley. The NWRO became the largest group advocating for welfare recipients in the nation. It took the lead on advocating for increasing welfare payments and making the system more responsive to the needs of recipients. But it struggled with internal dissension, poor management, and racial tensions. The mostly white, middle-class leadership and management of the NWRO clashed with the mostly nonwhite membership. Many of these members believed that welfare recipients should rightfully serve in leadership positions, and they resented the middle-class status of directors. In 1969, Wiley replaced the Caucasian leadership with African-American men. This did little to dampen dissension within the ranks, however. Wiley resigned in 1972 as the NWRO was reaching a financial crisis. The organization struggled for several more years and eventually folded in 1975.

## REPLACING THE WELFARE SYSTEM

In January 1968, President Johnson appointed the Commission on Income Maintenance Programs, also known as the Heineman Commission. The work of this body was to study poverty and resolve on a program for a federally guaranteed minimum income level. After nearly two years, the Heineman Commission concluded its work, recommending that the government operate through the income tax system. A "negative income tax" (NIT) would provide credits and refunds to those families that earned less than a certain annual income.

With this recommendation, the Heineman Commission was taking up a proposal that had already been in the works for years. The steep rise in "transfer payments" such as Social Security, Medicaid, and AFDC had since the 1950s been inspiring alternative schemes from lawmakers and economists. A proposal by economist Milton Friedman, laid out in his 1962 book *Capitalism and Freedom*, would replace the system of "progressive taxation" in the federal income tax, as well as all Social Security and Medicare taxes, with a simple flat tax (usually proposed at the rate of 25 percent). At the same time, the federal government would grant $10,000 annually to all adults. The intent of Friedman's proposal was to simplify the tax code, eliminate the welfare bureaucracy, and impose by federal law a minimum national standard of living. Proponents believed the NIT would also end "welfare dependency." In 1972, the presidential campaign of George McGovern took up the NIT idea; McGovern's proposal consisted of a grant of $1,000 per person, with benefits gradually reduced up to 33⅓ percent depending on income level.

The Johnson administration's Office of Economic Opportunity undertook experimental pilot programs—"income maintenance experiments"—to research the effects of a guaranteed income and the negative income tax. The programs were launched in 1968 in New Jersey and continued into the early 1970s in Denver and Seattle. After several years, however, researchers concluded that income maintenance by the federal government created as many problems as it solved. Rather than reducing dependency, the grants tended to disincentivize work. They also tended to break up marriages, because the payments reduced the pressure on breadwinners to remain with and provide for their families. There was also a problem of unreported income, which raised the need for a large policing and monitoring apparatus to prevent fraud.

No action was taken by Congress on these recommendations, but the concept of a federally guaranteed minimum income survived and was taken up again by the administration of Johnson's successor, Richard Nixon.

# A PROPOSAL FOR WELFARE REFORM

By the time Richard Nixon of California was campaigning for president in early 1968, the idealism of the decade was evaporating. Civil rights and antiwar demonstrations were breaking out frequently in inner cities and on college campuses. A few cities exploded in violence, with rioters battling police and causing widespread property damage, as well as fear and resentment. The nation was growing more polarized between economic classes and ethnic groups. Accusations of incompetence and dishonesty surrounded the conduct of a prolonged war in Vietnam.

The expansion of the federal welfare program and the turmoil in the inner cities fed the anger of the middle class, causing a backlash against a system that had been generally supported by the public since the 1930s. Reviewing the welfare program and the state of the urban underclass, Daniel Patrick Moynihan wrote *The Negro Family: The Case for National Action*, commonly called the Moynihan Report. In this document, Moynihan summoned federal statistics to support the now-prevailing view that welfare had become a symptom of a social malaise among African Americans, rather than a helping hand for broken families and the jobless:

> *The majority of Negro children receive public assistance under the AFDC program at one point or another in their childhood. At present, 14 percent of Negro children are receiving AFDC assistance, as against 2 percent of white children. Eight percent of white children receive such assistance at some time, as against 56 percent of nonwhites. . . . The steady expansion of this welfare program, as of public assistance programs in general, can be taken as a measure of the steady disintegration of the Negro family structure over the past generation in the United States.*[26]

The reaction against welfare was strongest among blue-collar workers, traditional Democratic voters who had supported Roosevelt's New Deal policies. These descendants of European immigrants, whose families had been urban and solidly Democratic for a century, were now moving out of the cities and into the suburbs—and the Republican Party. The racial conflict erupting in the urban centers of the United States catalyzed their opposition to welfare. They believed that the welfare program had become a waste of public money and a system that contributed to the same problems it was meant to correct.

Senator Russell Long, a member of the Senate Finance Committee, articulated the prevailing view that simple cheating and malingering were the prime culprits in rising welfare rolls. He made the following comment to this effect in 1972:

> *I am no newcomer to the welfare scene. My record on behalf of the poor is clear. But I am concerned—gravely concerned—that the welfare system, as we know it today, is being manipulated and abused by malingerers, cheats and outright frauds to the detriment not only of the American taxpayers*

*whose dollars support the program, but also to the detriment of the truly needy on whose behalf the Federal-State system of cash assistance is so important. There is no question in anyone's mind that the present welfare system is a mess.*[27]

Nixon rode this antiwelfare movement into office in 1968, handily defeating his Democrat opponent, Hubert Humphrey, who had come to stand for the Democratic tradition of an activist and idealist government. Nixon preached the virtues of hard work and self-reliance and disparaged government programs, holding himself up as an example of the self-made man. He derided the Great Society, played up the issue of welfare fraud, and criticized a federal government that in his opinion was growing bloated, corrupt, and ineffective.

Nixon's proposed solutions did not always match his conservative rhetoric, however. He suggested revamping the federal welfare system by making it not smaller but more equitable, with uniform eligibility standards, a guaranteed minimum income level, and rules that would force beneficiaries off the welfare rolls and into gainful employment. The Family Assistance Plan (FAP), conceived in large part by Daniel Patrick Moynihan, would guarantee a benefit level of $1,600 for every family of four either unemployed or working at wages that kept them below a certain income level. The proposal set this income level at $4,000 per year—notably, some $2,000 less than the federally established poverty level. The beneficiaries without work would have to enter a job training program, and eventually the federal government would turn over the entire program to the states to administer. Nixon's proposal was intended to end the state-to-state variations in existing welfare programs. Many Americans believed the state rules were leading poor people to migrate solely for the purpose of winning welfare benefits. Many states were countering this perceived trend by establishing residency requirements, which were being frequently challenged in the courts.

The FAP gained few supporters, however, either among members of Congress or the public at large. It was criticized largely for its work requirement. Forcing mothers with dependent children into work, critics feared, would lead to further family disintegration; it would also lead to labor-force competition in a national job pool threatened by inflation, overcapacity, and foreign competition. The FAP also drew criticism from welfare advocacy groups, in particular the National Welfare Rights Organization, whose leader, George Wiley, dubbed it the "Family Annihilation Plan." The proposal languished for a few years in a congressional committee and then died. But its basic tenets survived as guidelines for a successful welfare reform effort in the 1990s.

Moynihan himself analyzed the failure of the FAP in his book *The Politics of a Guaranteed Income*, concluding:

*The proposal of a guaranteed income predictably aroused opposition from groups that had reason to oppose income redistribution. . . . But* unpredict- ably *the competitive outbidding process among liberals set off by the proposal of a modest income guarantee ended with positions verging on the fantasized. The demand arose not for guaranteed income but for guaranteed wealth. . . . Upper middle-class liberals, having lost a sufficient awareness of the privi- lege—the singularity—of class position, now proposed privilege for all: an attractive thought, but as unattainable as it is illogical.*[28]

Congress did pass several other Nixon administration proposals, how- ever, including an increase in Social Security benefits and an expansion of the Food Stamp Program, which became mandatory for the states. Food stamps were now subject to expanded federal eligibility standards. In addi- tion, those receiving welfare benefits but no employment income could now obtain food stamps free of charge. The federal government also established national eligibility standards for Social Security payments to retirees, to the blind, and to the disabled. The Supplemental Security Income (SSI) pro- gram, which granted payments to those unable to work, became the first federal program to guarantee a minimum income level.

Nixon easily won reelection in 1972. The end of U.S. involvement in the Vietnam War in 1973, many Americans felt, promised a new emphasis on domestic social programs. But economic reality was darkening any rem- nants of 1960s idealism and experimentation. Increasing inflation was eating at the living standards of low-income and middle-class families. Economic competition from overseas was holding down U.S. wages. Because the wages of U.S. laborers did not keep pace with rising inflation, income in- equality increased during the 1970s. Many families found it necessary to work multiple jobs in order to afford rent, food, and basic necessities; in the meantime, both income and Social Security taxes were squeezing the middle class. Large companies were downsizing and outsourcing their jobs to coun- tries in Latin America and Asia, where they could pay the prevailing, lower wages. Increased racial tension fueled by desegregation, affirmative action programs, and court-ordered school busing prompted the migration of the middle class from the cities to the suburbs.

In these conditions, lawmakers forgot the concept of a guaranteed mini- mum income but held fast to the notions of reforming or eliminating the welfare system and promoting the entrance of welfare recipients into the workforce through mandated employment and/or job training. The Nixon administration turned to the income tax code to promote these goals. In a new version of the negative income tax, the administration proposed the Earned Income Tax Credit (EITC). This plan allowed families earning $4,000 or less per year a tax credit of 10 percent of their earnings. Congress approved the EITC bill in 1973. (The credit now amounts to 40 percent of the first $10,750 earned and ends at about $35,000 of earned income; the maximum credit is $4,400. At the federal level, EITC amounted to $36 billion in refunds in 2004; 11 states and three municipalities also have adopted the EITC.)

The Nixon administration also succeeded in having Congress pass a job program known as the Comprehensive Employment and Training Act (CETA). CETA granted public and private entities funds for low-wage service jobs as a means of training the young and unemployed for the job market. Title XX of the Social Security Act, passed in 1974, granted money to the states for various social welfare programs, to be tailored by the states to their local needs. Social Security retirement and disability payments were increased and indexed to inflation, with cost-of-living adjustments (COLA) to be made each year when inflation rose 3 percent or more.

The effect of these changes and adjustments was the opposite of Nixon's promises to scale back the welfare system—in fact, welfare spending expanded at a faster rate during the Nixon presidency than during that of Lyndon Johnson.

## WELFARE IN THE CONSERVATIVE AGE

The resignation of Richard Nixon in August 1974 was a watershed in American political history. The Watergate scandal that drove him from office was widely seen as a symbol of corruption at the highest levels of the federal government. Under the succeeding administration of Gerald Ford, welfare received little attention from the White House other than the work of the president's veto pen. Ford rejected an expansion in the federal school lunch program and a public works bill, and he cut the budget of the Department of Health, Education, and Welfare (soon to be renamed the Department of Health and Human Services).

In the meantime, unemployment increased while inflation rose. In 1973, an oil-price shock exacerbated the nation's economic problems, and an increasing number of families fell below the federal poverty level. Responding to criticism of welfare programs from both liberals and conservatives and encouraged by the presence of a cooperative Democratic Congress, Jimmy Carter, Ford's successor, proposed a sweeping reform of the welfare system. The Better Jobs and Income Program (BJIP) would end AFDC and food stamps, as well as the Supplemental Security Income program. It would set up a system of job training and work incentives for the employable and income maintenance for the permanently disabled, and it would expand the Earned Income Tax Credit as well.

The proposal failed in Congress, however, where it was criticized for its higher expenses, its public sector jobs, and its universal coverage. Carter was also unable to persuade Congress to pass a national health insurance program or to shore up Social Security's deteriorating finances with a higher rate of employer contributions and higher payments out of general tax revenue. In the meantime, the high inflation and unemployment inherited from the Ford administration continued. His presidency falling to a new low in approval ratings, Carter was handily defeated by Ronald Reagan in the 1980 presidential election.

Reagan, the former governor of California, came to office with the reputation of a steadfast welfare opponent. After his second election to the California governorship in 1970, he had proposed and persuaded the state legislature to pass a series of welfare reform laws that restricted eligibility for benefits and required benefit recipients to look for work. At the time of the 1980 presidential election, the federal welfare program and specifically AFDC were in very poor repute. The number of AFDC recipients had increased from 7.4 million in 1970 to 10.6 million in 1980, while funding for the program had risen from $4.1 billion in 1970 to $12 billion in 1980.[29] U.S. historian James T. Patterson, author of *Restless Giant*, explains how this came to be:

> *AFDC expanded because the number of single mothers, driven up by increases in out-of-wedlock pregnancies and in divorces, kept rising, and because activists—some of them welfare mothers, some of them liberals who staffed legal aid and legal services programs—at last enabled poor single mothers to become aware of their eligibility. By the 1960s, many more of these mothers were asserting their rights to aid, and receiving it.*[30]

In his speeches Reagan preached small government, low taxes, the free market, and an end to the welfare state. A president who had once been a supporter of Franklin Roosevelt and the Democratic Party now proposed throwing Roosevelt's New Deal into reverse. Like Nixon, Reagan advocated the return of welfare programs to the states and the dismissal of the federal government's role in them. He began this project by ending the CETA job-training program, begun in 1973, and cutting spending on food stamps and AFDC. He also proposed immediate cuts in Social Security payments, both for retirees and the disabled, and an eventual shift of all spending on AFDC and food stamps to the states, which would have the option of ending the programs altogether. As a concession to federal control of basic health benefits for the poor, he suggested that the federal government assume all Medicaid payments.

Early in the Reagan administration, the welfare scholars Frances Fox Piven and Richard Cloward argued that a built-in bureaucratic opposition with a national constituency would check the president's efforts to roll back the welfare state. "There now exists," they wrote, "an enormous array of agencies and programs oriented to popular grievances. . . . For all its zeal, [the Reagan administration] cannot simply eliminate the huge and intricate state apparatus. . . . Nor can that apparatus be effectively disciplined either, for much of it lies beyond federal reach. . . . It stands as a source of internal bureaucratic opposition."[31]

In fact, despite his election mandate to limit government and roll back the welfare system, Reagan did back down on several proposed welfare cutbacks in the face of public and congressional resistance. While funding for AFDC declined by 1 percent and food stamp spending by 4 percent throughout his two terms as president, welfare spending grew from $199 billion to $230 billion, and the budget for the WIC supplemental food program increased by 58 percent. The cost of the Earned Income Tax Credit more than doubled, rising by 102 percent.[32] Congress did try to make the welfare system more uniform. In 1984, federal law required states to provide benefits to the second parent in families with an incapacitated or unemployed parent; AFDC-UP, or aid to families of the unemployed, would become mandatory in 1990.

The issue of Social Security's finances, in the meantime, remained at the political front and center, challenging the depression-era system of a mandated, publicly financed social welfare system. With the gradual aging of the working population, and in particular the baby boom generation's approach to retirement, Social Security was headed for financial trouble. By the 1980s, some estimates predicted that the amount of payroll taxes paid in were not going to match the rising amount of benefits paid out. The problem was compounded by the fact that Social Security surpluses were being used for the government's general expenditures and not being saved. In 1983, Congress reached a consensus reform of Social Security. The amendments delayed a cost-of-living adjustment, began taxing Social Security benefits for higher-income beneficiaries, accelerated payroll tax increases, and began a gradual rise in the retirement age, from 65 to 67.

The Social Security Administration took steps on its own, encouraged by the new administration's emphasis on spending cuts. The SSA reviewed its disability cases and, in those cases where the medical record showed only that a person was able to work—and not necessarily any medical improvement—it simply dropped the beneficiary from the roll. Many of these beneficiaries appealed their cases before administrative law judges and federal courts, which overturned more than 50 percent of the SSA review decisions by 1984.[33] A public outcry ensued as disabled beneficiaries won popular support against the review process. By the 1984 Disability Reform Act, passed unanimously in both houses of Congress, the standard of review was returned to its previous status—the SSA would have to show medical improvement in order to drop a disabled beneficiary.

## WELFARE DEBATES

The issues of welfare fraud and abuse of the Social Security disability system gained the spotlight during the 1980s and early 1990s. Critics of SSI disability pointed out that drug and alcohol abuse qualified as a disabling condition. Such vices, said these critics, should not be rewarded with government benefit checks, regardless of accompanying factors such as mental illness, homelessness, and joblessness. Much later, in 1996, Congress agreed, cutting all SSI, Medicare, and Medicaid benefits to this category.

Another issue of prime importance to the welfare reform movement was fraud by families, specifically those with children. In 1985, the Supreme Court had decided in *Sullivan v. Zebley* that Social Security could apply adult "functional capacity assessments" to children to determine their eligibility (which previously had only been determined by medical condition). The result of this decision was the payment of back benefits to 141,000 newly eligible children and an increase in the SSI rolls. In addition, in 1990 Social Security further increased the number of mental, physical, and behavioral problems that made children eligible for SSI benefits.

Critics saw the SSI program spiraling out of control, rewarding parents for the disabilities of their children. They pointed out that SSI payments were intended to replace lost employment income, which—by law—children could not earn. Medicaid, in this view, was the appropriate vehicle for children's medical and disability benefits. Supporters of SSI benefits claimed that disabled children cost their parents income through the higher expenses of medical care, nursing, prescription drugs, and the like, and they argued that the point of the SSI program was to support needy families, not just individual wage earners.

Authors and researchers argued for the elimination of the entire system. One of the most prominent critics of welfare, author Charles Murray, insisted in his book *Losing Ground* that welfare only exacerbated the problems it was meant to solve. Murray believed that welfare benefits should be ended completely:

> *The first effect of the new rules was to make it profitable for the poor to behave in the short term in ways that were destructive in the long term. Their second effect was to mask these long-term losses—to subsidize irretrievable mistakes. We tried to provide more for the poor and produced more poor instead. We tried to remove the barriers to escape from poverty, and inadvertently built a trap.*[34]

A conservative alternative to the situation was suggested by columnist George Will in his book *Statecraft as Soulcraft:*

# Welfare and Welfare Reform

*A welfare state run on conservative principles will provide the poor with cash to buy necessities from the private sector, thereby reducing the need for an enormous social service bureaucracy. And a conservative welfare state will provide incentives—such as deductions from taxes for medical-insurance premiums—to cause the private sector to weave much of the net of security that people demand in every developed, industrial society.[35]*

The Family Support Act, passed in 1988, was an attempt to make "supported work programs" the new foundation of the welfare system. The Job Opportunities and Basic Skills Training Program (JOBS), the centerpiece of that legislation, required the states to establish job training and job-search programs and allowed the states to mandate that welfare recipients take part. Some recipients were also required to perform community service jobs before they could receive welfare benefits. The Family Support Act also enhanced child-support enforcement and provided health care for mothers enrolled in the job programs. Most important for the future of the welfare system, the bill provided funding for experimental programs by the states.

The Family Support Act was unsuccessful, however, in its stated mission of replacing welfare benefits with job training programs. Funding was inadequate, and many states lacked the will or the means to follow the federal guidelines. Several states, however, made innovations that would eventually be taken up as federal law in the 1990s. Challenged to respond with local solutions to local economic problems, Governor Tommy Thompson of Wisconsin and others created new structures and procedures that required work; set time limits; and virtually replaced the simple, federally funded handouts that by then had such a bad reputation.

The new buzzword for Thompson and other governors, including Bill Clinton of Arkansas, was "comprehensive." For Clinton, running for president as a "New Democrat" in 1992, the Family Support Act was a start to a sweeping change of economic policy that would "end welfare as we know it." His vision of comprehensive reform included a raise in the minimum wage, expansion of the Earned Income Tax Credit, expanded child-care and Medicare benefits for those leaving the welfare system, wage garnishment for child support, job training, education, and a "two years and out" policy. This last measure would end benefits for those born after 1972 and require them to go into job placement, training, or education, with public-sector and community service jobs serving as a last-resort alternative to welfare benefits.

In 1992, Clinton was elected president. Early in his first term, the administration approved changes in the states' welfare requirements, including the provision of workfare and time limits for receiving benefits. Clinton proposed, and Congress passed, an expanded Earned Income Tax Credit, the provision of tax credits to defray child-care costs, health insurance for children of low-income families, and a raise in the minimum wage. With these measures, the Clinton administration returned the government to a more active role in providing for social welfare.

But the key early priority of the Clinton administration was a reform of the nation's health care system. The administration set up a task force, headed by Hillary Clinton, which proposed a sweeping change in the way health insurance would function. The National Health Security Plan, unveiled in September 1993, would mandate health insurance coverage for everyone, requiring employers to provide it through health maintenance organizations (HMOs), whose rates and benefits would be regulated by federal law. The plan was a compromise between a single-payer system, in which the government would control and operate the health insurance system, and a free-market solution, in which health care would become more efficient through increased competition and the federal treasury would save money through a rollback of Medicare and Medicaid.

The compromise failed to convince critics from both sides or win over the general public. The Clinton plan ended up in the legislative scrap heap, and in the elections of 1994, Clinton's opponents in the Republican Party took control of Congress. In the meantime, Clinton did succeed in expanding the Earned Income Tax Credit, granting tax credits to families spending money on child care, and increasing the minimum wage, from $4.25 per hour to $4.75 per hour beginning in 1996 and $5.15 per hour in 1997.

With health care issues set aside as too politically troublesome and the administration still determined on a legislative agenda of reform and efficiency, the welfare system arrived on the table. The higher incidence of fraud in the Food Stamp Program made it the easiest welfare issue to bring to a compromise on reform. Congress proposed ending federally determined eligibility for the program, capping its cost, and gathering all federal money for the program into block grants to be turned over to the states to administer. The president opposed the idea of ending federal eligibility standards as well as using block grants, but he did agree to a cut in food stamp spending and work requirements in the reform bill of 1996.

A thornier issue was AFDC. By the early 1990s, the AFDC program was enrolling some 14 million people, including 9 million children. The program was costing about $22 billion per year, about 1 percent of the federal budget.

Clinton released his welfare reform plan in June 1994. The plan set a two-year time limit for receiving welfare benefits. Welfare recipients would take part in job training and/or education and at the end of the two years would either find private-sector jobs or be placed in community service jobs funded by the states, for an indefinite period of time. The proposal included higher spending for child care, tougher child support enforcement, and a requirement that unwed teenage mothers be required to live with their parents.

# THE 1996 WELFARE REFORM

The Republican Party responded to the Clinton plan with the Contract with America, the centerpiece of their campaign to win back Congress in 1994. As part of the contract, the Republicans promised the Personal Responsibility Act, an overhaul of the welfare system that would return its management, and funding in the form of block grants, to the states. The block grants would, in effect, end welfare as an entitlement program; spending on welfare would no longer rise with the number of people eligible to receive benefits. Republicans stated that their intention was to "discourage illegitimacy and teen pregnancy by prohibiting welfare to minor mothers and denying increased AFDC for additional children while on welfare, cut spending for welfare programs, and enact a tough two-years-and-out provision with work requirements to promote individual responsibility."[36]

The Republicans also campaigned on an end to the AFDC program, an end to federal mandates for school lunches, and the founding of orphanages to care for children of dysfunctional families. This latter proposal earned derision from the Clinton administration but, in hindsight, won support from the *National Review* in an editorial of December 2004:

> *The emerging consensus is that social policy has ignored the developmental needs of children. The safety net has been woven to support single mothers. But children need more than a family-assistance check if they are to escape joining the next generation of the hopeless. "Governments don't raise children," President Clinton said, "parents do." But if the parent is a teenage drug addict whose boyfriend beats her children, then she is not raising them to anything but woe, and an institution becomes a desirable alternative.[37]*

Finally, Republican candidates also ran against the effort on the part of the administration to reform the health care system. In the 1994 elections, welfare reform proved a winning issue for the Republicans, who won control of the House of Representatives for the first time since 1954. When the 104th Congress began in early 1995, both sides were pledging to address the issue, and welfare reform was ripe for a legislative compromise.

In 1995, AFDC, food stamps, and Supplemental Security Income amounted to 4.4 percent of the federal budget: 14 million people were receiving AFDC benefits, 27 million food stamps, and 6.5 million SSI.[38] The Republican-inspired welfare reform bill first passed the House of Representatives and then was changed in the Senate, which added a "maintenance of effort" requirement that required states to maintain at least 80 percent of their welfare spending; a child-care program was also added to the bill. Clinton vetoed the bill, however, and offered a compromise, which would allow the block grants but also increase funding for child-care and job-training programs.

In 1996, after years of debate, Congress passed the Personal Responsibility and Work Opportunity Reconciliation Act. This law repealed Title IV of the original Social Security Act. The stated intentions of the bill were to end dependence on welfare and to support innovation by the states in order to better tailor welfare programs to local needs. AFDC came to an end, replaced by a new program known as Temporary Assistance to Needy Families (TANF).

The federal government also began to shift the financial burden to the states. Entitlement to federal welfare benefits ended: All payments were made from state treasuries, with the federal contribution varying with a number of factors. The benefits were limited to a total of 60 months over the lifetime of the beneficiary, which could accumulate over separate periods of time. Benefits were denied to anyone convicted of a drug felony, and to teenaged parents not living under adult supervision. Welfare fraud was also addressed with a provision denying benefits for 10 years to anyone convicted of welfare fraud in two or more states. Any noncitizen arriving in the United States after the bill's passage in 1996 was also denied welfare benefits.

The states were required to enforce basic eligibility guidelines set down by the federal government. Each state had the power to set up its own guidelines, as well; in general, that meant that states with varying economic conditions and wage levels were free to set the income and asset level above which welfare would not be paid. The law required the states to file details of their benefit levels and eligibility standards with the Department of Health and Human Services and also to explain how their appeals process would operate.

The bill set a goal that one quarter of welfare beneficiaries would be working or in job training by 1997 and one half of them achieving this by 2002. States were granted lump sums to fund their welfare programs; the federal guarantee of cash assistance for poor children ended. A lifetime time limit of five years was placed on welfare benefits, with heads of welfare families required to find work within two years of receiving benefits. The SSI program was also subject to stricter eligibility standards.

Although the law was passed with the express purpose of reining in welfare spending, the U.S. welfare state—at least in comparison to Europe—remained limited in scope. In contrast to a common provision of the European "welfare state," there were no family allowances in the United States. There were fewer publicly supported job training programs. Budgets for welfare and Social Security payments were smaller. There was less public spending on retirement pensions, comparatively little public housing, and no national health insurance.

The issue gained importance in the first years of the 21st century. Health costs were rising, as was the cost of insurance. Uninsured families depended on Medicaid (the federal "payer of last resort") and visits to hospital emergency rooms when in need of ordinary medical care. The public costs of operating municipal hospitals and clinics were threatening to break the budgets in several states, as was the public provision of health care to uninsured, "undocumented" immigrants.

President Clinton returned to the issue in 2000, the last year of his presidency. His new proposal aimed to provide assistance to low-income families for health insurance, enroll children in state insurance programs funded by federal block grants, and extend insurance to adults who had been disqualified by private insurers. Meanwhile, presidential candidates George W. Bush and Al Gore proposed prescription drug programs and changes in the Medicare system. While Gore favored an expanded role for the federal government, Bush relied on tax incentives to boost the use of private sector insurance and also favored privatization of the Social Security system.

## REAUTHORIZATION

The welfare reform law expired after its initial five years and must be regularly reauthorized by the U.S. Congress. The law went through a series of temporary extensions before full reauthorization was achieved within the Deficit Reduction Act of 2005, which was signed into law in July 2006. This reauthorization went into effect on October 1, 2006, and extends the law until another expiration date in 2010.

The law now requires a higher percentage of TANF recipients to be participating in work activities, in order for states to be paid their due amounts of grants from the federal government. At least 50 percent of all adults receiving TANF assistance, and 90 percent of two-parent households, must now be participating in work-related activities.

To count toward work participation under TANF, a single-parent family with a child under six must be active in work-related activities for an average of 20 hours a week. Other single-parent families must be active for an average of 30 hours per week. For two-earner households, a family not receiving federally funded child care must be active for 35 hours a week; a family receiving federally funded child care must be active for 55 hours a week.

Work-related activities as defined by the TANF provisions include:

- Unsubsidized employment
- Subsidized private-sector employment

- Subsidized public-sector employment
- Work experience (such as internships)
- On-the-job training
- Job search and job readiness assistance, up to six weeks a year
- Community service programs
- Vocational educational training, for up to 12 months
- Child-care services for an individual who is participating in a community-service program.

After a TANF family has attained 20 hours per week of these nine "core activities," the state may also count the following "noncore" activities:

- Job skills training related to employment
- Education related to employment
- Attendance at secondary school or a GED (general equivalency diploma) course.

The requirements for work-participation rates are lower for states that lessen their caseloads below their 2005 levels. (Previously, the law considered the caseload level before 1995 in making this adjustment.) If the caseload has fallen 5 percent, for example, then its work participation requirement also falls 5 percent. But the cause of a caseload decline is key. Caseload decline is to come strictly from welfare leavers who have found employment or who have reached their (60-month) time limit. The state may not register caseload declines that result from stricter income and resource (savings) requirements, from time limits, from sanctions for not maintaining a "full family," for new enforcement methods, or for new methods of verifying a recipient's family status, income, and so on.

In addition, the law specifies that a state's "participation-rate calculation" is based on the combined number of families receiving assistance in TANF and state-funded programs that count toward the state's maintenance-of-effort (MOE) requirement. Previously, MOE programs funded by the states did not count toward work participation rates. Finally, to encourage compliance with Department of Health and Human Services guidelines for reporting and verifying work participation by TANF recipients, the law penalizes states up to 5 percent of their grants if they do not adopt the guidelines.[39]

## IMMIGRATION AND WELFARE REFORM

The general consensus among researchers is that the welfare reform of 1996 has been successful in lowering caseloads and getting welfare recipients into the workforce. Employment rates for single mothers, in particular, have increased, although they fell in the recession that began in 2000. In the first few years of the welfare reform era, there were declines in the number of TANF recipients in nearly all the states. In 1993, there were 14.1 million AFDC recipients; in March 1999, the federal government was counting 7.3 million TANF recipients. The percentage of the population receiving benefits had fallen from 5.5 percent to 2.6 percent.[40]

Over the same period, job participation by former welfare recipients rose. Many of the jobs found by welfare leavers, however, were low-wage positions that held little opportunity for advancement. In addition, mental health, drug addiction, and domestic violence continued to cause family disruption and bring new recipients into the welfare programs.

A controversy has also arisen surrounding the use of welfare benefits by immigrants, both legal and illegal. Welfare reform was being debated during the 1990s, just as immigration levels were rising sharply to rates not seen since the years before World War I—rates that represent the high tide of European immigration to the United States. Prompted by poverty in their home countries and a porous border between the United States and Mexico, illegal immigrants were flooding into the country from Latin America. Once arrived, they joined an "underground" economy dependent on low-wage illegal employment, in which workers lacked the Social Security and unemployment insurance—as well as health care benefits—normally granted to legal employees. Opposition to the use of welfare benefits by immigrants was a popular cause for Republicans and was ultimately reflected in the final version of the 1996 welfare reform bill.

One view of immigration honored new arrivals as a vital mainstay of American history. Seeking a new life in a land of opportunity, immigrants had left behind their homes and in many cases their families. They arrived to work, save money, and establish themselves as American citizens. They assimilated American culture, learned the English language, and gave their children a chance at the comforts and privileges of the middle class.

In reality, this classical view of immigration was never completely accepted—hostility to immigrants is a tradition going back to the early 19th century and the migration of Catholics into a largely Protestant nation. In the early 20th century, scholars and politicians railed against less-desirable southern Europeans. An important ingredient of this hostility was the view that immigrants were unskilled laborers who were stealing jobs from ordinary citizens and were likely to become a burden on public charities.

In the 1990s, author Georg Borjas supported the notion that the new wave of immigration was degrading wages and working standards for legal immigrants and citizens. In his article "New Economics of Immigration: Affluent Americans Gain, Poor Americans Lose," published in 1996, he maintained that immigrants were less skilled than previous arrivals and more likely to receive welfare benefits, causing a cultural and economic rift among members of the working class:

> *The new immigrants are more likely to receive welfare assistance than earlier immigrants, and also more likely to do so than natives: 21 percent of immigrant households participate in some means-tested social-assistance program (such as cash benefits, Medicaid, or food stamps), as compared with 14 percent of native households. The increasing welfare dependency in the immigrant population suggests that immigration may create a substantial fiscal burden on the most-affected localities and states.[41]*

One month after passage of the welfare reform bill, the Immigration Reform Act of 1996 went into effect. Both new federal laws introduced new restrictions on use of welfare benefits by immigrants—legal and illegal. The 1996 welfare reform law denied welfare benefits to immigrants (who had arrived before enactment of the law) during their first five years of residence in the United States. It also restricted eligibility for benefits by legal residents (those holding "green-card" permanent residency). The law enforced the "affidavit of support" feature of immigration, making sponsors of immigrants legally liable for those who became a "public charge" as determined by the Immigration and Naturalization Service (now the United States Citizenship and Immigration Service). The fear of deportation as a result of this public-charge determination prompted a wave of new citizenship applications on the part of legal permanent residents.

The law gave states the option to use federal funds for "pre-enactment" immigrants, and it required states to provide Social Security insurance and food stamps benefits for children, the elderly, and disabled immigrants. The states also have the option to provide benefits to "post-enactment" immigrants after five years of residency; to receive SSI and food stamps, post-enactment immigrants must become U.S. citizens.

The law set up two broad categories of "qualified" and "unqualified" immigrants. Qualified immigrants enjoy greater access to welfare benefits; this category includes lawful permanent residents, refugees (admitted under the U.S. Refugee Act of 1980), battered spouses and children, and members of the armed forces. Unqualified immigrants include everyone else: "undocumented" aliens, temporary residents (students, tourists, temporary foreign employees, and so on), and those applying for political asylum or status as a refugee.

Audrey Singer, in "Welfare Reform and Immigrants: A Policy Review," summed up the effect of the welfare reform law on immigration policy:

> *When welfare reform was debated prior to the passage of PRWORA, policy makers were motivated by the immense savings that would be had by excluding noncitizens from participation in all federal means-tested benefits. The welfare*

*law was projected to save the federal government $54.1 billion over six years. The largest savings—$23.8 billion or 44 percent of the net savings—was to come from slashing benefits to legal permanent residents (green card holders). . . . From the immigrant point of view, the passage of PROWRA and the anti-immigrant debates leading up to its enactment signaled a formalized complaint against immigrants. This exclusion—government sponsored—hastened a climate of confusion and fear within immigrant communities that had sweeping effects on immigrant behavior, including the use of benefits as well as migration and naturalization.[42]*

Ten years after its passage, the 1996 welfare reform law achieved general support and a consensus of its overall success. The issue of immigration continued to divide lawmakers, however, as the population of undocumented (illegal) immigrants continued to rise in the first years of the 21st century. In 2007, President Bush sponsored a new law that represented an attempt at legislating a "path to citizenship," but it was derailed by opponents determined to block any legal status for undocumented workers. The key issue, once again, was the public cost of social benefits such as medical care and income supports, while the post-9/11 issues of public safety and the threat of terrorism carried across the U.S. borders reinforced critics' resistance.

---

[1] Dorothy Marshall, *The English Poor in the Eighteenth Century: A Study in Social and Administrative History.* London: George Routledge and Sons, 1926, p. 17.

[2] Dave Hage, *Reforming Welfare by Rewarding Work: One State's Successful Experiment.* Minneapolis: University of Minnesota Press, 2004, pp. xi–xii.

[3] Frederic Cople Jaher, *The Urban Establishment: Upper Strata in Boston, New York, Charleston, Chicago, and Los Angeles.* Champaign: University of Illinois Press, 1982.

[4] Charles Warren, *Congress as Santa Claus: The Welfare Clause of the Constitution* (reprint). New York: Arno, 1978, pp. 62–63.

[5] John Iceland, *Poverty in America: A Handbook.* Berkeley, Calif.: University of California Press, 2003, p. 12.

[6] Jane Addams, *Twenty Years at Hull-House.* New York: Macmillan, 1963, p. 72.

[7] David T. Burbank, *The Reign of the Rabble: The St. Louis General Strike of 1877.* New York: A. M. Kelley, 1966, p. 4.

[8] Michael Kronenwetter, *Welfare State America: Safety Net or Social Contract?* New York: Franklin Watts, p. 36.

[9] Kronenwetter, *Welfare State America*, p. 36.

[10] Sylvester Schieber, *The Real Deal: The History and Future of Social Security.* New Haven, Conn.: Yale University Press, 1999, p. 18.

[11] Huey P. Long, "Every Man a King," American Rhetoric: Top 100 Speeches. Available online. URL: http://www.americanrhetoric.com/speeches/hueyplongking.htm. Accessed on August 22, 2007.

[12] Schieber, *The Real Deal*, p. 23.

[13] Franklin Roosevelt, "State of the Union 1935," From Revolution to Reconstruction: An. HTML Project, University of Groningen, Netherlands. Available online. URL: http://www.let.rug.nl/usa/P/fr32/speeches/su35fdr.htm. Accessed on March 31, 2008.

[14] Roosevelt, "State of the Union 1935."

[15] Roosevelt, "State of the Union 1935."

[16] T. H. Watkins, *The Hungry Years: A Narrative History of the Great Depression in America*. New York: Henry Holt and Company, 1999, p. 259.

[17] John Gunther, *Roosevelt in Retrospect: A Profile in History*. New York: Harper, 1950, p. 286.

[18] *United States v. Butler*. Available online. vLex. URL: http://vlex.us/vid/20017958. Accessed on February 7, 2008.

[19] Larry Witt, "The 1937 Supreme Court Rulings on the Social Security Act," Social Security Online. Available online. URL: http://www.ssa.gove/history/court.html. Accessed on August 22, 2007.

[20] *Steward Machine Company v. Davis*. Justia.com. Available online. URL: http://supreme.justia.com/us/301/548/case.html. Accessed on August 22, 2007.

[21] Michael Tanner, *The Poverty of Welfare: Helping Others in a Civil Society*. Washington, D.C.: The Cato Institute, 2003, p. 25.

[22] Gordon W. Gunderson, "The National School Lunch Program: Background and Development," United States Department of Agriculture Food and Nutrition Service. Available online. URL: http://www.fns.usda.gov/cnd/lunch/AboutLunch/ProgramHistory_5.htm. Accessed on August 22, 2007.

[23] Michael B. Katz, *The Price of Citizenship*. New York: Henry Holt, 2001, p. 7.

[24] Lyndon B. Johnson, "Great Society Speech." Cold War: Historical Documents, Episode 13: Make Love, Not War. Available online. URL: http://www.cnn.com/SPECIALS/cold.war/episodes/13/documents/lbj/. Accessed on August 22, 2007.

[25] Ronald Reagan, "A Time for Choosing." Ronald Reagan Presidential Library. Available online. URL: http://www.reagan.utexas.edu/archives/reference/timechoosing.html. Accessed on August 22, 2007.

[26] Daniel Patrick Moynihan, "The Negro Family: The Case for National Action." Available online. URL: www.dol.gov/oasam/programs/history/webid-meynihan.htm. Accessed on September 11, 2007.

[27] Joe R. Feagin, *Subordinating the Poor: Welfare and American Beliefs*. Englewood Cliffs, N.J.: Prentice Hall, 1975, p. 7.

[28] Daniel Patrick Moynihan, *The Politics of a Guaranteed Income: The Nixon Administration and the Family Assistance Plan*. New York: Vintage Books, 1973, p. 545.

[29] James T. Patterson, *Restless Giant: The United States from Watergate to Bush v. Gore*. New York: Oxford University Press, 2007, p. 49.

[30] Patterson, *Restless Giant*, p. 49.

[31] Michael B. Katz, *In the Shadow of the Poorhouse: A Social History of Welfare in America*. New York: Basic Books, 1996, p. 300.

[32] Tanner, *The Poverty of Welfare*, p. 29.

[33] Katz, *The Price of Citizenship*, p. 215.

[34] Charles Murray, *Losing Ground: American Social Policy 1950–1980*. New York: Basic Books, 1994, p. 9.

[35] George Will, *Statecraft as Soulcraft: What Government Does*. New York: Touchstone Books, 2002, p. 129.

[36] "Republican Contract with America," U.S. House of Representatives. Available online. URL: http://www.house.gov/house/Contract/CONTRACT.html. Accessed on August 23, 2007.

[37] "Scrooge Redivivus? Newt Gingrich's Call for Public Orphanages," *National Review*, December 31, 1994. Available online. URL: http://www.findarticles.com/p/articles/mi_m1282/is_n25_v46/ai_16388625. Accessed on September 11, 2007.

[38] Katz, *The Price of Citizenship*, p. 11.

[39] Center on Budget and Policy Priorities, "Changes to TANF Requirements Under the Deficit Reduction Act." Available online. URL: http://www.cbpp.org/5–9–06tanf-chap1.pdf. Accessed on February 7, 2008.

[40] Harrell R. Rodgers, *American Poverty in a New Era of Reform*. Armonk, N.Y.: M. E. Sharpe, 2000, p. 178.

[41] George J. Borjas, "New Economics of Immigration: Affluent Americans Gain; Poor Americans Lose," *Atlantic Monthly*, November 1996, p. 72.

[42] Audrey Singer, *Immigrants, Welfare Reform, and the Poverty of Policy*. Westport, Conn.: Praeger, 2004, p. 25.

# CHAPTER 2

---

# THE LAW OF WELFARE AND WELFARE REFORM

## LAWS AND REGULATIONS

President Franklin Roosevelt sent a message to Congress on June 8, 1934, urging the legislature to create a system to provide "security against several of the great disturbing factors of life. Fear and worry based on unknown danger contribute to social unrest and economic demoralization. If, as our Constitution tells us, our Federal Government was established among other things, 'to promote the general welfare,' it is our plain duty to provide for that security upon which welfare depends."[1] The president then created a Committee on Economic Security and asked it to come up with a workable plan for social security.

### THE SOCIAL SECURITY ACT OF 1935

The Committee on Economic Security was headed by Edwin Witte, an economist from Wisconsin. The group finalized its plan in January 1935, and its recommendations were sent to Congress. The bill was introduced by Robert F. Wagner of New York in the Senate and David Lewis of Maryland in the House of Representatives. The Social Security Act passed by a vote of 371 to 33 in the House and by 77 to 6 in the Senate, and it was signed into law on August 14, 1935. It is now officially titled Chapter 7 of Title 42 of the United States Code and is cited in court proceedings as 42 U.S.C. §301–§1397.

The introduction to the bill states that it would serve as "an act to provide for the general welfare by establishing a system of Federal old-age benefits, and by enabling the several States to make more adequate provision for aged persons, blind persons, dependent and crippled children, maternal and child welfare, public health, and the administration of their unemployment compensation laws; to establish a Social Security Board; to raise revenue; and for other purposes."[2]

# Welfare and Welfare Reform

The Social Security Act was divided by Titles, as follows:

| | |
|---|---|
| Title I | Grants to States for Old-Age Assistance for the Aged |
| Title II | Federal Old-Age, Survivors, and Disability Insurance Benefits |
| Title III | Grants to States for Unemployment Compensation Administration |
| Title IV | Grants to States for Aid and Services to Needy Families with Children and for Child-Welfare Services (ADC) |
| Title V | Maternal and Child Health Services Block Grant |
| Title VI | Temporary State Fiscal Relief |
| Title VII | Administration |
| Title VIII | Special Benefits for Certain World War II Veterans |
| Title IX | Miscellaneous Provisions Relating to Employment Security |
| Title X | Grants to States for Aid to the Blind |
| Title XI | General Provisions, Peer Review, and Administrative Simplification |
| Title XII | Advances to State Unemployment Funds |
| Title XIII | Reconversion Unemployment Benefits for Seamen (Repealed) |
| Title XIV | Grants to States for Aid to the Permanently and Totally Disabled |
| Title XV | Unemployment Compensation for Federal Employees (Repealed) |
| Title XVI | Grants to States for Aid to the Aged, Blind, or Disabled |

The law set out the initial appropriations for the fiscal year ending June 30, 1936, for unemployment compensation (in the amount of $4 million); for aid to needy dependent children (in the amount of $24,750,000); for maternal and child health services (in the amount of $3,800,000); for crippled children (in the amount of $2,850,000); for vocational rehabilitation (in the amount of $841,000) and for aid to the blind (in the amount of $3 million).

In order to win their appropriations, the states had to submit plans that would pass review by the Social Security Board. In the case of aid to dependent children, for example, the law set out the following requirements for states:

*A State plan for aid to dependent children must (1) provide that it shall be in effect in all political subdivisions of the State, and, if administered by them, be mandatory upon them; (2) provide for financial participation by the State; (3) either provide for the establishment or designation of a single State agency to administer the plan, or provide for the establishment or designation of a single State agency to supervise the administration of the plan; (4) provide for granting to any individual, whose claim with respect to aid to a dependent child is denied, an opportunity for a fair hearing before such State agency; (5) provide such methods of administration (other than those relating to selection, tenure of office, and compensation of personnel) as are found by the Board to be necessary for the efficient operation of the plan; and (6) provide that the State agency will make such reports, in such form and containing such information, as the Board may from time to time require, and comply with such provisions as the Board may from time to time find necessary to assure the correctness and verification of such reports.*

> *The Board shall approve any plan which fulfills the conditions specified in subsection (a) except that it shall not approve any plan which imposes as a condition of eligibility for aid to dependent children, a residence requirement which denies aid with respect to any child residing in the State (1) who has resided in the State for one year immediately preceding the application for such aid or (2) who was born within the State within one year immediately preceding the application, if its mother has resided in the State for one year immediately preceding the birth.*

The Social Security Act defined dependent child as "a child under the age of sixteen who has been deprived of parental support or care by reason of the death, continued absence from the home, or physical or mental incapacity of a parent, and who is living with his father, mother, grandfather, grandmother, brother, sister, stepfather, stepmother, stepbrother, stepsister, uncle, or aunt, in a place of residence maintained by one or more of such relatives as his or their own home."[3]

The federal government began collecting payroll taxes to finance Social Security in 1937. In that year, the first benefits were paid. In the meantime, the Social Security Act had weathered a serious legal challenge. Roosevelt had recently suffered a series of reverses on New Deal legislation, including a Supreme Court decision that struck down the Railroad Retirement Act in 1935 and soon afterward the National Industrial Recovery Act.

In response, Roosevelt proposed a new federal law that would give the president authority to force the retirement of judges at least 70 years of age. His threat to "pack the court" with his political allies convinced the Supreme Court to uphold the Social Security Act against its first and only significant legal challenges in the cases of *Steward Machine Company v. Davis* and *Helvering v. Davis*, both of which were decided on May 24, 1937. Payroll taxes were first collected and benefits first paid in 1937.

The original Social Security Act provided only retirement benefits, and only to the worker. The 1939 amendments greatly expanded the scope of the Social Security system. The new law allowed for "dependents' benefits," paid to the spouse and minor children of a retiree, as well as "survivors' benefits," which were paid to the family on the death of an eligible worker before retirement. Some medical costs incurred after retirement were also covered. Benefit amounts were increased, and the law brought forward the start of monthly benefit payments from 1942 to 1940.[4]

## WELFARE ADMINISTRATION

The Social Security Act decreed that the government make rules for the efficient administration of the Aid to Dependent Children (ADC) program. The Social Security Board issued "state letters," in which the act was interpreted for the state lawmakers and administrators. As far as benefit levels went, the states were required to establish a "standard of need," or a minimum monthly amount required for basic food, shelter, and clothing. They also had to set limits on the possession of property (such as savings and real estate) and rules on the treatment of earned or unearned income.

The federal payments of $6 per first child and $4 for subsequent children gradually rose, with the rate depending on the average spending of the recipient. In 1956, Congress established variable matching rates, and federal contributions rose faster in states with a lower per-capita income. In 1965 (by which time the ADC program had been renamed Aid to Families with Dependent Children, or AFDC), the federal government was matching AFDC spending by the states dollar for dollar, and the states had the option of adopting Medicaid and its new payment system. In this system, matching rates rose as state per-capita incomes fell. It set a floor on matching aid at 50 percent of the state payments, while the ceiling was set at 83 percent.

As a result, the benefit levels in the individual states diverged over time. By the 1970s, with the rise in the costs of living, it was common for the states to be paying out a certain percentage of the standard of need in order to save their welfare budgets, which were set at whatever level the state legislatures might approve.

Eligibility standards varied through the years as well. At first, children were eligible for ADC payments only through age 15. In 1940, children 16 and 17 became eligible, as long as they were attending school; this expanded to age 20 in 1964. Eligible education then included high school or vocational training, and in 1965, it broadened to include a college or university. The eligibility age dropped to 17 in 1981, although states had the option of extending eligibility to high school students through age 18.

The law also allowed AFDC recipients to receive food stamps. The Agriculture and Consumer Protection Act, passed in 1971, required the Food Stamp Program to be administered in all states in 1974. The states counted AFDC benefits as income in determining the amount of food stamps available to the family; extra AFDC income brought a reduction in food stamps. When AFDC benefits fell (through a penalty or some benefit adjustment rule), the family was eligible for more food stamps.

Beginning in 1952, the welfare system was also made an instrument of child-support enforcement. By the Notification to Law Enforcement Officials (NOLEO) of that year, which amended AFDC, states were required to notify law enforcement of the payment of any benefits to an abandoned child. In 1967, Congress required the states to begin locating absent parents and forcing them to pay support to their children. A "parent locator" program required the states to furnish any information on absent parents to the Department of Health, Education and Welfare, which would assist in locating the parents by requesting information from the Internal Revenue Service. Another such change to AFDC, the Child Support Enforcement program, was part of amendments to the Social Security Act passed in 1975. In order to become eligible for AFDC payments, applicants had to assign their rights to child support to the state and to cooperate in establishing the paternity of a child born out of wedlock. This meant that child support payments for children in AFDC went through the child-support enforcement agency, rather than directly to the family. Child support payments often put families above the eligibility threshold for AFDC, and the Child Support Enforcement program allowed the states to reduce AFDC payments to families receiving child support.

## WORK INCENTIVES

Federal law changed in the 1960s to introduce work incentives into the AFDC program. In 1961, Congress required the states to deny assistance to families if an unemployed parent refused to accept work without good cause. In 1962, Congress authorized funds for Community Work and Training programs for AFDC recipients 18 and older.

Job training became required in 1968 with the Work Incentive programs. These were training programs administered by the state welfare agencies for AFDC recipients, and all unemployed fathers receiving AFDC had to take part. In this program, Congress provided incentives in the form of "income disregards." That is, the program disregarded a portion of any earned income (the first $30 of any income plus one third of the remaining income) for the purpose of calculating a family's income and its benefit level. In 1981, this income disregard was limited to the first four months of employment, and a limit was set on gross income, which was not to exceed 150 percent of the "standard of need." Congress granted the states the authority to establish their own welfare-to-work programs and authorized funding for job search programs.

The Family Support Act of 1988 initiated the Job Opportunities and Basic Skills Training Program (JOBS), which became Title IV-F of the Social Security Act. To comply with this legislation, all states had to enroll mothers with no child younger than age three in education or job training. To support the new requirements, Congress increased funding for the welfare-to-work programs, but it also required the states to provide benefits to families of unemployed parents.

## THE WELFARE REFORM LAW

The Personal Responsibility and Work Opportunity Reconciliation Act of 1996 (Public Law 104–193) was signed into law on August 22, 1996. It included provisions that added funding for new initiatives as well as measures that cut funding for certain existing programs. The law's most important change was an end to cash welfare payments under Title IV of the Social Security Act. It created two block grants to provide states with welfare funds. The first block grant was to provide cash and other benefits to needy families and to encourage the formation and maintenance of two-parent families. The second provided funds to the states for child care, intended for families receiving welfare benefits, those leaving welfare, and those whose low incomes put them in danger of needing welfare.

The 1996 welfare reform law limited welfare benefits that could be paid to several categories of recipients, including noncitizens, families that had received welfare benefits for more than five years, and children who were disabled as a result of "age-inappropriate" behavior. The law also outlined new policies aimed at reducing out-of-wedlock births, and it changed federal guidelines for child support enforcement by the states, the Food Stamp Program, and child nutrition programs. In essence, food stamps and Medicare remained federal entitlement programs, while AFDC ended and was replaced by a provisional welfare benefit, Temporary Assistance for Needy Families (TANF). TANF was to be partially funded by the federal government but administered by the states—and limited to no more than 60 months of payments in the lifetime of any recipient. That same year, Supplemental Security Income payments to drug addicts and alcoholics were ended as part of the Contract with America Advancement Act (Public Law 104–121). The welfare reform law allowed states a degree of discretion to extend benefit payments.

States could exempt up to 20 percent of their cases from the 60-month limit. But welfare payments were contingent upon a work requirement: All adults who had received welfare benefits for at least two years were required to participate in a work-related activity. The states could reduce this two-year limit; they also had discretion to determine what "work-related" activities were. Except for single parents of a child under age six, adults receiving benefits for two months who were not working had to participate in community-service employment, with hours and tasks to be set by the state.

To receive full federal funding, states were required to have one half of all their recipients in work programs for at least 30 hours a week. The federal government could also reduce block grants if a state failed either to provide data to the federal government, to ensure that funds were spent on children and families, to enforce penalties against those who did not cooperate in establishing paternity, or to maintain specified levels of state spending.

Spending on the TANF block grants was capped at $16.4 billion per year. Each year between 1996 and 2002, the basic block grants provided each state with whichever of three amounts was highest: the amount of federal money it had received for the four constituent programs in fiscal year 1995, the amount received in fiscal year 1994, or the average for fiscal years 1992 through 1994. To receive each year's full TANF block grant, a state had to spend in the previous year on behalf of TANF-eligible families a sum equal to 75 percent of state funds used in fiscal year 1994 on the replaced programs ("maintenance of effort"). If a state failed to meet the required work participation rates, its required "maintenance of effort" spending rose to 80 percent.[5]

The 1996 reforms increased the total amount for child-care block grants by $4 billion. But they ended the automatic entitlement of children to Supplemental Security Income under the "Individualized Functional Assessment" process. The new process was designed to detect whether or not children receiving SSI benefits had engaged in "age-inappropriate" behavior.

To discourage illegitimacy and promote two-parent families, the law required teen mothers to live at home or with a responsible adult and to attend school, and it earmarked federal funds for abstinence education. Unmarried mothers who did not help establish paternity of their children were subject to a 25 percent benefit reduction. The law also required the Department of Health and Human Services to rank the states on their reduction of nonmarital birth rates, and appropriated $1 billion over five years to provide performance bonuses to states that reduced the rates of nonmarital births and increased the number of two-parent families. A total of $400 million in bonus payments was made available to states that reduced their illegitimacy rates.

Reforms to child support enforcement included the automation of enforcement procedures and establishment of uniform tracking procedures. In addition, enforcement reforms strengthened interstate child support enforcement, required the states to adopt stronger measures to establish paternity, and created new and strong enforcement tools to increase actual child support collections.

The 1996 welfare reform law banned benefits to noncitizens and illegal aliens, including means-tested benefits. It made exceptions, however, for certain emergency benefits, work training programs, and benefits that promoted public health. In addition, military veterans and families with work histories of 10 years or more were exempted from the ban. The law earmarked some TANF funds for direct administration by Indian tribes and Native Alaskan organizations. It entitled Puerto Rico, Guam, and the Virgin Islands to TANF grants plus reimbursement (at a 75 percent rate) for welfare outlays above the federal block-grant level, but below new funding ceilings.

In all, the Personal Responsibility and Work Opportunity Act of 1996 cut $55 billion from low-income programs other than AFDC, including the

Food Stamp Program, the Supplemental Security Income program, and assistance to legal immigrants. The states could avail themselves of contingency funds in case of need, and the bill set aside $2 billion for this purpose. States were also permitted to divert federal TANF block-grant funds for other purposes. Under these welfare reform provisions, any family or category of families could be denied aid; in addition, states were free to shorten the five-year time limit for receiving aid for any reason. Unemployed persons between 18 and 50 without children were limited to three months of food stamps while unemployed in any three-year period.

## IMMIGRATION RESTRICTIONS

Welfare reform is generally regarded by lawmakers of both parties as a success. The most controversial aspect of the new law remains its restrictions on immigrant eligibility. Until the welfare reform law was passed in 1996, legal immigrants were eligible for the same levels of welfare benefits, and with the same eligibility requirements, as full citizens. The 1996 law made citizenship a condition of eligibility and put legal immigrants on the same footing as "undocumented" or illegal immigrants as far as welfare benefits went.

Political leaders on both sides of the welfare debate have criticized this controversial provision of welfare reform. In subsequent years, the law was amended to restore Supplemental Security Income (SSI) to immigrants who were in the country before the 1996 bill became law; in 1998, food stamps were restored for immigrant children, elderly, and disabled persons with the same status. Congress has gradually restored welfare eligibility on a limited basis to other selected segments of the immigrant population.

The eligibility of immigrants for welfare benefits varies with the specific program (TANF, job training, child support, and so on), and with the candidate's immigration status, age, state of residence, employment history, and date of arrival. Except for refugees, those granted political asylum, and victims of domestic violence, legal permanent residents remain, for the most part, ineligible for benefits. Once candidates have accrued 40 quarters of work, however, they become eligible for food stamps and SSI. (Citizenship also makes them eligible.) They must wait five years after entering the country before receiving TANF and Medicaid; states have the option of requiring 40 quarters of work or citizenship. Legal residents in the country before August 22, 1996, however, are eligible for SSI and, at the option of the states, for TANF and Medicaid; they are ineligible for food stamps unless they are disabled, age 65 or older on August 22, 1996, or have accrued 40 quarters of work.

The 1996 reforms also affected the law on "sponsor deeming" in welfare benefits. In the context of immigration, a sponsor is a person who petitions the U.S. Immigration and Naturalization Service (INS) to bring an alien into the United States. The income of a sponsor was counted in determining eligibility for aid for a certain period. After the law's enactment, sponsors for immigrants entering the United States after December 1997 have their income counted until the immigrant either becomes a full citizen or has worked for 40 quarters. The sponsor deeming now extends to Medicaid eligibility. The welfare reform law also limited the provision of state benefits, including nonemergency health care, to undocumented immigrants, unless the state passes a law that provides for such eligibility. In addition, state welfare employees cannot be prevented from reporting undocumented immigrants to the INS.

## THE AMENDMENTS OF 2005–2006

The most recent amendments to the welfare law were signed into effect in October 2006 as part of the Deficit Reduction Act of 2005. These moved the base year for caseload reduction credits to 2005 (it had previously been 1995). They also provided for $150 million in funding for "healthy marriage" educational programs, which can include up to $50 million for "responsible fatherhood" programs. The amendments increased childcare funding from $4.8 billion to $5 billion per year and provided for $2 billion of contingency funds to help maintain welfare programs during a recession. Under the 2005–06 provisions, states are allowed to exempt up to 20 percent of their cases from the five-year lifetime limit on TANF cash assistance.[6]

# COURT CASES

Modern welfare law has been subject to a myriad of court decisions regarding eligibility, restrictions, and benefit levels, with many decisions leading to U.S. Supreme Court cases based on the Fourteenth Amendment's due process and equal protection clauses. The basic constitutionality of the system was challenged soon after the passage of the Social Security Act in 1935, in the cases of *Steward Machine Company v. Davis* and *Helvering v. Davis.* Deciding both of these cases on the same day, the high court established the right of the federal government to collect revenues in the interest of "promoting the general welfare." The welfare laws are written and amended by Congress, but the welfare system has always been administered by the states. As a result, the courts have heard many cases relating to the legality of state guidelines regarding who may receive benefits and what the proper benefit levels are. Some of the more important court decisions follow.

## STEWARD MACHINE COMPANY V. DAVIS, 301 U.S. 458 (1937)

### Background

This case came as new laws were dealing with the problem of massive unemployment during the Great Depression. President Franklin Roosevelt's New Deal legislation had set up a myriad of programs and agencies to deal with the jobless, mainly by creating public works programs that, in the view of many, served merely as a stopgap measure. A new scheme of social insurance, paid for by taxes levied on employees and employers (with eight or more employees), came into being with the Social Security Act of 1935.

The new taxes were subject to a challenge in the Supreme Court. Its opponents found no provision for a Social Security program in the Constitution and cited the provisions of the Tenth Amendment, which reserves powers not specifically granted to Congress to the states. The petitioner in the case of *Steward Machine Company v. Davis* was an Alabama company that filed suit for the recovery of $46.14 paid to the Internal Revenue Service under the Social Security Act, Title IX (for unemployment compensation benefits). The suit was dismissed by a district court, and the decision was affirmed by a federal appeals court. The Supreme Court then heard the case in the spring of 1937 and gave its decision on May 24, 1937.

### Legal Issues

The new Social Security payroll tax mechanism was challenged on several grounds: that it was coercive on state governments, that it was an unconstitutional excise on the inalienable right of employment, that it was not uniform, that it had arbitrary exceptions, and that it invaded powers reserved to the states.

### Decision

The Supreme Court affirmed the appeals court decision and upheld the constitutionality of the new Social Security system, which was essentially a new method of directed taxation. The decision, written by Justice Benjamin Cardozo, laid out a variety of arguments in support of the system, including the opinion that an "excise [tax] . . . extends to vocations or activities pursued as of common right. What the individual does in the operation of a business is amenable to taxation just as much as what he owns. . . . Employment is a business relation, if not itself a business. It is a relation without which business could seldom be carried on effectively. The power to tax the activities and relations that constitute a calling considered as a unit is the power to tax any of them. The whole includes the parts."[7]

The lengthy decision then reviewed the circumstances surrounding the creation of the Social Security system:

> *During the years 1929 to 1936, when the country was passing through a cyclical depression, the number of the unemployed mounted to unprecedented heights. Often the average was more than 10 million; at times a peak was attained of 16 million or more. Disaster to the breadwinner meant disaster to dependents. Accordingly the roll of the unemployed, itself formidable enough, was only a partial roll of the destitute or needy. The fact developed quickly that the states were unable to give the requisite relief. The problem had become national in area and dimensions. There was need of help from the nation if the people were not to starve.*[8]

The decision concluded that, as relief of the unemployed is a proper function of local governments, a system of uniform federal taxation was a constitutional method of bringing about the desired result:

> *The Social Security Act is an attempt to find a method by which . . . public agencies may work together to a common end. Every dollar of the new taxes will continue in all likelihood to be used and needed by the nation as long as states are unwilling, whether through timidity or for other motives, to do what can be done at home. . . .*
>
> *Who . . . is coerced through the operation of this statute? Not the taxpayer. He pays in fulfillment of the mandate of the local legislature. Not the state [of Alabama]. Even now she does not offer a suggestion that in passing the unemployment law she was affected by duress. For all that appears, she is satisfied with her choice, and would be sorely disappointed if it were now to be annulled. The difficulty with the petitioner's contention is that it confuses motive with coercion. . . . To hold that motive or temptation is equivalent to coercion is to plunge the law in endless difficulties. The outcome of such a doctrine is the acceptance of a philosophical determinism by which choice becomes impossible. Till now the law has been guided by a robust common sense which assumes the freedom of the will as a working hypothesis in the solution of its problems. The wisdom of the hypothesis has illustration in this case.*[9]

### *Impact*

*Steward Machine Company v. Davis* was one of a series of important Supreme Court decisions in the Roosevelt-era "constitutional revolution." It gave Congress broad powers to mandate tax collection by the states in order to fund social benefit programs—in this case, unemployment compensation. In the

Social Security Act, Congress had given the states incentives to pass their own unemployment compensation plans. In each state that had such a plan, the taxpayers were permitted to credit 90 percent of the federal unemployment tax paid to the unemployment fund established by the state. The Supreme Court found that this method was not coercive, or in violation of "states' rights" or the Tenth Amendment. By permitting this scheme of tax collection, the decision rendered the Social Security program constitutional and laid the groundwork for the modern era of federally mandated social welfare programs.

## *HELVERING V. DAVIS*, 301 U.S. 619 (1937)

### *Background*

*Helvering v. Davis* and *Steward Machine Co. v. Davis* were both decided on May 24, 1937. In *Steward*, the Supreme Court upheld Title IX of the Social Security Act, which imposed a tax on employers of eight or more. In *Helvering v. Davis*, Titles VIII and II were at issue. Title VIII levies a tax on employers in addition to the one imposed by Title IX (though with different exemptions). It lays a special income tax upon employees to be deducted from their wages and paid by the employers. Title II provides for the payment of Social Security retirement benefits.

The case against this scheme of taxation was brought by a shareholder of the Edison Electric Illuminating Company of Boston. The shareholder sought to restrain the corporation from making the payments and deductions, claiming that these payments were unconstitutional. The suit charged that the deductions would produce unrest among the employees, followed by demands that wages be increased. The payments would also cause the corporation and its shareholders an irreparable loss, leading to a loss in the value of the corporation's shares.

### *Legal Issues*

The United States Commissioner of Internal Revenue and the United States Collector for the District of Massachusetts then intervened on the grounds that Title VIII is valid law and that an employer who is not directly subject to a tax may not challenge it. The Internal Revenue claimed even less standing for the shareholder. A federal district court upheld the tax on employers and denied the suit.

On appeal to the federal appeals court, the decree was reversed. The court held that the taxes were an invasion of powers reserved by the Tenth Amendment: "The powers not delegated to the United States by the Constitution, nor prohibited by it to the States, are reserved for the States respectively, or to the people." The appeals court also held that the Social Security tax was not an excise as excises were understood when the Constitution was adopted. The case was then brought to the Supreme Court.

### Decision

The Supreme Court decided that the benefits conferred by Title II were constitutional because, according to Article I, Section 8 of the Constitution, Congress may spend money in aid of the general welfare. The opinion, written by Justice Benjamin Cardozo, stated that "the line must still be drawn between one welfare and another, between particular and general. Where this shall be placed cannot be known through a formula in advance of the event. . . . The discretion belongs to Congress, unless the choice is clearly wrong, a display of arbitrary power."[10]

The opinion surveyed the historical background to the Social Security legislation in this way:

> . . . *the purge of nationwide calamity that began in 1929 has taught us many lessons. Not the least is the solidarity of interests that may once have seemed to be divided. Unemployment spreads from State to State, the hinterland now settled that, in pioneer days gave an avenue of escape. . . . Spreading from State to State, unemployment is an ill not particular, but general, which may be checked, if Congress so determines, by the resources of the Nation. . . . The hope behind this statute is to save men and women from the rigors of the poorhouse, as well as from the haunting fear that such a lot awaits them when journey's end is near.*[11]

### Impact

*Helvering v. Davis* decided the constitutionality of the Social Security Act and its scheme of mandatory taxes on employers and employees. More broadly, the decision affirmed the responsibility of the federal government for welfare benefits that had previously been the business of state and local governments. An important basis for the decision was the contention that when individual states levy taxes and distribute benefits, they place themselves in competition with other states and often put local interests over the interest of those in need. Thus, local charity prompted migration and disruption, and only a federal scheme could equitably serve the interest of all the citizens.

## CARMICHAEL V. SOUTHERN COAL & COKE COMPANY, 301 U.S. 495 (1937)

### Background

The Southern Coal & Coke Company brought suit in the District Court for the Middle District of Alabama in an effort to restrain the state from collecting contributions to the federal Unemployment Trust Fund. By the Social Security Act, the funds were then requisitioned by the state in order to pay unemployment benefits. The Alabama Unemployment Compensation Act and the unemployment collections had been approved by the Social Security Board. The district court granted the suit, which was then appealed to the Supreme Court.

### Legal Issues

In this case, the Supreme Court had to decide whether the Unemployment Compensation Act of Alabama infringed the due process and equal protection clauses of the Fourteenth Amendment, and whether it was invalid because its enactment was coerced by the Social Security Act. Those opposed to the unemployment compensation scheme claimed that it unlawfully discriminated against larger employers (the tax was levied only on employers of eight persons or more), that it discriminated among classes of employers (certain professions were exempt), and that it involved an unconstitutional surrender to the national government of the sovereign power of the state.

### Decision

On May 24, 1937, the Supreme Court found the Alabama statute and unemployment tax constitutional. According to the opinion, "such levies . . . were known in England and the Colonies before the adoption of the Constitution, and must be taken to be embraced within the wide range of choice of subjects of taxation, which was an attribute of the sovereign power of the states. . . . As the present levy has all the indicia of a tax, and is of a type traditional in the history of Anglo-American legislation, it is within state taxing power."[12] As for the assertion that the tax unfairly discriminated against larger employers, the Court held that "neither due process nor equal protection imposes upon a state any rigid rule of equality of taxation."[13] The states had the right to make this distinction for the sake of reducing administrative costs, or for any other reason. In addition, the states had the right to tax or not tax particular classes of employers.

### Impact

This was one of several key Supreme Court decisions, including *Steward Machine Company v. Davis*. It established the constitutionality of both the Social Security system and its scheme of federally mandated state levies on employees and employers for the purposes of financing the federal Social Security trust funds.

## KING V. SMITH, 392 U.S. 309 (1968)

### Background

This case tested the definition of "dependent child" under the Aid to Families With Dependent Children program (AFDC). By the Social Security Act, a "dependent child" has been deprived of "parental" support by reason of the death, continued absence, or incapacity of a parent. AFDC funds were provided only if the parent was continually absent from the home. In 1964, the state of Alabama passed a "substitute father" regulation, which denied AFDC payments to the children of a mother who cohabits in or outside her home with an able-bodied man, whether or not the man was the father of the children. This substitute father was considered a nonabsent parent. Over the three years following passage of the substitute father rule, the welfare rolls in Alabama declined by 20,000 persons.

Ms. Sylvester Smith, a widow since 1955, and her four children were residing in Dallas County, Alabama. They received AFDC benefits until October 11, 1966, when the county terminated benefits on the grounds that a paramour who visited Ms. Smith on weekends was now serving in the role of a substitute father. The children were otherwise eligible for benefits, and were not receiving any welfare benefits outside of AFDC payments. The alleged substitute father was legally married and had nine children of his own, all of whom were dependent on him for support. Mr. Williams, the substitute father, was not legally obligated to provide any form of support to the children of Ms. Smith.

### Legal Issues

The state contended that the regulation simply defines who is a nonabsent "parent," which the Social Security Act does not precisely define. Alabama saw it as a legitimate way of allocating limited resources available for AFDC assistance, which the Supreme Court had already found was a legitimate effort on the part of the states. The regulation, by the state's argument, also discouraged illicit sexual relationships and illegitimate births, which it held was one of the prime causes of the increase in the welfare rolls, and it treated informal "married" couples like ordinary married couples who were ineligible for AFDC aid so long as the father was in the home. The district court, which overturned the regulation, found it inconsistent with the Social Security Act and the equal protection clause.

### Decision

On June 17, 1968, the Supreme Court found that Alabama's substitute father regulation was invalid, as it defines "parent" in a manner inconsistent with Section 406 (a) of the Social Security Act. In denying AFDC assistance to appellees on the basis of the invalid regulation, the Court held that "Alabama breached its federally imposed obligation to furnish aid to families with dependent children with reasonable promptness to all eligible individuals." By the term "parent," Section 406 indicated an individual with a legal obligation to provide support to the child, and Alabama could not disqualify a child from AFDC based on the presence of an individual who had no such obligation. The Social Security Act was meant to provide for the needs of dependent children regardless of the behavior of their parents, whether absent or "substitute."[14]

### *Impact*

This decision disposed of the question of providing AFDC benefits to two-parent households where one of the parents had no legal obligation to provide for the welfare of the children. Under the "Flemming Rule" passed by Congress for the Department of Health, Education, and Welfare, lawmakers determined that harmful behavior should be dealt with through rehabilitative measures rather than through rules that punish AFDC recipients.

## *Shapiro v. Thompson*, 394 U.S. 618 (1969)

### *Background*

In three cases consolidated for a Supreme Court decision in 1969, the Court took on the matter of residency requirements for welfare recipients. One of the respondents in this case, Vivian Marie Thompson, was an unwed mother of one child and pregnant with her second when she moved from Massachusetts to Connecticut in June 1966. Unable to work, she applied for Aid to Families with Dependent Children in August, but she was denied in November on the basis of a state law mandating one year of residency before any applicant could receive welfare benefits. (Similar one-year requirements were being challenged in Pennsylvania and the District of Columbia.) The states and Washington, D.C., argued that the requirement was necessary to maintain fiscal solvency; that those who apply for welfare benefits within a year of arrival are more likely to remain burdens on the state; that they had the right to discourage people coming in the hope of securing higher AFDC benefits; and that residents can legally be classified on the basis of the contributions they make to the community in the form of taxes. The residency requirement was also supported on the basis that it discouraged fraud and encouraged new arrivals to find gainful work as soon as possible.

## *Legal Issues*

The respondents challenged the residency requirement—passed by a state legislature in Connecticut and Pennsylvania and by the U.S. Congress in Washington, D.C.—on the grounds that it created a classification of two groups who do not enjoy the equal protection of the laws, in violation of the Fourteenth Amendment to the Constitution, which declares: "No State shall make or enforce any law which shall abridge the privileges or immunities of citizens of the United States; nor shall any State deprive any person of life, liberty, or property, without due process of law; nor deny to any person within its jurisdiction the equal protection of the laws."

In addition, the residency requirement was challenged on the grounds that it interferes with interstate movement, that it violates the precedent that the states may not apportion benefits to residents on the basis of their greater or lesser tax payments, and that there was no provision for such a residency requirement within the original Social Security Act.

## *Decision*

The Supreme Court agreed with the respondents, stating that Connecticut, Pennsylvania, and Washington, D.C., had created an illegal distinction among residents and that they did not have any compelling administrative or social reasons for their residency requirements. By discouraging poor people from arriving, the requirements also violated a constitutional right to interstate travel. In its decision of April 21, 1969, the Court stated, "We do not perceive why a mother who is seeking to make a new life for herself and her children should be regarded as less deserving because she considers, among others factors, the level of a State's public assistance. Surely such a mother is no less deserving than a mother who moves into a particular State in order to take advantage of its better educational facilities."[15]

## *Impact*

Although this decision struck down residency requirements, the issue of "welfare migration" remained. The tendency of states with higher welfare benefits to attract indigent newcomers has been under almost constant scrutiny since *Shapiro v. Thompson*. Most studies found some correlation between level of benefits and the arrival of new residents who are welfare applicants. The conclusions, however, were obscured by the fact that states with higher levels of economic activity tend to have higher welfare benefits, and thus job-seekers as well as welfare-seekers will arrive in search of improved economic security. After the passage of the welfare reform law in 1996, the issue again came into the Supreme Court's jurisdiction, and again residency requirements were struck down in 1999. In effect, the Temporary

Aid to Needy Families (TANF) program reduced the impact of residency requirements by its federally mandated five-year time limit for the receipt of welfare benefits, as well as its incentives for job-training and job-placement programs to be implemented by the states.

## GOLDBERG V. KELLY, 397 U.S. 254 (1970)

### Background

In a case decided in March 1970, the state of New York appealed a federal court decision that required it to provide a hearing to welfare recipients whenever their benefits were terminated. Before the recipients brought the federal suit on the matter, New York had no law requiring such a hearing, and welfare recipients could have their benefits terminated without notice. After being challenged in court, the state commissioner of social services promulgated a new procedure for local communities. It provided the recipient a written notice and a chance for an appeal.

New York City's Department of Social Services, the benefits administrator concerned in this case, adopted Procedure 68–18 in response. The procedure allowed a caseworker, after discussion with the recipient, to recommend termination of benefits to a supervisor, who would send notice to the recipient. The recipient then had seven days to request a review. The respondents in this case challenged the new system as inadequate. It still allowed them no right to oral argument, no right to bring evidence, and no right to cross-examine witnesses on their own behalf.

### Legal Issues

This case tested the application of the Fourteenth Amendment rights of due process to the procedures for granting or denying public welfare benefits, and it explored the legal nature of those benefits: either privileged or a form of "new property." While welfare applicants might have some constitutional right to an evidentiary hearing on the matter, a state government such as New York's also could claim a public interest in saving costs, expediting decisions on welfare benefits, and not burdening the welfare system with lengthy appeals.

### Decision

By a vote of 7–2, the Supreme Court agreed with those claiming a constitutional right to a full evidentiary hearing when welfare benefits are terminated. The opinion stated, in part:

> *The city's procedures presently do not permit recipients to appear personally with or without counsel before the official who finally determines continued eligibility. Thus a recipient is not permitted to present evidence to that official*

*orally, or to confront or cross-examine adverse witnesses. These omissions are fatal to the constitutional adequacy of the procedures. . . . In almost every setting where important decisions turn on questions of fact, due process requires an opportunity to confront and cross-examine adverse witnesses.*[16]

The Court concluded that the interest of an individual in maintaining a minimum standard of living outweighed a public agency's interest in limiting its fiscal and administrative burdens. The welfare recipient had the right to a timely notice and to a hearing in which he or she could present contrary evidence and cross-examine witnesses. He or she also had the right to bring an attorney, although one did not have to be provided to them by the state. Dissenters, including Justice Hugo Black, believed the states had an overriding interest in protecting themselves from welfare recipients who had no legal claim on public funds.

### Impact

Before this case, public welfare benefits were considered a form of charity, not a legal right. The decision set the precedent that individuals have a property interest in welfare benefits granted to them by statute and have the right to prior notice and a hearing when those benefits are denied.

## DANDRIDGE V. WILLIAMS, 397 U.S. 471 (1970)

### Background

This case tried Maryland's "maximum grant regulation." Like many states, Maryland paid AFDC benefits according to a calculated minimum-income level known as a "standard of need." However, the state imposed a ceiling of about $250 per month on AFDC grants regardless of the size of the family. Welfare beneficiaries brought suit in the District Court for the State of Maryland, seeking to have this practice struck down. These plaintiffs pointed out that the maximum amount denied them the state's own calculation of their minimum standard of need, based on the size of their families, and thus discriminated against them.

### Legal Issues

According to the plaintiffs in the state case, the Maryland regulations violated the Social Security Act of 1935 as well as the due process clause of the Fourteenth Amendment. The plaintiffs also noted that the system gave them an incentive to place their children in other households, contradicting a stated purpose of the AFDC program to hold families intact. For its part, the state argued that it had an overriding interest in limiting AFDC payments and a right to balance welfare benefits with the interest of the public at large, who supported the AFDC program with tax payments. The suit succeeded in the district court; the decision was then appealed to the Supreme Court.

### *Decision*

The Supreme Court overturned the district court's decision on April 6, 1970. The justices found that the Maryland regulation was not prohibited by the Social Security Act or by the Constitution. "Given Maryland's finite resources available for public welfare demands, it is not prevented by the Act from sustaining as many families as it can and providing the largest families with somewhat less than their ascertained per capita standard of need." Although the Social Security Act mandates that aid "shall be furnished with reasonable promptness to all eligible individuals," the Maryland regulation did not deprive *individuals* of their aid but rather reduced grants to *families* as a whole. In addition, by the amendments to the Social Security Act passed in 1967, Congress explicitly recognized the lawfulness of maximum grant regulations; the Maryland regulations had thus been approved by the federal Secretary of Health, Education, and Welfare (as similar regulations had been approved in other states).

The Supreme Court dismissed the "overreaching" grounds as irrelevant to state regulation in the social and economic field:

> *The regulation is rationally supportable and free from invidious discrimination, since it furthers the State's legitimate interest in encouraging employment and in maintaining an equitable balance between welfare families and the families of the working poor. . . . We do not decide today that the Maryland regulation is wise, that it best fulfills the relevant social and economic objectives that Maryland might ideally espouse, or that a more just and humane system could not be devised. . . . But the intractable economic, social, and even philosophical problems presented by public welfare assistance programs are not the business of this Court.*[17]

### *Impact*

The decision found legal the practice of capping maximum grants regardless of family size, in the interest of limiting the overall cost of the public welfare system.

## *GRAHAM V. DEPARTMENT OF PUBLIC WELFARE,* 403 U.S. 365 (1971)

### *Background*

This case tried the constitutionality of denying welfare benefits to resident aliens. Since the 18th century, laws have been in place denying entry to the

United States of any immigrant likely to become a "public charge," and dependent on either private or public charity. The expansion of the welfare system in the 1950s and 1960s put the issue of immigrant access to welfare benefits again in the judicial spotlight.

The Supreme Court hearing followed arguments in three consolidated cases, one in Arizona and two in Pennsylvania. In July 1969, Carmen Richardson was a 64-year-old, lawfully admitted resident alien. Since emigrating from Mexico, she had resided continuously in Arizona. She met the requirements for Arizona's Assistance to Persons Permanently and Totally Disabled (APTD) benefits. The state, however, set a 15-year residency requirement, which denied her benefits. Mrs. Richardson instituted a class action suit, claiming that Arizona's alien residency requirements violated the equal protection clause of the Fourteenth Amendment as well as other provisions of federal law. She won the suit, which was then appealed to the Supreme Court.

Respondent Elsie Mary Jane Leger was a resident alien, originally from Scotland, who arrived in the United States in 1965. She worked as a domestic servant for a family in Havertown, Pennsylvania, and resided continuously in Pennsylvania as a taxpaying resident. In 1967, she moved to Philadelphia, where she entered into a common-law marriage with a U.S. citizen. In 1969, due to illness, Mrs. Leger applied for public assistance, which was denied based on her status as a resident alien. She instituted a class-action suit, which succeeded. In its decision the district court noted that "aliens, like citizens, pay taxes, and may be called into the armed forces . . . aliens may live within a state for many years, work in the state and contribute to the economic growth of the state." The decision was appealed by the state.

Beryl Jervis had been added as a plaintiff to the Leger action. Born in Panama in 1912, she came to the United States in 1968 to take domestic work in Philadelphia. In February 1970, she quit her job due to illness; her request for aid was turned down on the basis of her status as a resident alien.

### *Legal Issues*

This case tested the constitutional merits of denying welfare benefits on the basis of national origin and citizenship. The grounds for opposing this practice rest on the Fourteenth Amendment, which provides, "[N]or shall any State deprive any person of life, liberty, or property, without due process of law; nor deny to any person within its jurisdiction the equal protection of the laws." By long-established precedent, this "equal protection" clause of the Fourteenth Amendment applies to lawfully admitted resident aliens as well as citizens. In Arizona, however, resident aliens had to live in the United States for 15 years to qualify for benefits. United States citizens living in Pennsylvania, unable to meet the requirements for federally funded benefits, might have been eligible for state supported general assistance, but resident aliens as a class were not. The states claimed a "special public interest" in favoring citizens in the payment of limited resources such as welfare benefits.

The petitioners, who supported the restriction, argued that the denial of benefits involved no discrimination on the basis of sex, race, or nationality. They also argued that the states, in making the distinction between citizens and resident aliens, were pursuing a legitimate public interest, and that in the questions of certain privileges (namely, welfare benefits) the states had a right to discriminate between citizens and noncitizens. The Supreme Court had earlier found that states could restrict access by aliens to natural resources and to land. Noncitizens were also prohibited from basic rights of citizenship, such as voting, sitting on juries, and holding public office.

### Decision

In its decision of June 14, 1971, the Supreme Court disagreed with the arguments put forward by the states. The opinion, written by Justice Harry Blackmun, stated in part: "Whatever may be the contemporary vitality of the special public interest doctrine . . . we conclude that a State's desire to preserve limited welfare benefits for its own citizens is inadequate to justify Pennsylvania's making noncitizens ineligible for public assistance, and Arizona's restricting benefits to citizens and longtime resident aliens." A state may attempt to limit its expenditures for any reason, but may not do so by making "invidious" distinction between classes of citizens. "Since an alien, as well as a citizen, is a 'person' for equal protection purposes, a concern for fiscal integrity is [not] a justification for the questioned classification in these cases. . . . We hold that a state statute that denies welfare benefits to resident aliens and one that denies them to aliens who have not resided in the United States for a specified number of years violate the Equal Protection Clause."[18]

### Impact

This decision made resident aliens eligible for welfare benefits on the same basis as citizens. The passage of the welfare reform law in 1996, however, returned these restrictions to the law. The law set up two classes of immigrants: those arriving before and after August 22, 1996. Those arriving before were to lose their right to SSI benefits and food stamps; those arriving afterward lost their right to any form of federally funded assistance until they became citizens. Recent immigrants as well as longtime resident aliens remain ineligible for a wide range of benefits that are funded by the federal block-grant system; however, the law was neutralized to some extent by the passage of legislation by the states setting up welfare programs for immigrants. In addition, refugees and those seeking political asylum were made exempt from the new restrictions.

## TOWNSEND V. SWANK, 404 U.S. 282 (1971)

### Background

This case was originally brought by two college students and their mothers in the federal District Court for the Northern District of Illinois. The plaintiffs alleged that state welfare regulations violated the equal protection clause of the Fourteenth Amendment, the Social Security Act, and the supremacy clause of the Constitution. Under the Illinois regulation, needy dependent children 18 through 20 years of age who attended high school or vocational training school were eligible for benefits under the AFDC program, but such children who attended a college or university were not.

### Legal Issues

The original action in this case was brought on the basis that the Illinois regulations violated the due process clause of the Fourteenth Amendment and the "supremacy clause" of the Constitution, stated in Article VI, which renders the federal constitution and federal statutes and treaties as the supreme law of the land. The Social Security Act, a federal statute, defines "dependent child" to include a child "under the age of twenty-one and (as determined by the State in accordance with standards prescribed by the Secretary) a student regularly attending a school, college, or university, or regularly attending a course of vocational or technical training designed to fit him for gainful employment."[19]

A three-judge district court dismissed the plaintiff's constitutional arguments and upheld the Illinois statute and regulation, based on the assumption that Congress had granted the states authority to vary eligibility requirements of school-attending AFDC recipients as they saw fit, so long as the program otherwise conformed to guidelines set down by the federal government.

### Decision

The Supreme Court ruled on the case on December 20, 1971. In this decision, the justices cited *King v. Smith*, in which the Court overturned an Alabama regulation excluding from benefits children who had a man living in the household who was not their natural father. (The Social Security Act originally granted aid to dependent children only if a parent was continually absent from the home.)

The original Social Security Act provided aid only to dependent children under the age of 16. A 1939 amendment extended aid to children age 16 to 17 "regularly attending school." The aid to this group was optional at the states' discretion. But nothing in the law prescribed the type of school or allowed the states to exclude children on the basis of the type of school they were attending. As to the intent of Congress, the Court wrote, "Congress meant to continue financial assistance for AFDC programs for the age group only in States that conformed their eligibility requirements to the federal eligibility standards."[20] The student only had to be regularly attending a bona fide school.

In 1956, Congress deleted the school attendance requirement and provided for benefits for all dependent children of the 16–17 age group. In 1964, Congress authorized benefits for the 18–20 age group but limited them to children attending high school or vocational school. In 1965, the law was further amended to extend aid to children under 21 who were attending a "school, college, or university." The states had to conform their eligibility standards to federal law in order to receive AFDC grants-in-aid from the federal treasury.

Thus, the Supreme Court held the Illinois regulations to be a violation of the supremacy clause, Article VI, Paragraph 2 of the Constitution:

> *This Constitution, and the Laws of the United States which shall be made in Pursuance thereof; and all Treaties made, or which shall be made, under the authority of the United States, shall be the supreme Law of the land; and the Judges in every State shall be bound thereby, any Thing in the Constitution or Laws of any State to the Contrary notwithstanding.*

The justices also noted "there is a serious question whether the Illinois classification can withstand the strictures of the Equal Protection Clause. . . . We are not told what basis in practical experience supports the proposition that children with a vocational training are more readily employable than children with a college education. And a State's interest in preserving the fiscal integrity of its welfare program . . . may be protected by the State's 'undisputed power to set the level of benefits.'"[21]

### Impact

This decision limited the ability of states to set down restrictions regarding welfare eligibility, and was seen as further expansion and protection of the federal welfare system by the Supreme Court at the expense of the states. The tide began to turn with local welfare reform measures passed in the 1980s and early 1990s, when states began innovating in the face of the system's perceived failures and rising costs. The principle that states and not the federal government knew best when it came to tailoring welfare benefits was enshrined in the welfare reform act of 1996 and its subsequent reauthorizations. The law now tends to punish states by withholding block-grant funds for not conforming to more restrictive *federal* guidelines.

## *JEFFERSON V. HACKNEY*, 406 U.S. 535 (1972)

### Background

The appellants in this case were Texas AFDC recipients. They brought class-action suits against state welfare officials for a system of setting a "standard of need" in order to meet a ceiling set on overall welfare spending set by the Texas state constitution. The standard of need resulted in lower payments through the AFDC program than for other assistance programs.

When the beneficiary had outside income, the state computed the percentage by first applying the recipient's standard of need, then subtracting any outside income dollar-for-dollar from the benefits paid. (Other states first subtracted outside income from the standard of need, in order to determine the recipient's "unmet need." The latter system results in a relatively higher benefit level for those with outside income.) The appellants claimed that the Texas method violated the provisions of the Social Security Act and discriminated against them. The Supreme Court ruled on the case on May 30, 1972.

### Legal Issues

The appellants claimed the violation against Section 402(a)(23) of the Social Security Act, which required the states to make adjustments to reflect changes in the cost of living. The Texas method resulted in lower payments compared to a method used in other states. Opponents claimed a violation of the equal protection clause of the Fourteenth Amendment, as minority groups were adversely affected by it, and other programs benefiting groups such as the blind and disabled—with a lower percentage of minorities on their rolls—were not subject to the same calculation.

### Decision

In this decision, the Supreme Court noted that the Social Security Act required the states to make cost-of-living adjustments to their standards of need, thereby serving two purposes: "First, to require States to face up realistically to the magnitude of the public assistance requirement and lay bare the extent to which their programs fall short of fulfilling actual need; second, to prod the States to apportion their payments on a more equitable basis."

The Supreme Court noted that effective May 1, 1969, the standard of need for AFDC recipients in Texas was raised 11 percent to reflect the rise in the cost of living, and the state shifted to its percentage-reduction system. "In this way, the State has fairly recognized and exposed the precise level of unmet need, and by using a percentage-reduction system it has attempted to apportion the State's limited benefits more equitably."

The complaint alleged that, as a result of earned outside income, the Texas system provided only 75 percent of its standard of need to AFDC recipients, while paying 100 percent of recognized need to the aged (who generally do not earn outside income), and 95 percent to the disabled and the blind (who very rarely do). They argued that if the state adopts a per-centage-reduction system, it must apply the same percentage to each of its welfare programs. The Supreme Court disagreed, finding that each state had the discretion to set a standard of need as it saw fit to meet budgetary constraints.

As for the equal protection claim, the Court stated:

> *The number of minority members in all categories is substantial. The basic outlines of eligibility for the various categorical grants are established by Congress, not by the States; given the heterogeneity of the Nation's population, it would be only an infrequent coincidence that the racial composition of each grant class was identical to that of the others. The acceptance of appellants' constitutional theory would render suspect each difference in treatment among the grant classes, however lacking in racial motivation and however otherwise rational the treatment might be. Few legislative efforts to deal with the difficult problems posed by current welfare programs could survive such scrutiny, and we do not find it required by the Fourteenth Amendment.[22]*

## CARLESON V. REMILLARD, 406 U.S. 598 (1972)

### Background

This case involved a woman whose husband had enlisted in the United States Army and was serving in Vietnam. She applied for Aid to Families with Dependent Children (AFDC) benefits. At the time, the benefits she received as a wife of a serviceman were less than her "standard of need" as computed by the California welfare agency, and less than the monthly AFDC grant an adult with one child received in California. Her application was denied by the state. The Supreme Court heard the case, giving its ruling on June 7, 1972.

### Legal Issues

The Social Security Act granted aid to families with "dependent children," and included in the term "dependent child" one "who has been deprived of parental support or care by reason of . . . continued absence from the home." California did not count absence due to military service as legitimate "continued absence." The state stopped the husband's allotment check; when the mother again applied for AFDC benefits, the state again denied them, on the same grounds: that AFDC benefits were prohibited to needy families where the absence of a parent was due to military service. The beneficiary joined a class-action suit seeking to overturn the regulation on the grounds that it violated the Social Security Act and the due process and equal protection clauses of the Fourteenth Amendment. A federal district court agreed with her; the state then appealed the decision to the Supreme Court.

In its decisions in *King v. Smith* and *Townsend v. Swank*, the Supreme Court had held that state AFDC eligibility standards could not exclude persons eligible for assistance under federal standards. Any variation in the standards had to be set down expressly by Congress. In this case, the Court noted that the Department of Health, Education, and Welfare (HEW) included "service in the armed forces or other military service" as an example of a situation falling under the definition of "continued absence" in the original Social Security Act, which did not specify that "continued absence" had to come about through divorce or desertion or any other single reason.

### Decision

The Supreme Court upheld the district court decision to grant AFDC aid to the family. The opinion in this case concluded the following:

> *The presence in the home of the parent who has the legal obligation to support is the key to the AFDC program. . . . Congress looked to "work relief" programs and "the revival of private industry" to help the parent find the work needed to support the family . . . and the AFDC program was designed to meet a need unmet by depression-era programs aimed at providing work for breadwinners. . . . It is clear that "military orphans" are in this category, for, as stated by the Supreme Court of Washington, a man in the military service "has little control over his family's economic destiny. He has no labor union or other agency to look to as a means of persuading his employer to pay him a living wage. He is without access to collective bargaining or any negotiating forum or other means of economic persuasion, or even the informal but concerted support of his fellow employees. He cannot quit his job and seek a better paying one. . . . There is no action he could lawfully take to make his earnings adequate while putting in full time on his job. His was a kind of involuntary employment where legally he could do virtually nothing to improve the economic welfare of his family.*
>
> *We are especially confident Congress could not have designed an Act leaving uncared for an entire class who became "needy children" because their fathers were in the Armed Services defending their country.[23]*

### Impact

This decision confirmed the general precedent that eligibility for AFDC benefits was set by federal regulations, and the states could not deny benefits to an entire class of families in contravention of the language of the Social Security Act. Upon enactment of the welfare reform law of 1996, the determination of eligibility began passing to the states, with the federal government encouraging the states' conformity to federal guidelines by paying or withholding block-grant funding.

## *NEW JERSEY WELFARE RIGHTS ORGANIZATION V. CAHILL*, 411 U.S. 619 (1973)

### Background

This case dealt with a New Jersey statute that limited benefits of the state's "Assistance to Families of the Working Poor" program to those households in which the parents were ceremonially married and had at least one minor child who was the natural child of both, the natural child of one and adopted by the other, or a child adopted by both. Thus, common-law parents with only illegitimate children were ineligible. The appellants contended that the requirement discriminated unlawfully against illegitimate children. In the district court, a three-judge panel disagreed, finding that the state had a legitimate and lawful interest in "preserving and strengthening family life."

### Legal Issues

The denial of welfare benefits to illegitimate children was held by the petitioners in this case to violate the equal protection clause of the Fourteenth Amendment. The respondents, on the other hand, maintained that New Jersey had a right to encourage the formation of traditional families and thus discourage behavior that leads to greater expense on the part of the general public.

### Decision

In its opinion, dated May 7, 1973, the Supreme Court cited the case of *Weber v. Aetna Casualty and Surety*, in which the Court had held that under the equal protection clause a state may not exclude illegitimate children from sharing equally with other children in the recovery of workmen's compensation benefits for the death of their parent:

> *The status of illegitimacy has expressed through the ages society's condemnation of irresponsible liaisons beyond the bonds of marriage. But visiting this condemnation on the head of an infant is illogical and unjust. Moreover, imposing disabilities on the illegitimate child is contrary to the basic concept of our system that legal burdens should bear some relationship to individual responsibility or wrongdoing. Obviously, no child is responsible*

*for his birth and penalizing the illegitimate child is an ineffectual—as well as an unjust—way of deterring the parent.*

The Court held *Weber* as precedent for this case and in its opinion supported the appellants' claim that they had been denied equal protection, "for there can be no doubt that the benefits extended under the challenged program are as indispensable to the health and well-being of illegitimate children as to those who are legitimate." The opinion also cited the case of *Levy v. Louisiana*, in which it had held that a state may not create a right of action in favor of children for the wrongful death of a parent and exclude illegitimate children from the same right, as well as *Gomez v. Perez*, which had established that a state that mandates child support from a natural father cannot deny the natural father's illegitimate offspring the right to this support.

Justice William Rehnquist dissented from this decision:

*The New Jersey program for assistance to the working poor does not provide financial grants to classes of children as such, as is the case under various federal plans. Instead, it provides grants to classes of families as units. . . . The New Jersey Legislature has determined that special financial assistance should be given to family units that meet the statutory definition of "working poor." It does not seem to me irrational . . . to condition the receipt of such grants on the sort of ceremonial marriage that . . . the New Jersey Legislature is trying to protect from dissolution due to the economic vicissitudes of modern life. The Constitution does not require that special financial assistance designed by the legislature to help poor families be extended to "communes" as well.*

*In the area of economics and social welfare the Equal Protection Clause does not prohibit a State from taking one step at a time in attempting to overcome a social ill, provided only that the classifications made by the State are rational. Here the classification is based on a particular type of family unit, one of, if not the, core units of our social system. . . . I would affirm the judgment of the District Court.*[24]

### Impact

By this time, the Supreme Court was accepting the equal protection clause as the proper basis for dealing with welfare rights cases and determining the distribution of welfare benefits among various enumerated classes, including (in this case) illegitimate children. Judge Rehnquist's dissent, however, countered this trend. As Americans increasingly viewed the welfare system as overburdened and inefficient, and states began exercising more discretion in paying benefits and determining eligibility, appeals such as this one grew more infrequent, and the attempt to engineer family life and personal behavior through welfare incentives gained acceptance.

## *BURNS V. ALCALA*, 420 U.S. 575 (1975)

### *Background*

This decision arose from the case of three Iowa residents. The plaintiffs were pregnant at the time they filed a class-action suit against the state's welfare system. Their children would have been eligible for AFDC benefits upon birth; however, when the plaintiffs applied for welfare assistance they were refused on the ground that they, as yet, had no "dependent children" eligible for the AFDC program. The plaintiffs held that this refusal was at odds with the standard of eligibility under the Social Security Act and that they had thus been denied due process and equal protection under the Fourteenth Amendment.

The district court accepted the plaintiffs' reasoning, declaring that unborn children are "dependent children" under the Social Security Act. An appeals court affirmed the decision, which was then appealed to the Supreme Court.

### *Legal Issues*

The Supreme Court looked at the original intent of the Social Security Act, which defines dependent child as:

> *a needy child (1) who has been deprived of parental support or care by reason of the death, continued absence from the home, or physical or mental incapacity of a parent, and who is living with his father, mother, grandfather, grandmother, brother, sister, stepfather, stepmother, stepbrother, stepsister, uncle, aunt, first cousin, nephew, or niece, in a place of residence maintained by one or more of such relatives as his or their own home, and (2) who is (A) under the age of eighteen, or (B) under the age of twenty-one and (as determined by the State in accordance with standards prescribed by the Secretary) a student regularly attending a school, college, or university, or regularly attending a course of vocational or technical training designed to fit him for gainful employment.*

The act makes no mention of pregnant women or unborn children as such.

The Iowa suit cited ambiguous definitions of "child." Ambiguous definitions justify the interpretation of legislative intent by the Supreme Court. The suit further argued that paying benefits to needy pregnant women would further the purpose of the AFDC program, as it would help the women to pay for prenatal care and adequate nutrition and thus help them to care for their children. The plaintiffs noted that for over 30 years the Department of Health, Education, and Welfare (HEW) had offered the states an option to claim federal matching funds for AFDC payments to pregnant women.

### Decision

The Supreme Court disagreed and reversed the appeals court decision on March 18, 1975, giving the following opinion:

> *The AFDC program was originally conceived to substitute for the practice of removing needy children from their homes and placing them in institutions, and to free widowed and divorced mothers from the necessity of working, so that they could remain home to supervise their children. . . .*
>
> *Our analysis of the Social Security Act does not support a conclusion that the legislative definition of "dependent child" includes unborn children. Following the axiom that words used in a statute are to be given their ordinary meaning in the absence of persuasive reasons to the contrary. . . . We conclude that Congress used the word "child" to refer to an individual already born, with an existence separate from its mother.*[25]

The Court found that needs of pregnant women were met elsewhere in the Social Security Act, specifically Title V, which granted federal funding for prenatal and postnatal health services to mothers and infants in order to reduce infant mortality.

### Impact

This case turned on the Court's willingness to allow the Department of Health, Education, and Welfare to make the final decision regarding welfare rights and eligibility. It set the precedent that the plain meaning of the term "child" did not include an unborn child, a determination that would come into play in abortion cases. In addition, the Court decreed that the needs of unborn children, as far as the AFDC and other federal benefit programs were concerned, were to be met by prenatal care programs, publicly funded clinics, and the like, and not by direct payments to expectant mothers.

## MILLER V. YOUAKIM, 440 U.S. 125 (1979)

### Background

Section 408 of the amended Social Security Act covers AFDC grants made by the federal government to children in foster homes ("AFDC-FC"), paid under several conditions, including one that states "the child must be placed in a foster family home or child-care institution."

In 1969, Illinois made four children wards of the state, removing them from their mother's home and placing them in "unrelated" foster care facilities (that is, facilities not operated by relatives of the children). The children received full AFDC-FC benefits in the amount of $105 every month. In 1972, two of the children were placed with Linda and Maurice Youakim, who were under no legal obligation to accept or support them. The Youakim home was designated as an unrelated foster home, but the state refused to make foster care payments because the children were related to Linda Youakim. Under federal rules, this disqualified the Youakim household as a "foster home."

Illinois did provide each child basic AFDC benefits of $63 a month, less than the applicable $105 AFDC-FC rate. Claiming these payments were insufficient, the Youakims declined to accept the other two children, who continued to receive AFDC-FC benefits and live in unrelated foster care facilities.

In 1973, the Youakims and the four foster children brought a class action suit challenging Illinois's distinction between related and unrelated foster parents as violating the equal protection clause of the Fourteenth Amendment. A three-judge federal district court denied the suit. While the appeal of this decision was pending in the Supreme Court, the Department of Health, Education, and Welfare (HEW) issued new guidelines providing for the foster-care rate of payment when a court removes a child from the home and places it in a foster home, whether or not the foster care is provided by a relative.

In light of this new interpretation, the Supreme Court vacated the judgment and directed the district court to reconsider its original decision. The district court did so. It found for the plaintiffs, a decision that was affirmed in the federal appeals court. The case then arrived at the Supreme Court.[26]

## *Legal Issues*

As in many other welfare cases heard by the Supreme Court, the plaintiffs in *Miller v. Youakim* argued this case on the basis of the equal protection clause of the Fourteenth Amendment to the Constitution.

## *Decision*

The Supreme Court upheld the decisions of the district and appeals courts, directing Illinois to pay related and unrelated foster care benefits at the same rate. The opinion, dated February 22, 1979, noted that "Congress manifestly did not limit the term to encompass only the homes of nonrelated caretakers. Rather, any home that a state approves as meeting its licensing standards falls within the ambit of this definitional provision. That Congress intended no distinction between related and unrelated foster homes is further demonstrated by the AFDC-FC definition of 'aid to families with dependent children,' which includes foster care for eligible children who live 'in the foster family home of any individual.'"[27]

### Impact

The Supreme Court noted that the legislative history of the AFDC and Social Security programs generally supported "kinship care" by caregivers having some family relationship to foster children. The Temporary Assistance to Needy Families (TANF) program, which replaced AFDC in 1996, still authorizes payments to both related and unrelated foster homes on the part of the states.

## *BLUM V. BACON*, 457 U.S. 132 (1982)

### Background

This case began with a simple theft, which took place on June 1, 1977. After having her wallet and food stamps stolen, Jeanne Bacon reported the theft to the New York Department of Social Services (DSS). Without money for food and other essential items, she requested emergency assistance (EA) under New York's federally funded Emergency Assistance Program. The DSS denied her request, because of a recent state law. The law disqualified persons receiving or eligible for AFDC from receiving any cash EA and precluded the use of cash EA to replace a lost or stolen public assistance grant, including AFDC.

Another appellee, Gertrude Parrish, lost her AFDC funds to a burglar. She applied for EA; the DSS denied her request. Two other appellees, Linda Selders and Freddie Mae Goodwine, were also denied EA after they cashed their AFDC checks and suffered the loss of their money. The Supreme Court decided the case on June 14, 1982.

### Legal Issues

The appellees brought a class-action suit to halt enforcement of the state law. They argued that the law conflicted with the Social Security Act and violated the equal protection clause because it discriminated against AFDC recipients, both by providing EA itself to all eligible recipients other than AFDC recipients and by providing EA to replace lost or stolen public benefit grants to all public benefit recipients (such as recipients of Social Security and Supplemental Security Income) *other* than those on public assistance (including AFDC recipients).

### Decision

The Supreme Court decided the case on the basis of the supremacy clause of the Constitution, which holds that federal laws override conflicting state regulations in matters concerning federal spending. The Court found that the New York rules conflicted with federal regulations promulgated by the secretary of health, education, and welfare, which banned inequitable treatment under the EA program: "The eligibility conditions imposed [by a state welfare program] must not exclude individuals or groups on an arbitrary or unreasonable basis, and must not result in inequitable treatment of individuals or groups in the light of the provisions and purposes of the public assistance titles of the Social Security Act."[28]

### Impact

In this and similar welfare cases, the Supreme Court was now giving substantial weight to the rules and procedures of agencies such as HEW charged with administering the Social Security Act, on the basis of the supremacy clause of the Constitution (see also the cases of *Townsend v. Swank* and *Carleson v. Remillard*). By the 1990s, this precedent would be widely viewed as one cause of the increasing inefficiency of the welfare system, and a new trend arose of allowing states greater latitude in how welfare dollars would be spent.

## BOWEN V. ROY, 476 U.S. 693 (1986)

### Background

Steven J. Roy and Karen Miller received benefits under the AFDC and food stamp programs. They refused, however, to furnish their Social Security numbers and those of each member of their household, although federal regulations required it. They contended that obtaining a Social Security number for their two-year-old daughter, Little Bird of the Snow, would violate their Native American religious beliefs. Roy asserted that use of the unique Social Security number to identify and control his daughter would rob her spirit. The Pennsylvania Department of Public Welfare halted the child's AFDC benefits and prepared to reduce the level of food stamps that the household was receiving.

### Legal Issues

Roy and Miller then filed suit in district court, claiming that the free exercise clause of the First Amendment entitled them to an exemption from the Social Security number requirements. During trial, it was revealed that a Social Security number had already been assigned involuntarily. The court held that the Social Security number was not required to maintain the benefits system, and it barred the secretary of health and human services from using the child's Social Security number. The defendants were also enjoined from denying benefits until the child's 16th birthday despite her parents' refusal to provide a Social Security number.

### Decision

By a vote of 8 to 1, the Supreme Court overturned this decision on June 11, 1986. As recorded in the opinion written by Chief Justice Warren Burger, the justices found that the free exercise clause "affords an individual protection from certain forms of governmental compulsion but does not afford an individual a right to dictate the conduct of the Government's internal procedures. The Government's use of a Social Security number for appellees' child does not itself impair appellees' freedom to exercise their religion."[29] The Court found that the requirement applies to all welfare recipients, does not discriminate and is neutral on religious grounds, and promotes a legitimate public interest: the prevention of fraud.

### Impact

Outside of its application to welfare administration, *Bowen v. Roy* carried interesting implications for the principle of "freedom of religion." This First Amendment right does not, by this opinion, extend to requiring the government to suspend normal procedures in the administration of welfare benefits, nor does the First Amendment require the government to enhance the spiritual development of its citizens. The Supreme Court, however, did remand the case to federal district court in Pennsylvania, which was to determine whether the government agency had violated the Privacy Act by issuing a Social Security number that the recipient had not requested.

## *Bowen v. Gilliard*, 483 U.S. 587 (1987)

### Background

In 1975, federal welfare laws provided that any applicant for AFDC benefits must assign the state the right to receive child support payments, if any, for any family member included in the family unit. A recipient of aid, however, could exclude a child from the family unit if it was to their financial advantage, even though the child continued to live with the family. In 1984, by the Deficit Reduction Act (DEFRA), the rules were changed to require families applying for benefits to include all children living in the same home, including those for whom support payments were being received.

The law required the state to remit the first $50 per month of child support to the family; this payment was not to be counted as income.

## *Legal Issues*

A federal district court in North Carolina found that the 1984 statutory scheme violated the due process clause of the Fifth Amendment and its equal protection component, as well as the takings clause of that amendment. The case was then appealed to the Supreme Court, which Court decided the case on June 25, 1987.

## *Decision*

The Supreme Court justices found that the DEFRA amendment "rationally serves both Congress' goal of decreasing federal expenditures, and the Government's separate interest in distributing benefits among competing needy families in a fair way. It was also rational for Congress to adjust the AFDC program to reflect the fact that support money generally provides significant benefits for entire family units."

Further, according to the Supreme Court, the DEFRA law did not violate the takings clause of the Fifth Amendment, as the families had "no protected property rights to continued ADC benefits at the same level as before the [DEFRA] amendment."[30]

## *Impact*

This case set out an important principle in welfare law: that the government is not forced to continue or enhance a social benefit program once it has put one in place and has some discretion in administering such a program in order to maximize fairness and minimize public expenditures.

## *ANDERSON V. EDWARDS*, 514 U.S. 143 (1995)

### *Background*

The federal "family filing unit rule" groups cohabiting nuclear family members into a single "assistance unit" (AU) to determine their eligibility for AFDC. California's "non sibling filing unit rule" (the California Rule) grouped needy children living in the same household—whether or not they were siblings—into the AU if there was only one adult caring for them. The California Rule resulted in a decrease in the AFDC benefits due Verna Edwards and her minor granddaughter and two grandnieces, who were living in her household and dependent on her for support. A class-action suit was brought against the state officials charged with administering California's AFDC program.

### Legal Issues

This case was a simple test of the meaning of the AFDC regulations as written and amended within the Social Security Act. These regulations prohibited the states from reducing the amount of assistance solely because of the presence in the household of an individual who was not legally responsible for their care. In addition, the case tested the AFDC rule that prohibited the states from assuming that a cohabitant's income was available to a needy child. The district court granted summary judgment against the suit, thus upholding the California Rule, and a federal appeals court affirmed the decision. The plaintiffs in the original suit them appealed to the Supreme Court, which ruled on the case on March 22, 1995.

### Decision

The Supreme Court upheld California's method of determining need. The Court found, unanimously, that federal law does not prohibit California from grouping into a single AU all needy children living in the same household under the care of one relative. As stated in the opinion of the Court, written by Justice Clarence Thomas:

> *Respondents are simply wrong when they contend that . . . it was solely the arrival in Mrs. Edwards' home of her grandnieces that triggered a decline in the per capita benefits that previously were paid to her granddaughter; rather, it was the grandnieces' presence plus their application for AFDC assistance through Mrs. Edwards. Had the grandnieces, after coming to live with Mrs. Edwards, either not applied for assistance or applied through a different caretaker relative living in the home, the California Rule would not have affected the granddaughter's benefits at all. . . .*
>
> *[The AFDC] statute is reasonably construed to allow States, in determining a child's need (and therefore the amount of her assistance), to consider the income and resources of all cohabiting children and relatives also claiming assistance.*[31]

### Impact

The Supreme Court's decision in *Anderson v. Edwards* confirmed that the states had wide latitude to determine the income of all individuals in a household while setting AFDC payment levels.

## BLESSING V. FREESTONE ET AL., 520 U.S. 329 (1997)

### Background

Five mothers in Arizona sued the state's child support agency for failure to enforce a child support order, according to the terms of Title IV-D of the

Social Security Act as amended in 1996, which states: "The State will provide services relating to the establishment of paternity or the establishment, modification, or enforcement of child support obligations, as appropriate . . . [and] enforce any support obligation established with respect to (i) a child with respect to whom the State provides services under the plan; or (ii) the custodial parent of such a child."[32] The plaintiffs claimed an enforceable right to "substantial compliance" of the state's program to achieve the requirements of Title IV-D. The federal Ninth Circuit Court of Appeals agreed; the decision was then appealed to the Supreme Court.

### Legal Issues

This case treated the yet-unresolved question of whether federal regulations in the area of child support created enforceable individual rights for AFDC beneficiaries. While some courts saw Title IV-D as creating a general right to sue for compliance on the part of the states, others found that individuals could only bring a private suit for specific relief, such as monetary relief.

Beneficiaries of child support assign their child support rights to the state; the state may keep most of the support payments collected on behalf of AFDC families to offset their costs. Child-support recipients who do not collect welfare benefits have all collected funds paid to them. State child-support enforcement programs seeking AFDC funds must establish paternity, locate absent parents, and help families obtain support orders. The system must be in place statewide, and child-support recipients must be notified monthly of the amount collected on their behalf. These services must be free of charge. The federal Office of Child Support Enforcement (OCSE) oversees compliance. If a state does not comply with Title IV-D, the HHS reduces its AFDC grant by up to 5 percent.

Arizona had a poor child-support collection record, failing to collect sufficient back payments even to cover the costs of the Title IV-D program. Less than 5 percent of eligible parents were receiving regular payments. The OSCE regularly penalized the state with a fine of 1 percent of its AFDC grant. When the state submitted a plan for corrective action, the penalty was usually suspended.

The mothers had applied to the state for assistance with the collection of child support, but, they claimed, the state agency had failed to assist them effectively due to shortages in staff, a backlog of cases, and poor accounting and recordkeeping practices; by this failure the agency had violated their federal rights under Title IV-D, they said. The suit asked the Supreme Court to make a declaratory judgment that the Arizona child-support collection violated federal law and to require the state's compliance. The Arizona program director argued that Title IV-D creates no enforceable individual rights.

## Decision

The Supreme Court agreed with the Arizona state child support agency. In its decision of April 21, 1997, the Court stated that Title IV-D of the Social Security Act did not confer enforceable rights upon recipients of child support. Those plaintiffs suing child-support programs must demonstrate the violation of a federal right, not merely a violation of federal law:

> *As an initial matter, the lower court's holding that Title IV-D "creates enforceable rights" paints with too broad a brush. It was incumbent upon respondents to identify with particularity the rights they claimed, since it is impossible to determine whether Title IV-D, as an undifferentiated whole, gives rise to undefined "rights." . . . Title IV-D contains no private remedy—either judicial or administrative—through which aggrieved persons can seek redress. The only way that Title IV-D assures that states live up to their child support plans is through the [HHS] Secretary's oversight.[33]*

## Impact

After the *Blessing* decision, lower courts generally followed suit in rejecting claims that federal statutes such as Title IV-D created a right of individuals to sue for general compliance but permitting plaintiffs to sue for relief under specific provisions of state plans developed under the Social Security Act.

## MALDONADO ET AL. V. PENNSYLVANIA DEPARTMENT OF PUBLIC WELFARE, 97-1893 U.S. COURT OF APPEALS (THIRD CIRCUIT, 1998)

### Background

This case arose from an application for TANF benefits by Edwin Maldonado, a mechanic from Puerto Rico who supported his family partly with nutritional and medical assistance. In May 1997, Maldonado lost his job. Due to health problems, he moved with his family from Puerto Rico to Philadelphia, Pennsylvania, where he sought better health care.

In Pennsylvania, the Maldonados applied for TANF benefits; their application was approved by the Pennsylvania Department of Public Welfare (DPW), which also certified that both husband and wife were unable to work. The Maldonados qualified for $304 per month cash, as well as $720 in food stamps, medical benefits of $1,483.60, and a one-time grant for a job search in the amount of $213. As residents of Pennsylvania for at least 12 months, however, they would have qualified for $836 in monthly cash benefits per month. Thus, their actual benefits represented a reduction of almost 64 percent.

In a class-action suit, the Maldonados claimed that Pennsylvania's reduced benefits violated their constitutional rights to travel, to equal protection, and to nondiscriminatory treatment. The district court agreed, holding that the state scheme lacked a rational basis and thus violated the equal protection clause, and ordered the state to stop its enforcement of the two-tier benefits scheme. Pennsylvania appealed to the federal appeals court, which decided the case on September 9, 1998.

### Legal Issues

Pennsylvania had amended its welfare law in 1996 to change the amount of assistance that an eligible family arriving from another state could receive during the first 12 months of residence. As a result of the amendment, such a family would receive either the same benefits available to residents of at least 12 months or benefits equal to the benefit level the family had been eligible for before moving into the state, whichever amount was lower. Because Pennsylvania was granting relatively high cash benefits at the time of the suit, under this scheme, a typical eligible family moving to the state would experience a drop in their cash benefits for the first 12 months that they resided in the state.

Several months after the state changed its law, in August 1996, Congress passed the Personal Responsibility and Work Opportunity Reconciliation Act of 1996 (PRWORA). The PRWORA encouraged states to adopt restrictive cash benefit programs for those relocating from another state. The new law changed the basic funding to block grants and authorized two-tier systems such as Pennsylvania's that awarded lower benefits to newer residents.

In the appeals court, Pennsylvania argued that its residence requirement did not penalize the plaintiffs' fundamental right to travel or their right to equal protection. Instead, it argued, the court erred in holding that the scheme was unconstitutional when it found that it was not related to a legitimate governmental interest. The state contended that the statute furthered its legitimate interest in fostering the self-sufficiency and work ethic of its citizens, including its newest citizens. In this way, the two-tier system encouraged beneficiaries to seek work rather than increased benefits.

### Decision

The appeals court affirmed the district court decision in this case and declared Pennsylvania's two-tier welfare system unconstitutional. The court referred to *Shapiro v. Thompson*, the landmark Supreme Court case that struck down residency requirements for welfare recipients. In this decision, the Court had found that "any classification which serves to penalize the exercise of [the] right [to travel], unless shown to be necessary to promote a compelling governmental interest, is unconstitutional."[34] In the *Shapiro* decision, the Supreme Court had concluded that the one-year residence requirement discriminated based solely on duration of residency in the state and thus obstructed the fundamental right to interstate travel and migration.

The appeals court also referenced *Memorial Hospital v. Maricopa County*, in which the Supreme Court had ruled on an Arizona law that required one-year residency in a county as a prerequisite to receiving free nonemergency hospital or medical care. The Court found that medical care is as much a basic necessity of life to an indigent as welfare assistance and that the classification penalized those persons who had exercised their constitutional right of interstate migration.

Taking these Supreme Court opinions into account, the appeals court stated the following in its opinion in the *Maldonado* case:

> *The appropriate comparison is between those persons subject to the classification and those persons who are similarly situated but for the classification. Here, whether Pennsylvania's two-tier scheme amounts to a penalty must be determined by comparing new residents of Pennsylvania and other similarly situated longer-term Pennsylvania residents, and not by comparing new residents of Pennsylvania and those of their former state. . . . Residents of Puerto Rico have no claim to Pennsylvania welfare benefits or to equal protection under Pennsylvania's welfare laws until they move from Puerto Rico and establish a bona fide residence in Pennsylvania. Only once those persons reside in Pennsylvania is the classification applicable to them. . . .*
>
> *From a constitutional standpoint, it is of no consequence that the Maldonados receive the same benefits that they would have received in Puerto Rico. Pennsylvania's two-tier welfare scheme penalizes the Maldonados for having exercised their right to travel by treating them significantly less favorably than other similarly situated longer-term Pennsylvania residents solely because they exercised that right more recently. . . . The $532 monthly reduction in the Maldonados' Pennsylvania benefits, based solely on their newly arrived status, amounts to a 64 percent reduction in cash benefits and plainly penalizes them for having exercised their right to migrate into the state. . . . The Commonwealth [of Pennsylvania] has not demonstrated that this is a compelling interest or that a two-tier scheme is necessary to achieve that end.[35]*

## Impact

The *Maldonado* case decided residency requirements *after* the passage of the PRWORA law in 1996. It confirmed the 1960s-era Supreme Court decision in the case of *Shapiro v. Thompson*, striking down any "welfare magnet" laws that provided lower benefits to more recent residents. Although the welfare reform law was designed to give states more flexibility in how they administer their welfare programs, setting up two-tier benefit levels in this manner was still found to be unconstitutional.

## SAENZ V. ROE, 526 U.S. 489 (1999)

### Background

Before and after the passage of the welfare reform law in 1996, California was providing higher welfare benefits than most other states. In 1992, the California legislature enacted §11450.03 of the state Welfare and Institutions Code. Like the Pennsylvania system in contention in the case *Maldonado v. Pennsylvania* (see above), the California law limited new residents to the benefits they were entitled to in their prior state. Three newer California residents—having moved from Louisiana, Oklahoma, and Colorado—challenged the constitutionality of the system, each alleging abusive family circumstances as the reason for their move. Louisiana and Oklahoma provided $190 and $341, respectively, for a family of three (as opposed to full California benefits of $641); the former Colorado resident was limited to $280 a month, as opposed to the full California grant of $504 for a family of two.

### Legal Issues

The 1992 suit was successful in federal district court and was upheld in the Supreme Court. Then Congress enacted the Personal Responsibility and Work Opportunity Reconciliation Act of 1996, which replaced AFDC with Temporary Assistance to Needy Families (TANF). The new law expressly authorized any state receiving a TANF grant to pay the benefit amount of another state's TANF program to residents who had lived in their new state for less than 12 months. California then announced that enforcement of its 12-month residency requirement for full benefits would return on April 1, 1997.

On that date, the law was challenged again. The district court again issued an injunction. An appeals court affirmed the injunction, and the case arrived at the Supreme Court.

### Decision

The Supreme Court rejected the appeal by the State of California and declared the state's two-tier system of benefits unconstitutional, giving the following opinion on May 17, 1999:

*The right to travel embraces a citizen's right to be treated equally in her new State of residence, [thus] a discriminatory classification is itself a penalty. California's classifications are defined entirely by the period of residency and the location of the disfavored class members' prior residences. Within the category of new residents, those who lived in another country or in a State that had higher benefits than California are treated like lifetime residents; and within the broad subcategory of new arrivals who are treated less favorably, there are 45 smaller classes [i.e., from 45 other states] whose [lesser] benefit levels are determined by the law of their former States. California's legitimate interest in saving money does not justify this discriminatory scheme.[36]*

### Impact

The *Saenz v. Roe* decision deemed an important provision of the 1996 welfare reform law to be unconstitutional: It struck down the 12-month residency requirement, which had been a serious bone of contention in the writing and passage of the new federal law. The vote was 7-2, with Chief Justice William Rehnquist and Justice Clarence Thomas dissenting. In his dissent, Thomas invoked the original intent of the framers Constitution:

*The Articles of Confederation . . . [in Article IV] guaranteed that "the free inhabitants of each of these States, paupers, vagabonds and fugitives from justice excepted, shall be entitled to all privileges and immunities of free citizens in the several States." . . . [A]t the time the Fourteenth Amendment was adopted, people understood that "privileges or immunities of citizens" were fundamental rights, rather than every public benefit established by positive law. Accordingly, the majority's conclusion—that a State violates the Privileges or Immunities Clause when it "discriminates" against citizens who have been domiciled in the State for less than a year in the distribution of welfare benefit [sic] appears contrary to the original understanding and is dubious at best.[37]*

## LEGAL SERVICES CORPORATION V. VELASQUEZ, 531 U.S. 533 (2001)

### Background

This case involved the Legal Services Corporation (LSC), a public agency authorized to distribute funds appropriated by Congress to organizations providing free legal assistance to indigent clients. There are restrictions on the funds, however. By federal law, recipients cannot give the money to any political party or campaign or use it to advocate or oppose any ballot measure. Nor can the funds be paid to lawyers or groups in criminal proceedings or in litigation involving nontherapeutic abortions, school desegregation, military desertion, or violations of the Selective Service (military draft) statutes.

Since 1996, Congress has also prohibited Legal Services funding of any organization that seeks to challenge the welfare laws. Organizations and attorneys that receive the funds cannot represent clients in a welfare matter that challenges these laws—even when the challenge becomes apparent after representation is under way. The respondents were lawyers employed by LSC grantees who challenged this restriction. A federal appeals court invalidated the restriction, finding it in violation of the First Amendment. The case then went to the Supreme Court.

## *Legal Issues*

In this case, the LSC and the federal government cited *Rust v. Sullivan*. The Supreme Court had upheld a prohibition barring doctors employed by federally funded family-planning clinics from discussing abortion with their patients. The counseling activities covered by the *Rust* decision were judged to be governmental speech, as doctors were giving information on government programs. In a welfare suit, by contrast, an attorney representing a petitioner is opposing a government policy, regulation, or decision.

## *Decision*

The Supreme Court affirmed the lower court decision, holding that the LSC's restriction on funding violates the First Amendment. The restriction, said the Court, distorts the judicial system by limiting the advocacy of private, independent attorneys who may be arguing on behalf of their clients and against a decision of a government agency. It also unfairly insulates the laws of the government from challenge. This is especially true in cases when an indigent client has no alternative in seeking representation—in contrast to a medical patient, who can more easily find an alternative, private-sector clinic or doctor. The majority opinion of February 28, 2001, written by Justice Anthony Kennedy, states the following:

> *Although the government has the latitude to ensure that its own message is being delivered, neither that latitude nor its rationale applies to subsidies for private speech in every instance. . . . The LSC program was designed to facilitate private speech, not to promote a governmental message. An LSC attorney speaks on behalf of a private, indigent client in a welfare benefits claim, while the Government's message is delivered by the attorney defending the benefits decision. The attorney's advice to the client and advocacy to the courts cannot be classified as governmental speech even under a generous understanding of that concept.*[38]

### *Impact*

The decision in this case allowed indigent clients a wider latitude of argument in their appeals on welfare law to the courts: LSC-funded attorneys may challenge the laws in the context of an argument over the delivery of welfare benefits. However, the LSC still restricts certain political activities of the organizations and attorneys they fund. Banned activities include lobbying lawmakers and representing any client that is making a direct effort to amend the welfare laws or regulations.

## *BARNHART V. THOMAS*, 540 U.S. 20 (2003)

### *Background*

The respondent in this case, Pauline Thomas, had worked as an elevator operator at a time when the profession was long obsolete. In August 1995, her job was eliminated. At the age of 53, she applied for Title II benefits (for disability) and Supplemental Security Income under Title XVI of the Social Security Act, claiming disability by reason of heart disease and cervical and lumbar radiculopathy. An administrative law judge (ALJ), a type of judge who is responsible for deciding appeals to the Social Security Administration, accepted that Thomas was impaired. But the judge also found that her disability did not prevent her from working as an elevator operator and rejected the argument that the job of elevator operator no longer existed in significant numbers in the national economy. The ALJ's decision was upheld by the district court, which affirmed that job obsolescence is irrelevant under the regulations of the Social Security Administration (SSA). A federal appeals court reversed the decision, which was then brought to the Supreme Court.

### *Legal Issues*

The Social Security Administration (SSA) pays benefits and Supplemental Security Income to persons with a "disability." A person qualifies as disabled, and thereby eligible for such benefits, "only if his physical or mental impairment or impairments are of such severity that he is not only unable to do his previous work but cannot, considering his age, education, and work experience, engage in any other kind of substantial gainful work which exists in the national economy."[39]

### *Decision*

The Supreme Court held that the SSA, in reaching its finding on Thomas's case without investigating whether the job still exists in significant numbers, made a reasonable interpretation of the Social Security law. Writing for the majority on November 12, 2003, Justice Antonin Scalia explained,

*[The Social Security guideline] establishes two requirements: An impairment must render an individual "unable to do his previous work" and must also preclude him from "engag[ing] in any other kind of substantial gainful work." The clause "which exists in the national economy" clearly qualifies the latter requirement. The SSA may find "not disabled" a claimant who can do his previous work, without inquiring whether that work exists in the national economy. Rather, it reserves inquiry into the national economy for the last step in its evaluation process, when it considers vocational factors and determines whether the claimant can perform other jobs in the national economy.*

*Congress could have determined that an analysis of a claimant's capacity to do his previous work would in most cases be an effective and efficient administrative proxy for the claimant's ability to do some work that exists in the national economy. . . .*

*When a statute speaks clearly to the issue at hand we "must give effect to the unambiguously expressed intent of Congress," but when the statute "is silent or ambiguous" we must defer to a reasonable construction by the agency charged with its implementation.[40]*

In this case, the Supreme Court found that the Social Security Administration had made a reasonable decision: The scarcity of a given occupation does not qualify an otherwise able worker as disabled. Rather than being qualified for SSA and SSI benefits, the worker can reasonably be expected to engage in a similar but different occupation.

### Impact

The decision in this case narrowed the scope of arguments for disability claims under the Social Security Act. Engaging in an obsolete occupation does not contribute to one's inability to carry out a different occupation that is more current in the national economy.

---

[1] Franklin Roosevelt, "Message to Congress Reviewing the Broad Objectives and Accomplishments of the Administration." Social Security Online. Available online. URL: http://www.ssa.gov/history/fdrstmts.html#message1. Accessed on February 4, 2008.

[2] "Social Security Act 1935." Available online. URL: http://www.ourdocuments. gov/doc.php?flash=true&doc=68. Accessed on February 4, 2008.

[3] "Social Security Act 1935." Available online. URL: http://www.ourdocuments. gov/doc.php?flash=true&doc=68. Accessed on February 4, 2008.

[4] "Historical Background and Development of Social Security: Pre-Social Security Period." Social Security Online. Available online. URL: http://www.ssa. gov/history/briefhistory3.html. Accessed on February 4, 2008.

[5] Vee Burke, et al., "New Welfare Law: The Personal Responsibility and Work Opportunity Reconciliation Act of 1996," CRS Report for Congress. Available on-

line. URL: http://digital.library.unt.edu/govdocs/crs/permalink/meta-crs-369:1. Accessed on February 4, 2008.

[6] "Welfare Reform: Deficit Reduction Act of 2005," U.S. Department of Health and Human Services, Administration for Children and Families. Available online. URL: http://www.acf.hhs.gov/programs/ofa/drafact.htm.

[7] *Steward Machine Company v. Davis*, 301 U.S. 548 (1937), The Oyez Project. Available online. URL: http://www.oyez.org/cases/1901-1939/1936/1936_837/>. Accessed on September 24, 2007.

[8] *Steward Machine Company v. Davis*, 301 U.S. 548 (1937), The Oyez Project. Available online. URL: http://www.oyez.org/cases/1901-1939/1936/1936_837/>. Accessed on September 24, 2007.

[9] *Steward Machine Company v. Davis*, 301 U.S. 548 (1937), The Oyez Project. Available online. URL: http://www.oyez.org/cases/1901-1939/1936/1936_837/>. Accessed on September 24, 2007.

[10] *Helvering v. Davis*. Social Security Online History Pages. Available online. URL: http:www.ssa.gov/history/supreme1.html. Accessed on September 24, 2007.

[11] *Helvering v. Davis*. Social Security Online History Pages. Available online. URL: http:www.ssa.gov/history/supreme1.html. Accessed on September 24, 2007.

[12] *Carmichael v. Southern Coal and Coke Co.* Social Security Online History Pages. Available online. URL: www.ssa.gov/history/supreme3.html. Accessed on September 24, 2007.

[13] *Carmichael v. Southern Coal and Coke Co.* Social Security Online History Pages. Available online. URL: www.ssa.gov/history/supreme3.html. Accessed on September 24, 2007.

[14] *King v. Smith*. Available online. URL: Justia.com http://supreme.justia.com/us/392/309/. Accessed on February 13, 2008.

[15] *Shapiro v. Thompson*. Cornell University Law School, Legal Information Institute. Available online. URL: http://www.law.cornell.edu/supct-cgi/get-us-cite/394/618. Accessed on September 24, 2007.

[16] *Goldberg v. Kelly*, 397 U.S. 254 (1970). FindLaw.com. Available online. URL: http://www.laws.findlaw.com/us/397/254.html. Accessed on September 24, 2007.

[17] *Dandridge v. Williams*, 397 U.S. 471 (1970). The Oyez Project. Available online. URL: http://www.oyez.org/cases/1960-1969/1969/1969_131/. Accessed on September 25, 2007.

[18] *Graham v. Department of Public Welfare*. Cornell University Law School, Legal Information Institute. Available online. URL: http://www.law.cornell.edu/supct/html/historics/USSC_CR_0403_0365_ZO.html.

[19] Social Security Act, 1939 Amendments. Social Security Administration. Available online. URL: http://www.ssa.gov/history/pdf/1939Act.pdf. Accessed on September 25, 2007.

[20] *Townsend v. Swank*. Justia.com. Available online. URL: http://supreme.justia.com/us/404/282/. Accessed on September 25, 2007.

[21] *Townsend v. Swank*. Justia.com. Available online. URL: http://supreme.justia.com/us/404/282/. Accessed on September 25, 2007.

[22] *Jefferson v. Hackney*, Justia.com. Available online. URL: http://supreme.justia.com/us/406/535/case.html. Accessed on September 25, 2007.

[23] *Carleson v. Remillard*, 406 U.S. 598 (1972). The Oyez Project. Available online. URL: http://www.oyez.org/cases/1970-1979/1971/1971_70_250/. Accessed on October 2, 2007.

[24] *New Jersey Welfare Rights v. Cahill*. Justia.com. Available online. URL: http://supreme.justia.com/us/411/619/. Accessed on October 2, 2007.

[25] *Burns v. Alcala*. Justia.com. Available online. URL: http://supreme.justia.com/us/420/575/. Accessed on October 2, 2007.

[26] *Miller v. Youakim*. FindLaw.com. Available online. URL: http://caselaw.lp.findlaw.com/cgi-bin/getcase.pl?court=US&vol=440&invol=125&friend=nytimes. Accessed on February 13, 2008.

[27] *Miller v. Youakim*, 440 U.S. 125 (1979). The Oyez Project. Available online. URL: http://www.oyez.org/cases/1970-1979/1978/1978_77_742/. Accessed on October 2, 2007.

[28] *Blum v. Bacon*, 457 U.S. 132 (1982). The Oyez Project. Available online. URL: http://www.oyez.org/cases/1980-1989/1981/1981_81_770/. Accessed on October 2, 2007.

[29] *Bowen v. Roy*. FindLaw.com. Available online. URL: http://caselaw.lp.findlaw.com/scripts/getcase.pl?navby=CASE&court=US&vol=476&page= 693. Accessed on October 2, 2007.

[30] *Bowen v. Gilliard*, 483 U.S. 587 (1987). The Oyez Project. Available online. URL: http://www.oyez.org/cases/1980-1989/1986/1986_86_509. Accessed on March 18, 2008.

[31] *Anderson v. Edwards*. Legal Information Institute, Cornell University Law School. Available online. URL: http://www.law.cornell.edu/supct/html/93-1883.ZS.html. Accessed on October 2, 2007.

[32] Social Security Act, at Social Security Online. Available online. URL: http://www.ssa.gov/OP_Home/ssact/title04/0454.htm. Accessed on September 27, 2007.

[33] *Blessing v. Freestone*, Cornell University Law School, Legal Information Institute. Available online. URL: http://www.law.cornell.edu/supct/html/95-1441.ZS.html. Accessed on October 2, 2007.

[34] *Shapiro v. Thompson*, Cornell University Law School, Legal Information Institute. Available online. URL: http:///www.law.cornell.edu/supct-cgi/get-us-cite/394/618. Accessed on September 24, 2007.

[35] *Maldonado et al. v. Pennsylvania Department of Public Welfare*. Available online. URL: http://vls.law.vill.edu/LOCATOR/3d/Jun2001/971893o.txt. Accessed on October 2, 2007.

[36] *Saenz v. Roe*, FindLaw.com. Available online. URL: http://caselaw.lp.findlaw.com/scripts/getcase.pl?navby=CASE&court=US&vol=526&page=489. Accessed on October 2, 2007.

[37] *Saenz v. Roe*, FindLaw.com. Available online. URL: http://caselaw.lp.findlaw.com/scripts/getcase.pl?navby=CASE&court=US&vol=526&page=489. Accessed on October 2, 2007.

[38] *Legal Services Corp. v. Velazquez*, 531 U.S. 533 (2001), The Oyez Project. Available online. URL: http://www.oyez.org/cases/2000-2009/2000/2000_99_603. Accessed on October 2, 2007.

[39] "Social Security and Acquiescence Rulings." SSR 85-28: Titles II and XVI: Medical Impairments That Are Not Severe. Available online. URL: http://www.ssa.gov/OP_Home/rulings/di/01/SSR85-28-di-01.html. Accessed on February 13, 2008.

[40] *Barnhart v. Thomas*, Cornell University Law School, Legal Information Institute. Available online. URL: http://www.law.cornell.edu/supct/html/02-763.ZS.html. Accessed on October 2, 2007.

# CHAPTER 3

## CHRONOLOGY

This chapter presents a chronology of significant events in the history of welfare law and government policy. Included are major legislation from precolonial times to the present, as well as court cases and various state and federal initiatives regarding the welfare system. Unless stated otherwise, the listed events occurred in the United States.

### 1601

- England passes a Poor Law, guiding local parishes in the provision of relief for children, the able-bodied poor, and the "impotent"—those suffering disability or sickness. The justices of the peace in each parish appoint overseers, who collect taxes for relief and distribute benefits.

### 1642

- The Plymouth Colony adopts a law, modeled on the English Poor Law of 1601, allowing for the collection of taxes by each town to provide for relief of the poor.

### 1657

- The Scots Charitable Society, the first private mutual-aid group organized to benefit the poor, is established by 27 men of Scottish heritage in Boston. Legally incorporated in 1786, the group served as a model for other private charitable groups in colonial America and has survived into the 21st century.

### 1664

- New Amsterdam becomes an English colony, ends its system of voluntary and church-sponsored poor relief, and adopts the English Poor Law model.

# Welfare and Welfare Reform

## 1672

- Virginia passes a statute directing justices of the peace to enforce the laws of England against vagrants and idlers and empowering the county courts to place children whose parents are unable to care for them as apprentices to tradesmen.

## 1701

- The colony of Massachusetts begins reimbursing towns for benefits extended to those "unsettled" persons (nonresidents) suffering contagious disease. This law, written to avoid the forced eviction of the sick from towns burdened with their care, is the first to establish a system of public welfare on a colony-wide basis.

## 1790

- A poor law based on the public welfare statutes of the northeastern United States is passed in the Northwest Territory, which on its organization in 1787 included what are now Ohio, Michigan, Indiana, Illinois, Wisconsin, and Minnesota east of the Mississippi River.

## 1797

- The Society for the Relief of Poor Women is founded in New York. It organizes home visits and other forms of outdoor relief for the poor.

## 1795

- The district of Speenhamland, England, guarantees a minimum income level for all workers, paying a regular benefit to relieve poverty among the rural poor. The Speenhamland system of "outdoor relief" endures until the passage of the Poor Law Amendment in 1834.

## 1805

- The Samaritan Society is founded in New York to provide emergency relief to poor citizens.

## 1821

- The Quincy Report is published in Massachusetts to analyze the growing incidence of pauperism. The report blames intemperance for the problem and identifies two general categories of the poor: the "able" poor who can work but are unwilling, and the "impotent" poor who are disabled, infirm, sick, or old.

# Chronology

## 1823

- The Yates Report is published in New York. It recommends a law banning public begging and a ban on outdoor relief to unemployed males between the ages of 18 and 50 who are physically capable of working.

## 1824

- By the County Poorhouse Act, the state of New York directs the founding of one or more workhouses in each county, to be funded by county-wide tax levies. Residence at the workhouses is mandatory for all those receiving public relief.

## 1834

- England's Poor Law Amendment, also known as the Poor Law Reform Bill, amends the Poor Law of 1601 and ends "outdoor relief" to the poor in England. The law sets up a Poor Law Board to oversee a system of public workhouses, which were to be so unpleasant that anyone able to work would not voluntarily choose to enter one.

## 1845

- The first chapter of the St. Vincent de Paul Society in the United States is formed in St. Louis, Missouri. Its goal is to organize relief for the poor among religious organizations.

## 1853

- The New York Children's Aid Society is founded to remove young beggars and runaways from the streets and place them in foster homes in western states.

## 1865

- Congress establishes the Bureau of Refugees, Freedmen, and Abandoned Lands, the first federal welfare agency, as a part of the War Department. The "Freedmen's Bureau" assists war refugees and freed slaves to find shelter, medical aid, food, and employment until it is closed down in 1872.

## 1872

- The New York State Charities Aid Association is organized by Louisa Lee Schuyler to advocate for improved public health and social welfare.

## 1877

■ The Reverend Stephen Humphreys Gurteen establishes the Charity Organization Society in Buffalo, New York, intended to coordinate and streamline the relief efforts of private and public welfare agencies. Within a few years, similar organizations are established in several other large American cities.

## 1889

■ Founding of Hull-House, the first "settlement house," is founded in Chicago by Jane Addams and Ellen Gates Starr. Eventually spreading over a large campus of more than a dozen buildings, Hull-House offered lectures, recreational activities, concerts, job referrals, and the first public playground in the city of Chicago.

## 1904

■ The first training colleges for social workers are founded in New York (The New York School of Philanthropy) and Boston (The Boston School of Social Work).

## 1910

■ Kansas City establishes its Board of Public Welfare, the first municipal welfare department in the United States. This agency begins a trend of cities and counties consolidating their various public charity departments into a single bureau that oversees welfare eligibility, benefit levels, and payments.

## 1921

■ Congress passes the Sheppard-Towner Maternity and Infancy Act, providing federal aid to the states to fund social welfare programs, including child health and maternity programs. The law will be repealed in 1927.

## 1929

■ ***October 29:*** The stock market crashes, bringing about a steep drop in economic activity, rising unemployment, and increasing demands on systems of local relief and private charities. Over the next few years, the Great Depression, as it comes to be called, causes mass poverty, hunger, and homelessness.

## 1931

■ The state of New York passes the State Unemployment Relief Act, also known as the Wicks Act, making New York the first state in the nation to provide unemployment benefits. The Wicks Act inspires similar legislation in 24 other states by the end of the year.

## 1932

- *January:* Wisconsin passes the first state unemployment law. By the "Wisconsin Plan" (also known as the "American Plan"), employers pay into a reserve fund, specific to each company; their tax rates are affected by the amount of unemployment claims filed against them. By the rival "Ohio Plan," employers pay into a common state fund rather than individual reserves.
- *June:* President Hoover signs the Emergency Relief and Construction Act, which sets up the Emergency Relief Administration (ERA). ERA offers loans to the states for unemployment relief, but few states borrow these funds.

## 1933

- *May 12:* Congress passes the Federal Emergency Relief Act, which makes $500 million of the federal budget available to the states as grants, rather than loans, for unemployment relief. The law sets up the Federal Emergency Relief Administration (FERA), the first national welfare bureau.

## 1934

- *June 29:* President Roosevelt creates the Committee on Economic Security, whose task is to study the issue of Americans' economic security and make recommendations on how to promote it. The committee's conclusions are drafted into the bill that becomes the Social Security Act.

## 1935

- *August 14:* President Franklin Roosevelt signs the Social Security Act, passed earlier that month by a vote of 371 to 33 in the House of Representatives and 77 to 6 in the Senate. It creates a system of unemployment insurance; grants-in-aid to the states to which employers are required to contribute a percentage of their payroll; and Aid to Dependent Children (ADC), relief paid to single-parent families with dependents.

## 1937

- *May 24:* The Supreme Court upholds the Social Security Act in the cases of *Steward Machine Company v. Davis* and *Helvering v. Davis.*

- *May 24:* The Supreme Court decides the case of *Carmichael v. Southern Coal and Coke Company*, finding state-administered payroll taxes for funding unemployment insurance to be constitutional.

## 1939

- *May 16:* The first Food Stamp Program is passed, allowing those on relief to purchase stamps and receive additional stamps for free. The free stamps are given at the rate of $0.50 for every $1 of "orange stamps" and can be used to buy foods determined by the Department of Agriculture to be in surplus.
- *August 11:* Amendments to the Social Security Act are approved, greatly expanding the scope of the Social Security system. The amendments increase Old Age Insurance benefit levels, extend unemployment benefits, include dependents and survivors as beneficiaries under the newly created Survivors' Insurance, and create a system of benefits to the disabled.

## 1940

- *January 31:* The first Social Security retirement pensions are paid out from the U.S. Treasury.
- Children ages 16 and 17 become eligible for ADC payments, as long as they are attending school.

## 1943

- The first Food Stamp Program, begun in 1939, ceases operation.

## 1946

- Congress passes the National School Lunch Program, the Full Employment Act, and the National Mental Health Act, increasing the scope of federal assistance to the states for social welfare programs.

## 1949

- By the Agriculture Act, Congress directs the Department of Agriculture to deliver surplus food and goods, which are acquired through federal price supports for agricultural commodities, to the poor.

## 1950

- Further amendments to the Social Security Act extend coverage to full-time farmworkers and domestics, the self-employed, state and local public employees, and employees of nonprofit agencies.

# *Chronology*

## 1952

- *July 1:* The Notification to Law Enforcement Officials (NOLEO) Amendment comes into effect. It requires states to notify law enforcement of the payment of any welfare benefits to an abandoned child.

## 1953

- The federal Department of Health, Education, and Welfare is established. The agency oversees federal social welfare programs.

## 1956

- Social services such as job training and family counseling are added to the AFDC program but are unfunded as distinct programs by Congress. In addition, Congress supplements Social Security with Disability Insurance (DI), which insures those unable to work due to a disabling condition.
- The federal government begins raising its contributions to state ADC payments. The original schedule paying $6 per first child and $4 for subsequent children now varies depending on the average spending of the recipient state. By this system, federal contributions to state welfare programs rise faster in states with lower per-capita income.

## 1961

- By the AFDC-UP (Unemployed Parent) law, AFDC benefits are extended to two-parent families in which the head of the household is unemployed and the family has exhausted unemployment benefits. This measure is intended to discourage unemployed fathers from abandoning their families.
- *May 29:* A pilot food stamp program begins, testing a new system for distributing food to low-income people. Like the program run during World War II, it requires food stamps to be purchased. But it eliminates the additional stamps to be used for surplus foods.

## 1962

- Aid to Dependent Children (ADC) is renamed Aid to Families with Dependent Children (AFDC).
- *July 25:* The Public Amendments to the Social Security Act, also known as the Social Service Amendments, are enacted. These amendments increase federal subsidies to state job retraining programs to up to 75 percent of the cost incurred by the states and extend the AFDC-UP program.

**101**

## 1964

- *January 8:* In his State of the Union message, President Lyndon Johnson urges Congress to pass a 13-point program that he calls the War on Poverty.
- *August 20:* President Johnson signs the Economic Opportunity Act, intended to replace direct welfare benefits with enhanced economic opportunity for the poor.
- *August 20:* President Johnson signs the Food Stamp Act, which allows qualifying families to buy food coupons at a discount to their face value and use them to purchase groceries. The states are allowed to set eligibility for the program, and participation by stores and local communities is voluntary.

## 1965

- *July 1:* AFDC eligibility for students expands. Beneficiaries aged 16 to 20 may receive welfare payments if they are attending college or a university.
- *July 30:* Amendments to the Social Security Act establish Medicare (Title XVIII) and Medicaid (Title XIX). Medicare provides medical and hospitalization insurance to those over 65 years of age, funded by participant premiums, Social Security payroll taxes, and federal subsidies. Medicaid is intended to provide medical services for people who qualify for welfare; it is funded by federal grants to the states.

## 1966

- The National Coordinating Committee of Welfare Rights Groups is formed. Its goals are a guaranteed minimum income for all families and a curb on investigative tactics used to determine eligibility for welfare benefits.

## 1967

- Responding to a sharp increase in the number of welfare recipients, Congress passes the Public Welfare Amendments to the Social Security Act. The Work Incentive Program (WIP) is established, disqualifying adults and older children from AFDC benefits if they do not accept jobs or job retraining.

## 1968

- *March 23:* In *King v. Smith*, the Supreme Court strikes down an Alabama statute that denied AFDC payments to households where the mother cohabits with a "substitute" father.

## 1969

- *April 21:* In the case of *Shapiro v. Thompson*, the Supreme Court decides that eligibility for public assistance cannot be restricted by duration of residency.
- *August 8:* President Nixon presents the Family Assistance Plan (FAP), which proposes a minimum federally guaranteed annual income of $1,600 for a family of four. Although Nixon presses for the legislation for the rest of his first term in office, the FAP is subject to criticism from conservatives and liberals alike and fails to pass Congress.

## 1970

- In the case of *Goldberg v. Kelly*, the Supreme Court decides that welfare beneficiaries who are denied benefits have the right to a full evidentiary hearing on the matter. The decision vests welfare recipients with a property right in their benefits.

## 1971

- *January 11:* Public Law 91-671 is enacted, giving the Food Stamp Program uniform national eligibility standards and work requirements. Participating states must provide stamps equivalent to the cost of a nutritionally adequate diet. Households are limited to food stamps valued at up to 30 percent of their income. The Food Stamp Program is expanded to Guam, Puerto Rico, and the Virgin Islands.
- *June 14:* By the decision in *Graham v. Department of Public Welfare*, the Supreme Court strikes down the denial of welfare benefits to resident aliens, on the grounds that this practice violates the Fourteenth Amendment's guarantee of due process and equal protection.
- *August 10:* The Agriculture and Consumer Protection Act is enacted; it requires states to implement the Food Stamp Program in all jurisdictions by July 1, 1974. It also adjusts the income calculation for beneficiaries and requires the Department of Agriculture to establish temporary eligibility for food stamps in case of natural disaster.
- *December 9:* President Richard Nixon vetoes the Comprehensive Child Care Act, passed by Congress to fund child-care, nutrition, and preschool programs.
- *December 27:* By the Talmadge Amendments, Congress mandates that all AFDC recipients must register for job training, except for mothers with children under six. States must place at least 15 percent of people registered into jobs or lose federal funding for AFDC benefits.

## 1972

- *October 30:* Congress raises Social Security benefits by 20 percent and expands federal funding for the Food Stamp Program. Through the Supplemental Security Income (SSI) program, the federal government establishes uniform guidelines for three categorical assistance programs: Old Age Assistance, Aid to the Blind, and Aid to the Permanently and Totally Disabled. Previously the states had set eligibility and benefit levels for these programs.

## 1973

- Congress passes the Earned Income Tax Credit, which provides a refund of income taxes up to $400 to those earning $4,000 a year or less.
- *May 7:* In *New Jersey Welfare Rights Organization v. Cahill*, the Supreme Court rules that federal regulations override competing state statutes, such as a New Jersey law that denied AFDC benefits to the illegitimate children of common-law parents.
- *December 28:* Congress passes the Comprehensive Employment and Training Act (CETA), by which the federal government funds public service jobs for the unemployed through nonprofit agencies.

## 1974

- *July 1:* All states are now required to participate in the Food Stamp Program. The program is to be implemented in Puerto Rico on November 1.

## 1975

- *January 4:* President Gerald Ford signs the Social Service Amendments of 1974. These amendments to the Social Security Act change the way the AFDC program deals with child support. Child support payments for children in AFDC must go through a state child-support enforcement agency, rather than to the family. In order to become eligible for AFDC payments, applicants must assign their rights to child support to the state and cooperate in establishing the paternity of a child born out of wedlock.
- *October 1:* By the Social Service Amendments (Title XX) to the Social Security Act, the federal government allocates $2.5 billion to the states for welfare services, to be determined by each state.

## 1977

- President Jimmy Carter proposes a Jobs and Income Security program, but the idea fails to gain any support in Congress.

- *September:* Congress passes and the president signs the Food Stamp Act of 1977. The law eliminates the purchase requirement, which had forced beneficiaries to buy food stamps (at a discount to their face value).

## 1980

- *June 17:* Congress passes the Adoption Assistance and Child Welfare Act. The law sets limits on the amount of time children must spend in foster care (18 months), and offers federal aid to subsidize adoption.

## 1981

- The newly inaugurated administration of President Ronald Reagan passes important changes to the federal welfare and Social Security systems. Disability Insurance (DI) cases are to be reviewed every three years, with those able to work in any capacity losing their eligibility; total family benefits are capped; the benefit calculation is reviewed and changed.
- The eligibility age for welfare beneficiaries is reduced to 17 years, with states having the option to extend eligibility to 18 years for those attending high school.

## 1984

- *October 9:* President Ronald Reagan signs into law the Disability Benefits Reform Act, designed to solve an administrative logjam and bitter debate between the Social Security Administration and the administrative law judges responsible for deciding disability review cases.
- Congress requires that, in all states, AFDC benefits be extended to two-parent families in which the second parent is disabled or incapacitated.

## 1987

- Governor Tommy Thompson of Wisconsin proposes a series of five major welfare reform initiatives known as "Wisconsin Works," or W-2. The proposed legislation (which passes in 1996) offers incentives for welfare recipients to end their benefits, extends work requirements for mothers of preschool children, and, through the Learnfare proposal, requires teenagers in the AFDC program to attend school in order to be counted in the calculation of the family's welfare benefit.

## 1988

- *October 13:* Congress passes the Family Support Act. The law sets work requirements for two-parent families receiving welfare benefits and sets up the JOBS program, a state employment and training program to move

AFDC clients from welfare to the workforce. It also requires states to extend AFDC-UP benefits to families with unemployed parents, effective 1990.

## 1990

- *October 1:* Federal requirements regarding AFDC-UP come into effect. By the Family Support Act of 1988, all states must extend AFDC eligibility to families with unemployed parents. Prior to this amendment, 22 states banned such AFDC-UP payments to two-parent families.

## 1992

- The states begin experiments with welfare reform measures, under a program of federal waivers of guidelines and regulations. The experiments set up work requirements, time limits, increasing income limits, and other measures designed to cap or lower welfare spending.

## 1993

- *August 10:* Congress expands the Earned Income Tax Credit, extending it to childless workers.
- *October 17:* The Mickey Leland Childhood Hunger Relief Act increases eligibility for food stamps. Among other provisions, the new law allows deductions for child support payments made to persons outside the household, and raises the cap on deductions for child care for children.

## 1995

- *February 10:* Governor William Weld of Massachusetts signs a landmark Welfare Reform Law. The Department of Public Welfare becomes the Department of Transitional Assistance, and the law sets work requirements for welfare families with children age six and older and time limits (two years) for families with children two years and older.

## 1996

- *April 25:* Governor Tommy Thompson of Wisconsin signs into law the W-2 program. The program is a harbinger of a sweeping welfare reform law to be passed later in the year by the U.S. Congress.
- *August 22:* President Clinton signs the Personal Responsibility and Work Opportunity Reconciliation Act (PRWORA), also known as the 1996 welfare reform bill. It replaces AFDC with Temporary Assistance for Needy Families (TANF) benefits can be paid to any individual for no more than five years (consecutive or nonconsecutive).

# *Chronology*

## 1997

- *May 2:* The federal government rejects a plan by Texas to fully privatize its welfare system.
- *August 5:* The Balanced Budget Act of 1997 is signed into federal law. The law restores SSI benefits to elderly immigrants, eases restrictions on food stamps, and allows food stamp recipients to take jobs and enter job training programs. It also includes a new $3 billion welfare-to-work grant.
- *August 5:* The Taxpayer Relief Act is signed into federal law. The act expands the Work Opportunity Tax Credit Program and creates the Welfare-to-Work Tax Credit, offered to employers who hire welfare beneficiaries.

## 1999

- *May 17:* In *Saenz v. Roe*, the Supreme Court strikes down a California provision that limited welfare benefits to residents within 12 months of taking up residency in the state. The decision invalidates residency requirements for full welfare payments in 14 other states.

## 2002

- *May:* Congress passes the Food Security and Rural Investment Act of 2002, which reauthorizes the Food Stamp Program. Eligibility for the program is restored for resident aliens who have lived in the United States for at least five years; there is no minimum residency requirement for immigrants receiving disability payments or for children.

## 2003

- According to the U.S. Census Bureau, 12.5 percent of the population are living below the poverty line, an increase from 12.1 percent, in 2002, with the greatest increase occurring among black children. In addition, welfare caseloads have dropped in nearly every state and overall by approximately 50 percent.

## 2005

- *December:* PRWORA, which has been temporarily extended in each of four years since its 2001 expiration, is revised and reauthorized by the Deficit Reduction Act of 2005. The law requires the states to have 50 percent of their cases meeting work requirements, in which TANF recipients participate for at least 20 hours a week in one or more of 12 work activities. The reauthorization remains in effect until 2010.

## 2006

- The federal government publishes new rules for TANF grants to the states. Among other guidelines, the rules (which take effect on October 1) require that at least 50 percent of welfare recipients work at least 30 hours a week.

## 2007

- Federal TANF spending reaches $16.5 billion.

## 2008

- A study published by the Rockefeller Institute of Government finds that welfare spending is diverging sharply between high- and low-income states. For example, while Connecticut spent $3,527 per beneficiary in noncash assistance in 2006, Mississippi spent $702 per person. From 1997 to 2006, the national average for AFDC/TANF assistance declined from $1,700 to $600 per beneficiary, with about 60 percent of the total money coming from the federeal treasury.

# CHAPTER 4

---

# BIOGRAPHICAL LISTING

Following are brief biographies of individuals who have played a significant role in the history of social welfare policy, and in the making of the current Social Security and federal welfare systems.

**Edith Abbott,** educator and author born in Grand Island, Nebraska. Abbott was the daughter of Othman Abbott, a Nebraska lieutenant governor. She studied at the University of Nebraska and earned a doctorate in economics at the University of Chicago. She served as dean of the School of Social Service Administration at that university from 1924 until 1942. Abbott supported expanded public welfare benefits and a federal welfare administration. She helped to found the Bureau of Public Welfare in Cook County (encompassing Chicago) and, along with her sister Grace Abbott, helped to write the Social Security Act of 1935. Edith Abbott was an influential figure in the days when the federal government was systematizing the national welfare program that is still in place. Her books include *The Tenements of Chicago 1908–1935*, *Public Assistance*, and *Social Welfare and Professional Education*.

**Grace Abbott,** social reformer and child-welfare advocate from Grand Island, Nebraska, who played an important role in child welfare and child labor issues. Abbott attended Grand Island Baptist College and afterward taught high school. She attended the University of Chicago from 1907 until 1909, when she received a master's degree in philosophy. She then began working at Hull-House, where she was a resident until 1917 and directed the Immigrants Protective League. In 1917, Abbott became a director of the Children's Bureau, a division of the Department of Labor, where she oversaw enforcement of child labor laws passed by Congress in 1916. She also supported provisions in the Sheppard-Towner Act, which set up the first federal grants for welfare benefits for children. Abbott became head of the Children's Bureau in 1921 and served in that post until 1934, when she became a professor of public welfare at the University of Chicago. She wrote *Child and the State*, a book on public aid to single mothers and children that had some influence on the founding of the ADC program under the Social Security Act of 1935.

**Jane Addams,** pioneer in the settlement house movement of the late 19th century. Addams was born into a Quaker family, the daughter of John Huy Addams, state senator from Illinois. A visit to Toynbee House in London inspired her to open Hull-House in 1889 in Chicago. Hull-House became a bustling social welfare workshop, where those in need of training and education could attend classes and find employment. It became a model for other such institutions at a time when private charity was promoted as the answer to corrupt and ineffective local administration of social welfare programs. Hull-House expanded in the following years to provide meals and temporary shelter to the homeless, a nursery, and a library; it offered lectures and welcomed foreign visitors interested in bringing the settlement house idea to their home countries. Addams helped found the National Progressive Party in 1912 and became president of the Women's Peace Party in 1915. She was awarded the Nobel Peace Prize in 1931. Two of her books describe *Twenty Years at Hull-House* and *The Second Twenty Years at Hull-House*.

**Arthur Altmeyer,** best known for his work writing and administering the Social Security Act. Born in DePere, Wisconsin, Altmeyer earned a doctorate from the University of Wisconsin in 1931 and then joined the administration of President Franklin Roosevelt. Altmeyer favored a greatly expanded federal role in providing benefits to the unemployed during the Great Depression. He served in the National Recovery Administration (NRA), the agency founded under Roosevelt to run a variety of job and training programs. In 1934, he was named to the Committee on Economic Security, which developed the Social Security Act of 1935, and he later served as chairman of the Social Security Board beginning in 1937. He became commissioner of the Social Security Administration but lost his job in 1953 at the outset of the Eisenhower administration; at that time, the Social Security program was coming under criticism as an illegal and unwise expansion of federal authority.

**William Beveridge,** a leader in British social welfare policy. Beveridge was born in Bengal, India. He studied law at Oxford but gave up his legal practice to work at Toynbee Hall, a settlement house in the poor East End of London. As a journalist for the *Morning Post*, he exposed working and living conditions of the poor, and he joined the British government in 1909 as director of Labour Exchanges, the department that administered Britain's public unemployment agencies. He became director of the London School of Economics and Political Science in 1919 and gained a reputation as one of the world's leading economists. Prime Minister Winston Churchill appointed Beveridge to chair a committee to study welfare policy in 1941. The ensuing report, *Social Insurance and Allied Services*, became a foundation for sweeping changes in British welfare policy after World War II. Beveridge suggested that Britain's private companies would benefit from shifting health insurance to the public sector, and that a national insurance system would provide the country with a healthier and more productive workforce. Under his prompting, Britain established a social security system, the National Health Service, and expanded public housing programs.

**Eveline Burns,** respected academic authority and one of the founders of the U.S. Social Security system. Burns was born in England and earned a Ph.D. at the London School of Economics. She moved to the United States in 1926 and began teaching at Columbia University in 1928. She taught economics and specialized in comparative study of the world's various social security systems. Burns joined the Committee on Economic Security in 1934 and helped to formulate the Social Security Act of 1935. She became a director of research for the Committee on Long-Range Work and Relief Policies, a part of the National Resources Planning Board. This body helped formulate postwar welfare and unemployment policy for the federal government. She wrote many prominent books and articles on the Social Security system; her *Social Security and Public Policy*, published in 1956, was the key textbook on the subject for many years.

**Harry Cassidy,** Canadian authority on social welfare policy who advocated a greatly expanded role for the federal government. Cassidy earned a doctorate from the Brookings School of Economics in 1926, after which he undertook comprehensive studies of unemployment, poverty, and homelessness in Canada. He taught at the University of Toronto in the early 1930s and became director of Social Welfare in British Columbia in 1934. He helped to found graduate schools at the University of Toronto and the School of Social Welfare at the University of California, Berkeley. His book *Social Security and Reconstruction in Canada*, published in 1943, influenced the establishment of a welfare system in Canada. Greatly influenced by the New Deal policies of the Roosevelt administration, Cassidy advocated a similar system for Canada in the years after World War II.

**Thomas Chalmers,** Scottish mathematician and church leader who undertook a change in the methods of public poor relief. Trained in mathematics at St. Andrews, he was ordained a minister in the parish of Kilmany in 1803 and then served the parish of St. John in Glasgow in 1820. Chalmers believed the system of mandatory tax levies for poor relief were counterproductive. He assigned the deacons of his church to visitation and oversight of the poor families in the parish, and to the task of encouraging them to productive employment. By this method of church involvement, Chalmers managed to reduce the levies for poor relief by a significant amount, and his approach was promoted in the following century by those advocating private solutions to poverty and unemployment.

**Bill Clinton,** president of the United States from 1993 until 2001, during whose administration the federal government passed the Personal Responsibility and Work Opportunity Reconciliation Act (PRWORA), also known as the welfare reform dawn of 1996. Clinton graduated from Georgetown University and earned a Rhodes scholarship to attend Oxford University, then earned a law degree at Yale University. He was elected governor of his home state of Arkansas in 1978 at the age of 32. During his term, he made reforms in Arkansas's educational and welfare systems. In 1992, Clinton successfully ran for the presidency as a moderate Democrat interested in a national overhaul of the AFDC program. The final welfare reform bill did not succeed until 1996, however, after Republicans had taken a majority in Congress. The new law eliminated AFDC entirely, replacing it with federal block grants for Temporary Assistance for Needy Families (TANF) programs. It also set up work requirements for welfare recipients and offered performance bonuses to the states for meeting certain goals in reducing illegitimacy and moving beneficiaries into the workforce.

**Wilbur Cohen,** welfare and Social Security administrator born in Milwaukee, Wisconsin. Cohen attended the University of Wisconsin, after which he moved to Washington, D.C., and took part in drafting the Social Security Act of 1935. He joined the Social Security Administration on its founding and helped to amend the Social Security law in the next decades, gradually broadening the act and expanding eligibility and benefits. President John Kennedy named him to the Task Force on Health and Social Security and assistant secretary in the Department of Health, Education, and Welfare (HEW). Cohen was responsible for guiding the Medicare and Medicaid laws to passage in 1965 and served HEW as full secretary in the Johnson administration. Seeing the Social Security system under threat, Cohen founded Save our Security in 1979 and fought reductions in the act's coverage during the Reagan administration.

**Robert DeForest,** social reformer and philanthropist born in New York City. DeForest studied law at Columbia University and was named general counsel of the Central Railroad of New Jersey, a post in which he served for 50 years. He took part in several Progressive-era reforms, including a New York tenement-house law in 1901, which he helped to write. His 1903 book *The Tenement-House Problem* spurred lawmakers to action and brought about greater public awareness of the condition of the poor. DeForest helped found the New York School of Philanthropy and the Russell Sage Foundation, and took part in the founding of the Red Cross disaster-relief program.

**Dorothea Dix,** 19th-century activist for better treatment of the mentally ill. Born in Hampden, Maine, Dix established a private girls' school in Boston and later a school for the poor. While working as a Sunday school teacher in the East Cambridge jail, she was horrified by the cruel treatment of the prisoners, many of whom suffered from mental illness. She helped to establish new institutions in several states and foreign countries. She persuaded Congress to pass a measure in 1854 expanding the federal government's role in providing land and money for public welfare. The new law was vetoed by President Franklin Pierce, who saw Congress overstepping its constitutional authority.

**Martha Eliot,** child-welfare administrator and educator born in Dorchester, Massachusetts. Eliot attended Radcliffe College and Johns Hopkins University, where she earned a medical degree. She joined the federal Children's Bureau in 1924 and rose to chief of that agency in 1951. As a delegate to the conference establishing the World Health Organization in 1946, Eliot was the only woman to sign the group's founding charter. She taught at the Yale University School of Medicine and the Harvard School of Public Health, and she led efforts against birth defects, rickets, and childhood diseases. She ran the federal program granting money to the states for families and dependent children, allowing the states much greater leeway in shaping these programs to suit local conditions and needs.

**John Engler,** governor of Michigan from 1991 until 2003 who oversaw an important state welfare reform law. Born in the town of Mt. Pleasant, he attended Michigan State University. He was first elected a member of the state legislature at the age of 23 and served as a Republican member of that body for 20 years. In 1991, his first year as governor, Michigan ended its general assistance program. Michigan lawmakers passed the To Strengthen Michigan Families law in 1992, which takes advantage of federal waivers to allow welfare recipients to earn more money and work longer hours. In 1995, Governor Engler signed another welfare reform law, which set up a Work First program. Work First required a minimum number of weekly hours of work by welfare recipients and required teenage parents to live in adult-supervised settings in order to receive benefits. The goal was to move welfare recipients into the workforce. This popular Michigan law was later used as a model by many states coping with the new mechanism set up by Congress with the 1996 welfare reform law.

**Abraham Epstein,** advocate of social security. Born in Russia, Epstein arrived in the United States in 1910 and attended the University of Pittsburgh. As director of the Pennsylvania Commission on Old Age Pensions, he led the drive for public old-age pensions in that state. He founded the American Association for Old Age Security in 1927, and in the following years fostered public support for a federal social security and pension system. Epstein became a consultant to the Social Security Board in the 1930s and wrote several books on the topic of old-age pensions.

**Homer Folks,** leader in Progressive-era child welfare reform. Folks was born in Hanover, Michigan, and studied at Albion College and Harvard. He served as director of several public welfare agencies, including the State Charities Aid Association of New York and Public Charities of New York City. As superintendent of Pennsylvania's Children's Aid Society, he focused on public support and training of destitute and abandoned children. Folks helped to found the National Child Labor Committee, under the administration of President Theodore Roosevelt, and led a Conference on Dependent Children and the founding of the U.S. Children's Bureau in 1912. He administered Red Cross efforts in Europe after the American entry into World War I in 1917. In New York, he helped to write the Public Health Law and the Public Welfare Act, important precursors to welfare legislation later passed under Governor Franklin Roosevelt.

**Newt Gingrich,** politician and legislator who served as Speaker of the House of Representatives from 1995 to 1999 and presided over the passage of the welfare reform law. Gingrich was born in Harrisburg, Pennsylvania. He earned a bachelor's degree from Emory University in Atlanta and a doctorate at Tulane University in New Orleans. He was a history professor at the University of West Georgia before winning his first election as a congressman from Georgia in 1978. In 1994, during the congressional campaign season, the Republicans released the Contract with America, a plan detailing actions the Republicans would take if they should attain majority status in the House. The document, written in part by Gingrich, proposed the Personal Responsibility Act, which would cut welfare spending by prohibiting welfare to mothers under age 18, by denying additional AFDC payments when new children are born into a welfare family, and by setting down work requirements and a "two years and out" limit on welfare payments, which would have to be followed by entrance into the job market or job training. These proposals were amended and adopted in the Personal Responsibility and Work Opportunity Reconciliation Act that was signed into law in 1996.

**Stephen Humphreys Gurteen,** 19th-century founder of the charity organization society movement in the United States. Gurteen was born in England and attended Cambridge University. He left for the United States soon afterward, becoming a lawyer and teacher. Appointed a minister to St. Paul's Church in Buffalo, New York, he led the church's public charity work during an economic depression. Returning to England, he observed the work of the London Charity Organisation Society and emulated this effort in Buffalo in 1877. The Buffalo Charity

Organization Society gathered community leaders and coordinated efforts of private charities, directing the needy to particular services and programs. Gurteen moved to Chicago in the 1880s and there served as director of the Chicago Charity Organization Society. These groups paved the way for reforms of private charity work and the public oversight of welfare programs in the early 20th century.

**Harry Hopkins,** leader of federal relief efforts during the Great Depression. Hopkins was born in Sioux City, Iowa. He attended Grinnell College, after which he served as the director of a settlement house on the Lower East Side of New York City. In 1915, he was named director of the city's Bureau of Child Welfare. In 1924, he was appointed by Governor Franklin Roosevelt director of the New York Temporary Emergency Relief Administration. After Roosevelt was elected president in 1932, he brought Hopkins to Washington, D.C., to serve in his administration. Hopkins helped to organize the Federal Emergency Relief Administration and was the first director of the Works Progress Administration, which during the depression was the largest employer in the nation. He was named secretary of commerce in 1938. He was Roosevelt's chief relief administrator and during World War II served as a diplomat, negotiator, and presidential right-hand man.

**Oliver O. Howard,** head of the Freedmen's Bureau from 1865 until the bureau was disbanded in 1872. A graduate of West Point, Howard fought for the Union and reached the rank of general during the Civil War. As head of the Freedmen's Bureau, he oversaw the distribution of food rations to the hungry; assistance with housing, jobs, and education for freed slaves; operation of a public health system; and a court system that decided cases involving ex-slaves.

**Josephine Shaw Lowell,** social reformer and leading advocate for the poor and low-income workers, born into a wealthy Boston family. In 1876, she was appointed the first woman commissioner of the New York State Board of Charities. In this post, she became a leading advocate of improved public care for the disabled and for benefits for dependent children and widows. Lowell also supported the settlement house movement, in which volunteers set up small institutions in the cities to help immigrants make the transition to American work and life. Like many in the settlement house movement, she was a critic of charities that simply fed and clothed people without giving them the means to self-sufficiency. She founded the Consumer's League in 1890 to promote better wages and working conditions for women.

**Thomas Robert Malthus,** English economist of the late 18th and early 19th centuries best known for his theories on population growth. Malthus was an important voice against the English poor laws that had been in effect for hundreds of years. He believed that population growth would eventually outstrip the food supply, and he argued that sustained social welfare policies, which were designed to help the poor survive, were counter to the national interest. He advocated greater moral responsibility on the part of the poor to resist burdensome population growth and also favored abolition of all public welfare programs. Malthusian ideas formed an important philosophical core of opposition to welfare in the 19th and early 20th centuries.

**Daniel Patrick Moynihan,** politician and leading researcher in welfare issues. Moynihan was born in Tulsa, Oklahoma, and raised from the age of six in New York City. He served in the U.S. Navy from 1944 to 1947, after which he studied at Tufts University and the London School of Economics. He served on the staff of New York governor Averell Harriman and joined the Kennedy administration as assistant secretary of labor. Moynihan's 1965 report *The Negro Family: The Case for National Action* made his reputation as an expert on issues of race and welfare policy. Noting that welfare rolls were expanding even as unemployment was on the decline, Moynihan called for further government action to address the problem. His observation of the breakdown of the nuclear family in the African-American community and the rise of out-of-wedlock births, however, earned him sharp criticism from welfare advocates, who contended that he was "blaming the victim." Moynihan advocated a period of "benign neglect" as a member of the Nixon administration, believing that the administration should attempt to tone down the rhetorical battle on race and welfare; he also strongly disagreed with the welfare reforms of 1996 under the Clinton administration.

**Charles Murray,** noted author and critic of the modern welfare system. Murray was born and raised in Iowa, graduated from Harvard in 1965, and served in the Peace Corps in Thailand for six years. His ideas about social policies in that country and about the negative influence of bureaucratic mechanisms meant to improve the lives of the poor formed his general outlook on welfare programs in the United States. He joined the American Institutes for Research in 1974 and the American Enterprise Institute in 1990. His 1984 book *Losing Ground: American Social Policy 1950–1980*, which denounced the expansion of the welfare system in the 1960s, became a touchstone study for the welfare reforms of 1996. Murray's 1994 work *The Bell Curve*, however, attracted criticism for its correlation of intelligence and socioeconomic status.

**Jacob Riis,** journalist whose muckraking exposés of slum conditions in New York were a key impetus of Progressive-era labor and social welfare reforms. Riis immigrated to the United States at the age of 21 and experienced firsthand the conditions in New York City's public poorhouses. He became a police reporter for the *New York Sun* and later for the *New York Tribune*. His photographs of the poor and the slums of lower Manhattan were collected into *How the Other Half Lives.* This book prompted the closing of poorhouses and began the era of muckraking journalism, which targeted poverty and unsanitary conditions of the urban immigrant milieu.

**Isaac Rubinow,** leading teacher and writer on the subject of public social insurance. Rubinow immigrated from Russia in 1893 and earned a doctorate in economics from Columbia University. He published *Social Insurance* in 1913 and *The Quest for Security* in 1914, two books in tune with the new Progressive party and its call for a national social welfare mechanism. Rubinow's work strongly influenced the generation of economists and politicians who created a new, federally guaranteed safety net with the Social Security Act of 1935.

**Mary Elizabeth Switzer,** noted public administrator who was a key figure in the expansion of federal funding of services to the disabled. Switzer attended Radcliffe College, graduating in 1921, and was employed by the Department of the Treasury and the Public Health Service. She became director of the Office of Vocational Rehabilitation in 1950 and helped to write the 1954 Vocational Rehabilitation Act. The federal building in Washington, D.C., that houses the Social Security Administration and the Department of Health and Human Services is named after Mary Switzer to commemorate her work.

**Tommy Thompson,** Wisconsin governor who pioneered an important welfare reform effort in his state. Thompson was born in Elroy, Wisconsin, the son of a small-town store owner. He earned a law degree from the University of Wisconsin and was elected representative to the Wisconsin Assembly in 1966. Thompson was first elected Wisconsin governor in 1987 and served in that office for four terms, through 2001. He initiated the Wisconsin Works program, which guided welfare beneficiaries into the labor force; it provided an important model for the federal welfare reform of 1996. Thompson was appointed secretary of the Department of Health and Human Services by newly elected President George W. Bush in 2001. In that role, he spearheaded the Medicare insurance reforms of 2003.

**Wayne Vasey,** welfare and social work administrator who was an important figure in the mid-20th century, as social work was making the transition to the public administration of welfare programs. Vasey was a dean of several academic social work departments, at the University of Iowa, Rutgers, and Washington University in St. Louis. His ideas on social work and welfare went into a report that formed the basis for the 1962 Social Service amendments to the Social Security Act.

**William Weld,** Republican governor of Massachusetts from 1991 to 1997 who passed an important welfare reform law. Weld graduated from Harvard College and Harvard Law School and served as a federal prosecuting attorney during the 1980s. In 1995, during his second term as governor, he signed the state's Welfare Reform Law. The law renamed the state welfare department the Department of Transitional Assistance. It set work requirements and placed a time limit of two years of benefits on all recipients able to work and with children at least two years old. Those with children age six and up were required to perform 20 hours per week of community service, and teenage parents had to live at home and complete high school. The law also ended the practice of increasing welfare payments to families with new children. Massachusetts immediately lowered its welfare rolls and became a model state for the welfare reform law passed by Congress in 1996.

**George Wiley,** a leading activist on behalf of the poor. Wiley earned a Ph.D. in organic chemistry from Cornell University and worked as a chemistry professor at the University of California–Berkeley in 1958 and then at Syracuse University in 1960. At the same time, he took part in a number of political causes, serving on a national council of the Congress of Racial Equality (CORE) and founding a CORE chapter in Syracuse. In 1966, Wiley founded the Poverty Rights Action Center in Washington, D.C., and the next year he established the National Welfare Rights Organization (NWRO), in which he served as its first director. These groups worked for improved benefits and an improved standard of living for the poor and unemployed. Wiley was developing a new group, to be known as the Movement for Economic Justice, when he drowned in an accident in 1973.

# CHAPTER 5

## GLOSSARY

The following is a short glossary of terms of interest to the researcher of welfare topics. It includes legislative and administrative terms and program and organization acronyms, as well as some historical phrases that are relevant to the study of private and public charity, the settlement house movement, and the Social Security program.

**AFDC–Unemployed Parent (AFDC-UP)**   A provision of Title IV of the Social Security Act, which came into effect in 1961, that provided welfare benefits to the unemployed parents of a minor already receiving ADC benefits.

**Aid to Dependent Children (ADC)**   A benefit program established as Title IV of the Social Security Act of 1935, and which provided for federal payments as a one-third share of state welfare benefits to children. The name of the program was changed to Aid to Families with Dependent Children (AFDC) in 1962.

**Aid to Families with Dependent Children (AFDC)**   Welfare benefits established by the federal government in the Social Security Act of 1935; originally called Aid to Dependent Children (ADC). AFDC was superseded by Temporary Aid to Needy Families (TANF) in the welfare reforms of 1996.

**block grants**   Money distributed without restrictions to a statewide or local entity for the purpose of funding an entire class of benefits.

**caretaker relative**   A person (not a parent) designated as the individual responsible for the care of a dependent child. The federal government began providing welfare benefits for caretaker relatives through the ADC program in 1950.

**cash grant**   A payment, such as Temporary Assistance to Needy Families (TANF) or Supplemental Security Income (SSI), to those unable to support themselves or their families and meet everyday expenses.

**categorical aid**   Welfare benefits targeted to a specific class of individuals, such as the elderly, the blind, and the disabled.

**charity organization society**   Organizations formed in the late 1800s to offer a variety of services to those on public relief and to provide for more efficient administration of public and private charities. The charity organization societies promoted self-sufficiency on the part of the poor and a scientific approach to philanthropy.

**Child and Adult Care Food Program (CACFP)**   A program managed by the U.S. Department of Agriculture that provides grants to schools and child-care centers to support milk, snacks, and balanced meals.

**Child Care and Development Fund (CCDF)**   A federal program authorized by the welfare reform law of 1996 that funds child care for low-income families.

**Civilian Conservation Corps (CCC)**   A work relief program established in 1933 during the Great Depression to assist unemployed men by providing public-works employment.

**Community Services Block Grant (CSBG)**   A federal program that funds local service providers, known as community action agencies, to benefit low-income families or communities.

**Community Work and Training (CWT)**   A program of federally funded job training programs that are provided to welfare recipients 18 years and younger. The CWT was authorized by Congress in 1962.

**Comprehensive Employment and Training Act (CETA)**   A law passed in 1973 intended to provide employment to the unemployed and work training for high school students. CETA provided full-time jobs for one to two years, with the intention of providing a marketable skill. The program was discontinued in 1982.

**Department of Health and Human Services (HHS)**   The federal department that oversees the administration of state welfare and social service programs.

**devolution**   A term for the transfer of control over welfare programs to states, counties, and municipalities. Devolution is based on the principle that local agencies are better able to address local needs than the federal government.

**discouraged worker**   A category of unemployed person. By the definition of the federal Bureau of Labor Statistics (which calculates the official national unemployment rate), a discouraged worker is an unemployed person who is available for work and has looked for work in the past 12 months, but who is not currently looking for work because they believe there are no jobs available or none for which they would qualify. Different agencies calculating local unemployment rates use different lengths of time to define when an unemployed person who has stopped actively looking for work has become a discouraged worker.

**Earned Income Tax Credit (EITC)**   An income-tax credit for low-income wage earners, first made part of the federal tax code in 1975. The credit is calculated as a percentage of wages earned, up to a maximum amount, and is subtracted directly from the amount of income tax owed. The maximum increases with the number of children in the family. Those with income below the threshold of taxation receive the credit as a payment from the U.S. Treasury. Before the welfare reform of 1996, the credit was not considered income for the purpose of calculating welfare eligibility; the new law allowed the states to determine if and how the EITC would be figured as income for TANF beneficiaries. Other federal benefits, including Medicaid and Supplemental Security Income, ignore the EITC in figuring family income.

**Economic Opportunity Act**   Federal legislation passed in 1964 that formed the centerpiece of the Great Society effort of the Johnson administration. The law set up the federal Office of Economic Opportunity to administer new federal welfare, jobs, and housing programs.

**entitlement program**   A public program that provides financial benefits, or goods and services, to eligible individuals as a legal right. An "open-ended" entitlement requires the government to offer benefits to all qualified individuals. "Closed-ended" entitlements put a cap on total spending for the program.

**essential person**   An individual designated as someone not in the immediate family but essential for the health, welfare, and upbringing of a child on the AFDC program. Benefits were extended to "essential persons" starting in 1968.

**Family Assistance Plan**   A proposal by President Richard Nixon to replace the federal welfare system, notably the AFDC program, with a federally guaranteed annual income. The plan died in Congress but generated considerable debate over the merits of simply dropping eligibility/work/education requirements and transferring money directly to families in need.

**family cap**   A provision in some state welfare laws that eliminates additional payments to families that gain members while on the welfare rolls.

**Family Support Act of 1988**   A revision in the federal welfare law that increased work requirements for those on AFDC and increased funding of child-care, job training, and transportation subsidies for welfare recipients.

**Federal Insurance Contributions Act (FICA)**   A payroll tax imposed in equal amount on employees and employers to finance Social Security and other benefit programs for the disabled, the elderly, and survivors. In 2006, the tax was set at 1.45 percent for Medicare and 6.2 percent for Social Security. In 2008, the Social Security tax was capped at $102,000 in annual income; this amount is reset upward each year. Medicare contributions have no cap.

**Federal Poverty Level**   A statistical method of determining the nation's poverty threshold, which is set every year by the Department of Health and Human Services; also called Federal Poverty Guidelines. The poverty level varies with family size and location. (Alaska and Hawaii have higher poverty levels, reflecting the higher cost of living in those states.) A multiple or percentage of the poverty level is used in setting benefit levels in various federally funded programs.

**Food Stamp Program**   A program overseen by the Food and Nutrition Service of the U.S. Department of Agriculture that provides coupons (food stamps) to low-income people for the purpose of buying food. It has been in effect since the passage of the Food Stamp Act of the early 1960s.

**formula grants**   Federal grants that are provided to the states and calculated on the basis of the population, income level, unemployment level, and other statistical measures of the state's general need.

**general assistance**   A program that provides benefits to families and individuals who are in need but who do not meet the criteria or eligibility standards for more specifically targeted welfare benefits.

**grants-in-aid**   Direct payment from one government to another, or from government to a private entity, to fund a specific program. State welfare benefits are partially funded by federal government grants-in-aid.

**Housing Choice Vouchers**   A program administered by the Department of Health and Human Services that provides low-income families, the elderly, and disabled persons with rent subsidies in order to secure decent market-rate housing; also known as "Section 8."

**income disregards**   Money earned by a family receiving welfare benefits but not counted toward the ceiling on their income established by state welfare guidelines; also known as "disregards."

**Individual Development Account (IDA)**   A personal savings account authorized by the Personal Responsibility and Work Opportunity Responsibility Act of 1996 that is administered by state and county agencies. Typically IDA money can be used for starting a business, buying a first home, or paying for postsecondary education. Individuals can contribute earned income, and those contributions are not counted toward the income or asset ceilings that limit eligibility for TANF or any other welfare benefits. The funds are matched by public and private agencies depending on the terms of the IDA.

**indoor relief**   Public welfare benefits dispensed through residential institutions such as orphanages, mental institutions, reformatories, workhouses, and almshouses.

**in-kind assistance**   A noncash benefit, such as food stamps, that must be used for a specific purpose.

**Job Opportunities and Basic Skills Training (JOBS)**   A program established by the Family Support Act of 1988 as Title IV-F of the Social

# Glossary

Security Act to replace the WIN program. The 1988 law required states to enroll all welfare mothers, except those with a child younger than age three, in education, work, or job training through the JOBS program. *See also* **Work Incentive (WIN) program.**

**Job Training Partnership Act**   A federal law enacted in 1982 that provided funds for job training programs for unskilled laborers and those facing barriers to employment. The law was repealed in 1998, and the federal job training mechanism was revised in the Workforce Investment Act of 1998.

**Low Income Home Energy Assistance Program (LIHEAP)**   A federal program that provides low-income families with assistance for their energy bills and costs.

**matching grants**   Money distributed by the federal government to the states, which the states must match at a certain percentage; also called matching funds. For some programs, matching grants are required in order for the state to receive funds.

**means testing**   A process for determining eligibility for and amount of benefits based on income level. AFDC and TANF benefits are means tested; their benefits are paid out only to those qualifying up to a maximum income level. Social Security, by contrast, is not means tested; all who pay in are eligible for benefits, based on the age at which they retire.

**Medicaid**   A health insurance program for low-income families established as Title XIX of the Social Security Act of 1965. Medicaid funding is shared by the federal and state governments, while benefits and eligibility are managed by the states. The program's eligibility standards and fee schedules are overseen by a federal agency known as the Centers for Medicaid Services (CMS). Participation by the states is voluntary; however, all 50 states have been taking part since 1982, when Arizona joined the program.

**Medicare**   A hospitalization and health insurance program for those at least 65 years of age, established as Title XVIII of the Social Security Act of 1965. Hospitalization insurance is financed by Social Security payroll taxes, while medical insurance is a voluntary program for which participants pay a low monthly premium that is subsidized by federal tax dollars. The Social Security Administration collects premiums from covered individuals, determines eligibility, and sets benefit levels.

**mothers' pensions**   Benefits provided to poor and widowed mothers by the states in the early 20th century. Mothers' pensions were the precursor to the Aid to Dependent Children program, part of the Social Security Act of 1935.

**Ohio Plan**   A 1930s-era scheme of state unemployment insurance in which employers' unemployment taxes are pooled into a common state fund.

**Old-Age Insurance (OAI)**   A system of relief for the elderly established by the Social Security Act. Employees would make compulsory regular contributions from their payroll (at the original rate of 1 percent) and would be entitled to regular fixed benefits, proportional to their salaries, after age 65.

**Old Age, Survivors, and Disability Insurance (OASDI)**   The name, since 1956, for the component of the Social Security Act of 1935 that collects premiums and pays benefits for retirees, survivors (widows and widowers), and the disabled.

**outdoor relief**   Public welfare benefits paid directly to recipients; also known as "home relief."

**Personal Responsibility and Work Opportunity Reconciliation Act of 1996 (PRWORA)**   The federal law (also known as Public Law 104-193) that ended the AFDC program, replaced it with Temporary Aid to Needy Families (TANF), and provided new guidelines for the states for providing welfare benefits.

**safety net**   A general term for the system of benefits and services that guarantee a basic minimum standard of living to the poor.

**Section 8**   *See* **Housing Choice Vouchers**.

**settlement house**   An institution, popular in the late 19th and early 20th centuries, that provided services such as education, job training, soup kitchens, and temporary shelter in low-income neighborhoods. The settlement house was originally meant to help new arrivals and immigrants adapt to a new urban environment.

**Social Security Act**   The 1935 law that established the modern Social Security system; also known as the Economic Security Act. The Social Security Act established Old-Age Insurance (later Social Security), federal Unemployment Insurance, and Aid to Dependent Children (later Aid to Families with Dependent Children, or AFDC), and it set up a mechanism for funding these systems through payroll taxes.

**Social Security Administration**   The federal department responsible for collecting Social Security taxes; paying out Social Security benefits; and determining eligibility for benefits for retired workers, the disabled, and survivors (widows and orphans).

**Social Security Disability Insurance (SSDI)**   A form of federal insurance, funded by Social Security payroll taxes, that offers benefits to those injured or otherwise incapacitated and totally unable to hold gainful employment. Recipients must be under the age of 65 and must have worked five out of the past 10 years.

**Special Supplemental Food Program for Women, Infants and Children (WIC)**   A federal program managed by the U.S. Department of Agriculture that provides food for pregnant and nursing women and for children under the age of five.

**standard of need** The maximum amount of income a family receiving welfare benefits can earn in order to be considered needy. The standard of need is a method of quantifying a state's poverty level for the purpose of setting welfare benefit amounts, which are usually figured as a percentage of the standard of need.

**State Letters** Rules and instructions provided by the Social Security Administration to the states for the implementation of their Social Security and ADC programs. The State Letters were gathered into a *Handbook of Public Assistance Administration* in 1945, and formal rules for state welfare administration were set down in the *Code of Federal Regulations* in 1967.

**Supplemental Security Income (SSI)** A benefit program intended to help blind, disabled, and poor persons to afford their basic needs of food, clothing, and shelter. Established in 1972, SSI is funded by general tax revenues and administered by the Social Security Administration.

**survivors** Widows (or widowers) and orphans.

**Temporary Assistance for Needy Families (TANF)** The federal welfare program that replaced Aid to Families with Dependent Children (AFDC) under the welfare reform law of 1996. TANF benefits are payable to an individual for a maximum of five years, either consecutive or nonconsecutive. The TANF program was reauthorized by the Deficit Reduction Act of 2005.

**waivers** Exemptions from certain federal guidelines and restrictions, for the sake of allowing states more flexibility in how they administer local welfare programs. Waivers became increasingly popular in the 1980s as lawmakers looked for ways of revising federal law to make the welfare system more effective.

**Wisconsin Plan** A 1932 scheme for state unemployment insurance in which employers' contributions are placed into individual reserve accounts for the purpose of paying claims against them. The state's unemployment tax is affected by the amount of unemployment benefits paid out to its former workers.

**Women, Infants, and Children (WIC)** *See* **Special Supplemental Food Program for Women, Infants and Children.**

**workfare** A general term for social welfare programs that require applicants to participate in the job market, either as an employee or trainee, in order to receive benefits. Workfare programs in some states make some form of community service, either paid or unpaid, an eligible form of employment.

**Workforce Investment Act (WIA)** A federal program that provides funding for job training and job placement services.

**Work Incentive (WIN) program**   A job-training program authorized by Congress in 1968. The states were required to implement the WIN program in order to prepare appropriate AFDC recipients for the workforce. Unemployed fathers receiving AFDC benefits had to enroll in the WIN programs from 1968, and in 1971, Congress required that all AFDC parents register for work or training.

# PART II

---

# GUIDE TO FURTHER RESEARCH

# CHAPTER 6

---

# HOW TO RESEARCH WELFARE AND WELFARE REFORM

The researcher of welfare topics has an abundance of information at hand. Welfare issues are fundamental to the nature of government and its constitutional limits—a question unresolved since James Madison was arguing the point with Alexander Hamilton. The subject of welfare is current and important for economists, public policy experts, sociologists, think tanks, public administrators, charities, and political observers. The topic will never be exhausted, as it is in the nature of poverty to remain unsolved and for its solutions to be a topic of debate across the political spectrum.

Having recently passed its 10th anniversary, the welfare reform law of 1996 provides a convenient topic of statistical study. In every state, and at the federal level, reports have been undertaken analyzing the effect of the law. The majority of these reports are available free of charge on the Internet. Others are condensed in books and articles, many of which are also available online.

Every set of statistics, however, is open to interpretation in light of the varying definitions of poverty, and the varying opinion of welfare's efficacy and propriety. The researcher should be aware at all times of the two fundamental positions on welfare: the stand of conservatives, who believe welfare to be harmful, unnecessary, and unconstitutional, and that of liberals, who believe the government should provide a minimum standard of living for all citizens. In the politically neutral field of pure economics, bias can be very easily hidden in the way simple numbers are presented, emphasized, and interpreted.

## TIPS FOR RESEARCHING WELFARE

With so much information available and so many perspectives to measure, the researcher is well advised to formulate a strategy for the investigation. Here are some tips for researching welfare-related issues:

- **Define the question at issue.** The researcher should develop a very specific issue or question before proceeding into books, periodicals, or reports. Most welfare topics are economic questions that address the system's efficiency and effectiveness. Others are more subjective matters, which gauge the morality and/or constitutionality of the welfare system. Researchers may take more interest in the history of public relief or charity. It is useful to begin by researching articles and books that have already been written on the specific issue, whether it is welfare-to-work programs, "devolution" of welfare to the states, welfare benefits for immigrants and noncitizens, or another specific issue. The researcher creates more effective and comprehensive work by grounding it in the findings of predecessors.

- **Use bibliographic resources.** The researcher of welfare issues should begin with public or university libraries. (Bookstores will have a limited number of titles on hand on this topic, although any book in print can usually be ordered.) A good academic library is the most useful research source of all, as the library will hold not only books and periodicals but also a variety of bibliographic resources such as catalogs, indexes, and bibliographies that can point the researcher in a specific direction. Many of these materials are available online; if the researcher does not belong to the university, he or she can usually pay an annual fee for library privileges or access online subscription services within an academic library.

- **Find timely statistics on the Internet.** Statistical information on welfare ages quickly, and the vast majority of books in a library are at least a few years old. For someone seeking the most recent numbers to ground a current research topic or opinion, the Internet and its wealth of free reports is the most useful medium of all.

# INTERNET RESEARCH

The Internet is a global network of computer servers that share TCP/IP, a "protocol" that allows the servers to communicate with each other. The World Wide Web is a method of sharing information over the Internet via a programming language known as hypertext markup language (HTML), which provides direct electronic links among "web pages" on the Internet. Most universities, public libraries, and government agencies have a presence on the Internet as well as a direct connection to it. Most states mandate that their human-service agencies provide up-to-date information on welfare services via the Internet to the public. Federal agencies, the Department of Health and Human Services (HHS), research institutes, think tanks, welfare advocacy groups, newspapers, periodicals, and prominent authors have their own web pages, accessible to all. The information provided on the Internet may be difficult to find in traditional print media such as books, magazines, and reports. However, since web pages carry no expiration date, the information may also be out of date and useless for any kind of research on current topics.

Searching the World Wide Web can be helpful or quite frustrating. A query for "welfare" or "welfare reform" through a search engine such as Google will return millions of results, unsorted, undated, and poorly described. A thorough researcher might have the time to open and examine a few hundred web sites of interest to the topic, but he or she must bring a critical eye to the content of these sites, as the creations of the World Wide Web range in quality from vital and comprehensive to useless.

There are several criteria to use when looking at a web page. Consider the author or organization that has created the web page. Points of view can be either expressed or hidden by proper names and acronyms. Researchers always must carefully examine any material presented for bias. The most important consideration is the relative expertise held by members of the group in the subject they purport to describe and analyze.

Generally, authoritative web sites will carry plentiful links to other sites (of varying viewpoints), and the links will operate properly (demonstrating that the URLs in use are still valid). A wider range of resources given—books, articles, reports, other web pages, and so on—marks the site as broadly useful rather than narrowly focused. Within the documents on the site, reference notes should be provided, with or without Internet links, and these sources should be easily verified.

Good web sites are updated frequently (the Last Updated date is frequently visible). Contact information will be provided: name, physical address or post office box number, phone number, e-mail address. Sponsorship of the site should be given, whether by governmental or nongovernmental organizations, academic institutions, or corporations. Advertising should be kept to a minimum.

Although a subjective consideration, the appearance and overall design of the web page is also a clue to validity. Links within the site should be logical and intuitive. Graphics should serve a useful function, rather than being presented as an end in themselves. A good design reflects careful programming, which in turn signifies a large investment in time and money by the individual or organization that created the page.

## WEB SITES OF INTEREST

Sites that offer a general background on the subject of welfare and welfare reform provide a good starting point for someone researching welfare topics. The following sites provide background as well as research reports and, in the case of the White House, official policy positions.

# Welfare and Welfare Reform

**Administration for Children and Families** (ACF) (http://www.acf.hhs.gov/index.html), part of the U.S. Department of Health and Human Services, provides policy direction and information services. ACF is the federal agency that, through congressional appropriation, funds state, territory, local, and tribal organizations to provide family assistance (welfare), child support, childcare, Head Start, child welfare, and other programs relating to children and families. Its site records the federal government's welfare law and regulations, official statistics, state program guidelines, and general information for beneficiaries. It is the single most useful Internet information source on welfare.

**American Bar Association Center on Children and the Law** (http://www.abanet.org/child/home.html) is a web site covering child abuse and neglect, as well as child welfare and protective services. This site contains child welfare laws, publications, and resource links.

**American Public Human Services Association** (http://www.aphsa.org/Home/home_news.asp) features welfare policy links, human service programs, child welfare resources, educational materials, and publications.

**Catalog of Federal Domestic Assistance** (http://12.46.245.173/cfda/cfda.html) gives access to a database of all federal program—including economic assistance—available to state and local governments; domestic public, quasi-public, and private organizations, both for-profit and nonprofit; specialized groups; and individuals.

**Center for Health Care Strategies, Inc.** (http://www.chcs.org/) is a policy resource center that promotes better public health care services for low-income families.

**Center for Law and Social Policy** (CLASP) (http://www.clasp.org/) is a national nonprofit group that provides assistance and educational guides to low-income families. CLASP offers research, policy analysis, and technical assistance to federal, state, and local policy makers; advocates; researchers; and the media.

**Center on Budget and Policy Priorities** (http://www.cbpp.org/) provides research and analysis on government policies and programs affecting low- and moderate-income families.

**Child Welfare Institute** (http://www.gocwi.org/) is a nonprofit organization that provides consultation and training services to state, local, and private child welfare and human service agencies.

**Child Welfare League of America** (http://www.cwla.org/) is an association of nearly 800 public and private nonprofit agencies that assist abused and neglected children and their families each year with a range of services.

**HandsNet** (http://www.handsnet.org/) provides daily news, training, online discussions, and Internet search tools for human services professionals working on a broad range of economic justice and antipoverty issues.

**Institute for Research on Poverty** (http://www.irp.wisc.edu/) is a university-based center for research into the causes and consequences of poverty and social inequality in the United States. It was established in 1966 at the University of Wisconsin-Madison by the U.S. Office of Economic Opportunity.

**Manpower Demonstration Research Corporation** (http://www.mdrc. org/), created in 1974 by the Ford Foundation and a group of federal agencies, is best known for mounting large-scale evaluations of real-world policies and programs targeted to low-income people. Its web site provides information on employment for welfare recipients, welfare-to-work programs, educational research on welfare programs, and links to related sites.

**Mathematica Policy Research** (http://www.mathematica-mpr.com/) offers policy makers a combination of evaluation expertise, direct data collection services, and insight into socioeconomic issues. Its areas of research include education, labor, health, disability, welfare, nutrition, and early childhood.

**National Center for Law and Economic Justice** (http://www.nclej. org/) works with public-interest advocates, private law firms, legal services lawyers, and grassroots groups on litigation, policy advocacy, and support for low-income organizing. Its web site offers case developments from 1996 to the present, case news, program resources, and related links.

**National Conference of State Legislatures** (http://www.ncsl.org/statefed/welfare/welfare.htm) is a bipartisan organization that serves the legislators and staffs of the nation's 50 states, commonwealths, and territories. It provides research and technical assistance to state policy makers on the implementation of federal law and regulations. The link provided here refers directly to the pages dedicated to welfare issues.

**National Indian Child Welfare Association** (NICWA) (http://www. nicwa.org/) is a comprehensive source of information on American Indian child welfare. NICWA provides public policy, research, and advocacy, as well as information and training on Indian child welfare. It also offers community development services to organizations, agencies, and professionals interested in the field of Indian child welfare, such as tribal governments and state child welfare agencies.

**Public Agenda Online** (http://www.publicagenda.org/), founded by social scientist Daniel Yankelovich and former secretary of state Cyrus Vance, provides research on issues ranging from education to foreign policy to immigration to religion and civility in American life. The web site offers recent stories, statistics, links, organizations, and public policy research relating to poverty and welfare in America.

**The Research Forum at the National Center for Children in Poverty** (http://www.researchforom.org) was created in January 1997 to facilitate relevant research about the effects of the new federalism on the poor. The web site features a searchable database of summaries of large- and small-scale welfare reform research projects.

**Rockefeller Institute of Government** (http://www.rockinst.org/) is the public policy research arm of the State University of New York. It conducts studies and special projects to help state governments meet their public policy challenges and deal with the federal government.

**Sargent Shriver National Center on Poverty Law** (http://www. povertylaw.org/clearinghouse-review) features articles from the monthly poverty law journal *Clearinghouse Review* and a searchable bank of poverty law case briefs.

**State Policy Documentation Project** (http://www.spdp.org/) can be regarded as a historical reference. From 1998 to 2000, the project tracked policy choices on Medicaid and the cash assistance programs of Temporary Assistance for Needy Families (TANF) in the 50 states and Washington, D.C.

**United Council on Welfare Fraud** (http://www.ucowf.org/) is devoted to fighting fraud and abuse of social service programs. It focuses on the prosecution of people who fraudulently obtain government benefits.

**Urban Institute** (http://www.urban.org/about/index.cfm), an independent policy analysis center, originated in 1968 to examine the problems facing America's cities. The Urban Institute describes its mission as promoting "sound social policy and public debate on national priorities." The organization evaluates policies and programs and shares its research findings with policy makers, program administrators, business, academics, and the public online and through reports and scholarly books. It also runs a useful web site offering a wealth of research papers and reports on the topic of welfare.

**Welfare Reform Academy** (http://www.welfareacademy.org/) is an organization at the School of Public Policy at the University of Maryland. It was created to help state and local officials, private social service providers, and other interested parties take advantage of the 1996 welfare reform law. The Welfare Reform Academy provides training in program design, implementation, and evaluation for a variety of public programs, including Temporary Assistance for Needy Families (TANF), food stamp, Medicaid, job training, child care, child welfare, and child support.

**The White House** (http://www.whitehouse.gov/infocus/welfarereform/) provides pages discussing welfare reform on its web site. These present the president's welfare policy initiatives—focusing on the reauthorization of the welfare reform law, which was accomplished in 2005—along with current news and briefings regarding welfare reform.

## THINK TANKS

Perhaps the most useful and abundant source of information on welfare issues is the traditional "think tank," or private nonprofit organization dedicated to research in one or more areas of public policy and socioeconomic issues. Think tanks are supported by donations from special interest and advocacy groups, private corporations, foundations, and individuals; some of them earn income from research projects and consulting.

Findings from the most prominent think tanks are often influential in the writing of new legislation. Most of these organizations have an ideological foundation and conduct their activities with a view toward supporting a certain political outlook. Nevertheless, the researcher who keeps this bias in mind will find think tank articles and reports very useful: Not only do they provide plentiful statistics and background research, but they also reveal philosophy or strategy from one side or the other on the topic of welfare. Several of the following think tanks have dedicated large regions of their web sites to welfare issues, welfare reform, and pending welfare legislation. All of their home pages prominently feature keyword search functions that will allow the researcher to select specific topics from their (sometimes very large) archives of articles and reports.

**American Enterprise Institute** (AEI) (http://www.aei.org/), a private, nonpartisan, not-for-profit institution, was founded in 1943 and is dedicated to research and education on issues of government, politics, economics, and social welfare. AEI research is conducted through three primary research divisions: Economic Policy Studies, Social and Political Studies, and Defense and Foreign Policy Studies. It also works through several specialized programs such as the Brady Program on Culture and Freedom, the AEI-Brookings Joint Center for Regulatory Studies, the National Research Initiative, and the Welfare Reform Academy (discussed in the previous section).

**Brookings Institution** (http://www.brook.edu/), one of the principal Washington-based think tanks, concentrates on research in economics, government, and foreign policy. Its stated mission is "to aid in the development of sound public policies and to promote public understanding of issues of national importance."

**Cato Institute** (http://www.cato.org/) is a libertarian think tank founded in 1977 by Edward H. Crane. It seeks to "broaden the parameters of public policy debate to allow consideration of the traditional American principles of limited government, individual liberty, free markets and peace." Its web site covers welfare issues in particular at http://www.cato.org/research/welfare/index.html.

**Center for American Progress** (http://www.americanprogress.org/), created in 2003 to counter the dominant conservative think tanks, bills itself as "progressive." The "Domestic & Economy" section of the organization's web site provides information on poverty, among other topics.

**Center for Economic and Policy Research** (http://www.cepr.net/) was established in 1999 by economists Dean Baker and Mark Weisbrot to "promote democratic debate on the most important economic and social issues that affect people's lives." The organization offers professional research on particular economic and social problems.

**Claremont Institute** (http://www.claremont.org/) is an organization founded in 1979 that sponsors scholarships for rising conservative leaders and operates public policy programs. The institute's stated mission is "to restore the principles of the American Founding," which it defines as "recovering a limited and accountable government that respects private property, promotes stable family life, and maintains a strong defense."

**Economic Policy Institute** (http://www.epi.org), established in 1986, identifies itself as a nonprofit, nonpartisan think tank that seeks to promote economic prosperity for all by highlighting the interests of low- and middle-income workers. The organization conducts original research on living standards and labor markets, government and the economy, globalization and trade, and the economy.

**Foundation for Economic Education** (http://www.fee.org/) was founded in 1946 by Leonard E. Read to advance the principles of private property, individual liberty, the rule of law, and free markets. Articles archived on the organization's web site address individual and corporate welfare, both of which the foundation adamantly opposes.

**Goldwater Institute** (http://www.goldwaterinstitute.org/) is an organization founded in Arizona in 1988 in honor of Senator Barry Goldwater (1909–98), an iconic conservative of the 20th century. The Goldwater Institute discourages excessive government reach, following the precept that "while the legitimate functions of government are conducive to freedom, unrestrained government has proved to be a chief instrument in history for thwarting individual liberty." It examines a variety of public policy areas, including welfare.

**Heritage Foundation** (http://www.heritage.org) is a conservative public policy research institute based in Washington, D.C. It aims to encourage public policy "based on the principles of free enterprise, limited government, individual freedom, traditional American values, and a strong national defense." The "Welfare Watch" feature on the foundation's web site (http://www.heritage.org/Research/Welfare/Welfare-Watch.cfm) offers information, guidelines, laws, regulations, government agency links, reports, and a forum all dealing with welfare-related issues.

**Hoover Institution for War, Revolution, and Peace** (http://www .hoover.org/) is a public policy research center on the campus of Stanford University. Devoted to politics, economics, and political economy—both domestic and foreign—as well as international affairs, the institution sponsors scholarly research that reflects its interest in representative government, private enterprise, and personal freedom.

**Hudson Institute** (http://www.hudson.org), founded in 1961 in Croton-on-Hudson, New York, was the first such organization to be called a "think tank." Its mission statement affirms its "commitment to free markets and individual responsibility, confidence in the power of technology to assist progress, respect for the importance of culture and religion in human affairs, and determination to preserve America's national security," and it sponsors research on each of these topics.

**Independent Institute** (http://www.independent.org/) is a nonpartisan organization committed to promoting government reform. In its scholarly research on public policy, including welfare issues, it aims to report "without regard to any political or social biases."

**Mises Institute** (http://www.mises.org/) is a research and educational center of classical liberalism, libertarian political theory, and the "Austrian School" of economics. Its web site offers several essays on welfare economics and the modern welfare state.

**National Center for Policy Analysis** (http://www.ncpa.org/), a nonprofit, nonpartisan public policy research organization, was established in 1983. Its stated goal is to "develop and promote private alternatives to government regulation and control, solving problems by relying on the strength of the competitive, entrepreneurial private sector." The center's web site covers health care, taxes, Social Security, welfare, criminal justice, education, and environmental regulation.

**New America Foundation** (http://www.newamerica.net/#) was established in 1999 as a "post-partisan" policy institute. It sponsors a wide range of policy research, conferences, and public outreach programs.

**Pacific Research Institute** (http://www.pacificresearch.org/) is a conservative think tank founded in 1979 that advocates free-market policies to achieve "freedom, opportunity, and personal responsibility for all individuals." Its web site is organized around the topics of business and economics, education, environment, health care, and technology.

**Progressive Policy Institute** (http://www.ppionline.org/) is a research and education institute that eschews the conflict between the political left and right and embraces the ideals of equal opportunity, mutual responsibility, and self-governing citizens and communities. The institute promotes a political "third way" in which an adaptive government is more responsive to the needs of citizens in the Information Age.

**Reason Foundation** (http://www.reason.org/), founded in 1968, espouses libertarian principles "including individual liberty, free markets, and the rule of law." The organization supports privatization of the welfare system.

## SEARCH ENGINES

The Internet has always been an often-incoherent mass of information. To make it a useful resource, the researcher can begin with a search engine, which requires the user to enter a word or phrase that will, with luck, return links to pertinent and useful sites. There are methods of narrowing the search. Surrounding a phrase with quotation marks, for example, assures that only the specific phrase, and not its components, will be used by the search engine. Entering "welfare reform," however, will return more sites than a user could ever hope to visit. Therefore, the search has to be further narrowed by adding places, dates, people, court cases, and so on.

Boolean operators allow the searcher to either expand or narrow the search. The operators are entered in capital letters: OR to broaden the search to include two or more terms, NOT to exclude terms, AND to instruct the search engine to return all sites that include both phrases. For example:

"welfare reform" AND "federal statutes"
"Bush administration" AND "welfare reauthorization"
"welfare policy" AND "Great Britain"

Seeking the web page of a certain organization can be accomplished by specifying "home page" after the name of the organization; for example:

"Administration for Children and Families" AND "home page"

There are web search tutorials offered online that will train the user in creating useful, targeted searches. The technology and methodology of search engines, however, is still evolving. Currently, searches can only be done using keywords, which quite often result in misleading or false links. (Simply entering "welfare" will return quite a few pages devoted to animal welfare, for example.) Some engines allow "proximity searches," in which the user limits the distance separating two or more search terms. This gives a more accurate list of returns than the default "whole page" search, which simply ranks the results by the number of occurrences of the term across the entire web site or page.

Anyone using search engines on the Internet should be aware that web page creators can purchase prominent listings and that organizations that operate search engines can feature (or filter out) certain sites according to their own criteria. Following are some of the most useful search engines on the World Wide Web.

- **Alta Vista** (www.altavista.com), one of the original crawler search engines, allows users to build very specific searches with the Advanced Search mode. A Boolean query feature allows expert searchers to enter complex queries; the user can translate text to or from 36 foreign languages.
- **Ask.com** (www.ask.com) is a search engine in which the user employs natural language to get responses to very specific requests. The response comes in the form of a list of sites that provide relevant information on

a subject phrase recognized by the engine. The search engine, however, is often busy.

- **Google** (www.google.com) is one of the most useful Internet search engines in existence thanks to a vast searchable database of web pages. The Advanced Search feature allows users to specify language, file format, date of the web pages, domains, and placement of the phrase searched for on the page. Users can also browse recent news stories on the topic. The user can have foreign language pages translated and also set the maximum number of results. Google now also offers a book search (http://books.google.com/), which allows the user to search the full text of books as well as articles and academic papers. (The number of page views in any single book, however, is limited.) In some cases, the book has gone out of copyright, or a publisher has given permission, and the user can read the entire volume online. Public domain books can be downloaded and printed out. Google Scholar (http://scholar.google.com/), which was in its beta (preliminary) phase in 2008, searches for academic papers and research reports.

- **WebCrawler** (www.webcrawler.com), which went live in 1994 and is trademarked by InfoSpace, Inc., was the first full-text search engine. It is a metasearch engine that combines sponsored and nonsponsored results from the top search engines, including Google, Yahoo!, Windows Live Search (formerly MSN Search), Ask.com, About.com, MIVA, and LookSmart. WebCrawler users can search for images, audio, video, and news.

- **Yahoo! Search** (www.yahoo.com) is the oldest and most popular web search engine, using a team of editors who constantly update and streamline its directories. Yahoo! provides users with an organized subject index, which makes it much easier to do targeted searches (for example, welfare reform statistics in Alabama, or early history of Social Security).

## LEGAL SEARCH ENGINES

There are two important search engines devoted to the subject of law, court cases, federal and state statutes, and the like: FindLaw (www.findlaw.com) and Westlaw (www.westlaw.com).

Like WestLaw, LexisNexis is a fee-based subscription services that allow users to search a constantly updated collection of state and federal statutes, court cases, regulations, public records, and international law. The LexisNexis database is located at www.lexis.com; Westlaw resides at www.westlaw.com. Other useful legal web sites include MegaLaw, where welfare is covered at http://www.megalaw.com/top/welfare.php.

## COURT CASES

Federal and state courts are the final arbiter of welfare law, as it is within these venues that the constitutionality of welfare statutes is finally decided. Court decisions are indexed according to a standard format, in which the title represents *Plaintiff v. Defendant*, *Petitioner v. Respondent*, or *Appellant v. Appellee* (in the case of appeals; the party bringing the appeal is the appellant). The citation then gives the volume number of the reporting publication, the starting page of the case, the venue (federal or state court), and finally the year.

A sample would be the citation "*Townsend v. Swank*, 404 U.S. 282." The case can be found in the 282nd volume of the *Supreme Court Reporter* (this publication name is simply designated as "U.S."), starting on page 404 (the case was decided in 1971). This publication gives only the opinion and dissent of the presiding justices—not the entire docket of evidence, briefs, oral arguments, or exhibits, which in some cases would fill a volume by themselves. For the legal researcher, opinions provide a useful feature in their citation of precedent cases, upon which the justices in the matter base their findings. (This system could be regarded as an early, hard-text form of hyperlinks.)

Many state supreme courts and appeals courts publish their full decisions online, and nearly all provide an index to the printed reporting source. There are also several useful private online sources of case law, used by legal scholars and researchers who can now avoid the laborious task of paging through the volumes owned by law libraries. These online sources include the Legal Information Institute, which publishes all Supreme Court decisions since 1990, plus more than 600 "historic decisions" at http://supct.law. cornell.edu/supct.

## THOMAS

The once-frustrating and time consuming process of tracking current legislative action by the U.S. Congress has been eased by the creation of the World Wide Web site THOMAS (http://thomas.loc.gov). Devoted to federal legislative information, THOMAS contains the *Congressional Record* and the full text of legislation available from 1989 to the present. In addition, the THOMAS page known as *Congressional Documents and Debates 1774–1873* offers a record of congressional proceedings from the legislature's first century.

The THOMAS homepage has two principal links to be used by researchers: Bill Text, and Bill Summary and Status. The searcher must specify the Congress by number. (Congressional sessions last two years and are consecutively numbered; the 2007–08 session is known as the 110th

Congress.) By default, the links go to the Congress currently in session. The Bill Text link can return bills dating back to the 101st Congress, or 1989–90. The Bill Summary and Status link can return bills dating back to the 93rd Congress, or 1973–74. Multiple Congresses search allows the user to search across more than one congressional session.

Bill Summary and Status presents related information: how the bill originated, who is sponsoring it, its status in committee, amendments attached to it, scheduled votes, and so on. In Bill Summary and Status, the researcher has several ways to search: Word/Phrase, Subject Term, Bill/Amendment Number, Stage in Legislative Process, Date of Introduction, Sponsor/Cosponsor, and Committee. The user can also browse by Popular and Short Titles, Public Laws, Private Laws, Vetoed Bills, and Sponsor Summaries. This link will not allow the researcher to read the full text of the bill, however; that is the work performed by the Bill Text search.

Researchers looking for legislative texts and documents prior to 1989 that are not available on the THOMAS site must locate a Federal Depository Library. There are approximately 1,250 of them in the United States and U.S. possessions, and at least one in each congressional district. A list can be accessed and searched at http://www.gpoaccess.gov/libraries.html.

## ONLINE BOOK CATALOGS

Retail book catalogs available online include Abebooks.com, Amazon.com, and Barnesandnoble.com. These sites can be quite useful, as they give not only title and publication information but, in many cases, selected reviews by readers and critics, as well as (limited) full-page views, tables of contents, copyright information, indexes, and the like. Google has entered the fray with Google Book (books.google.com), an online library with search functions, and with some public-domain books available in full. If the book has not yet been scanned into the site, Google Book provides links to online library catalogs that have the title, which is useful for tracking rare and out-of-print research materials that can be ordered through an interlibrary loan system. Google Scholar is a collection of academic articles and books, still in preliminary stages in the spring of 2007.

The most comprehensive online catalog is that of the Library of Congress, available at http://lcweb.loc.gov. This site offers useful guides and indexes for researchers, links to other library catalogs, access to foreign collections, interlibrary loan services, and a special section on law research.

Some subscription database services offer full-text of articles as well as books. These include Questia.com (http://www.questia.com), Project Muse (http://muse.jhu.edu/), Journal Storage (JSTOR; http://www.jstor.org/), and LexisNexis (http://www.lexisnexis.com/). Several online encyclopedias are collected at Answers.com, and a massive collection of articles exists at Wikipedia (http://www.wikipedia.com), a site that allows any and all users to edit online articles using whatever information they care to provide. Most online services can be searched by author, title, subject category, or keyword. The user can enter the words "welfare reform" for a list of books or articles with that exact phrase used. General subject headings are the most useful way to search an index or database. The heading might be "welfare fraud," "welfare reform," "private charity," "welfare economics," or "welfare rights movement."

Online databases can often be accessed free at subscribing public or university libraries. These databases offer indexes of books, periodicals, audiovisual materials, dissertations, government documents, law cases, online federal and state statutes, and the like, as well as indexes to reference works such as bibliographies, encyclopedias, and dictionaries. Among the most comprehensive are InfoTrac and Wilson SelectPlus. The LexisNexis database is a comprehensive online research tool, grouped into topical and state-specific libraries and subdivided into files that may be searched by keyword, author, title, date, and subject. The researcher may browse or search databases specific to a single state, as in Westlaw. Many newspapers and magazines also offer online databases and indexes through their own web sites.

# CHAPTER 7

## ANNOTATED BIBLIOGRAPHY

The following chapter presents a sample of available printed material, online documents, and audiovisual materials dealing with welfare policy and welfare reform. Web documents are freely available without subscription or purchase requirement. The material is broken down into the following general categories:

- historical perspectives
- private charity and public relief
- the New Deal and the Social Security law
- poverty and the Great Society
- the 1996 welfare reform law
- international perspectives on social welfare policy
- current issues and debate

These categories are further divided into books, periodicals, and Internet documents. The writings listed in this chapter fall into two general categories, either academic/analytical or general/polemical. Academic books and articles rely on statistics, case histories, and economic analysis to gauge the effectiveness and consequences of welfare policies. General interest books either give a historical account of welfare policy or take a philosophical/political stand on the welfare issue, advocating for a more generous welfare system, for or against welfare reform as it was passed into law in 1996, or against the welfare system in general. Many of the articles listed are also available online from subscription databases such as InfoTrac, LexisNexis, and Questia, and on the web sites operated by the periodicals themselves, which can often be accessed free of charge at public or university libraries.

# HISTORICAL PERSPECTIVES

## BOOKS

Brace, Charles Loring. "The Life of the Street Rats," from *The Dangerous Classes of New York and Twenty Years Work Among Them*. New York: Wynkoop & Hallenbeck, 1872. A book on the condition of homeless children in New York by the founder of the New York's Children's Aid Society, who established a program to send orphans to new families in the west.

Brown, Dorothy M., and Elizabeth McKeown. *The Poor Belong to Us: Catholic Charities and American Welfare*. 1st ed. Cambridge, Mass.: Harvard University Press, 1997. The authors describe the evolution of Catholic charities between the Civil War and World War II, when a large influx of Catholic immigrants gave rise to foundling homes, orphanages, reformatories, and foster care programs in New York City and other cities. Over the years, the small, local networks of volunteers were transformed into a professional and centralized organization that had a significant impact on welfare policy.

Crenson, Matthew A. *Building the Invisible Orphanage: A Prehistory of the American Welfare System*. Cambridge, Mass.: Harvard University Press, 1998. An account of the changing structure of child-welfare institutions, making a link between the decline of the traditional orphanage and the rise of the modern welfare state. The book also covers in detail the classic debate of family versus institutional care for dependent children. The debate concluded in favor of the private home and family, with the result that a single mother struggling to survive and raise children with minimal public support became the new paradigm of the needy.

Dinan, Susan. *Women and Poor Relief in Seventeenth-Century France: The Early History of the Daughters of Charity*. Aldershot, Hampshire, England: Ashgate Publishing, 2006. The author chronicles poor relief in the kingdom of France and the history of the Daughters of Charity, examining how the community's existence outside convents helped to change the nature of women's religious communities and the early modern Catholic Church.

Eden, Frederick. *The State of the Poor*. Salem, N.H.: Ayer Publishing, 1969 (reprint). A classic three-volume analysis of the poor, first published in 1797, that relies on thorough research, interviews, correspondence, personal investigations, and the interpretation of an impressive collection of facts and statistics. The author opposes the systems of public relief then in place and concludes that poor laws, rather than alleviating poverty, weaken society by removing the incentive to work and earn.

Fairchilds, Cissie C. *Poverty and Charity in Aix-en-Provence, 1640–1789*. Baltimore: Johns Hopkins University Press, 1976. A study of the system of charities in a southern French town under the Bourbon dynasty, up to the French Revolution. Nearly all charity administration was private and lay, a result of the Counter-Reformation and the notion that religious institutions were no longer capable of properly administering charitable works.

Farmer, Sharon A. *Surviving Poverty in Medieval Paris: Gender, Ideology, and the Daily Lives of the Poor*. Ithaca, N.Y.: Cornell University Press, 2002. A social history of poverty in the 13th and early 14th centuries. The author demonstrates that social class and gender played vital roles in the perception of the poor and in their own experiences and expectations. Medieval Paris provides a unique opportunity for the study of poverty; in the rest of Europe, the poor appeared only rarely in contemporary works of scholarship or literature.

Grell, Ole Peter, and Andrew Cunningham. *Health Care and Poor Relief in Protestant Europe, 1500–1700*. London: Routledge, 1997. The authors describe health care and poor relief in northern Europe in a period when urban poverty became a generally recognized problem for both magistracies and governments. The book includes contributions from international and leading scholars in the field, who draw on research into local conditions, map general patterns of development, and explore local and national approaches to health care provision and poverty.

Hands, A. R. *Charities and Social Aid in Greece and Rome*. Ithaca, N.Y.: Cornell University Press, 1968. A book on philanthropy and systems of public and private assistance in the ancient Mediterranean world.

Hosay, Philip M. *The Challenge of Urban Poverty: Charity Reformers in New York City, 1835 to 1890*. New York: Arno Press, 1980. This 1969 thesis examines the philosophies behind changing relief programs in New York through the 19th century. A moralistic approach, intending to improve the perceived personal defects of the poor, gradually gave way to an environmentalist approach, which emphasized job opportunity, better sanitation, housing, and other external factors.

Jutte, Robert. *Poverty and Deviance in Early Modern Europe*. Cambridge: Cambridge University Press, 1994. The author examines the causes and effects of poverty in historical Europe, giving details on the extent of poverty, the standard of living of the poor, and strategies of the state and individuals to relieve poverty. The book includes a chronology and biographies of leading European social reformers concerned with poor relief.

Lindenmeyr, Adele. *Poverty Is Not a Vice: Charity, Society, and the State in Imperial Russia*. Princeton, N.J.: Princeton University Press, 1996. A book describing traditional Russian views of poverty, charity, and salvation. The author explores private and public charity and public welfare in Russia to the early 20th century and covers the issue of post-Communist private charity.

Loewenberg, Frank M. *From Charity to Social Justice: The Emergence of Communal Institutions for the Support of the Poor in Ancient Judaism*. Piscataway, N.J.: Transaction Publishers, 2001. The author gives the definitions of "poor" in ancient Judaea and in the larger Greco-Roman world and describes the public systems, such as contractual slavery and mandated grain distribution by individual farmers, that arose to alleviate poverty. The book's central thesis is that modern welfare systems owe more to pre-Christian institutions in the Levant than to Greco-Roman society, through the influence of the Jewish tradition on early Christianity.

Riis, Jacob. *How the Other Half Lives*. New York: Penguin Books, 1997. A milestone in journalism and social commentary, this book caused a sensation when it first appeared in 1890. It describes, in eloquent words and photographs, the conditions in New York's Lower East Side tenements. The author does not spare the reader horrendous details of poverty, crime, disease, and general misery among the city's immigrants, who were exploited without mercy by their landlords and factory employers. The book helped to inspire the Progressive reform movement of the early 20th century.

Rose, Michael E., ed. *The English Poor Law, 1780–1930*. New Studies in Economic and Social History series. New York: Barnes & Noble, 1971. A survey of scholarly research on the English poor laws, the original welfare programs, that includes a useful checklist of the relevant statutes.

Rowntree, Benjamin Seebohm. *Poverty: A Study of Town Life*. New York: Macmillan, 1901. A classic study of poverty in the English city of York. The author interviewed hundreds of families and compiled an impressive array of statistical tables and maps in an effort to give a complete and accurate picture of the condition of the working class and the poor of his day. The book had considerable influence in England and played an important role in the eventual construction of that nation's 20th-century welfare state.

Safley, Thomas Max. *Charity and Economy in the Orphanages of Early Modern Augsburg*. Boston: Brill Academic Publishers, 1997. A book about charity and orphanages in the "Free Imperial City" of Augsburg. Germany. These market-oriented institutions employed business virtues: efficiency, long-term risk and reward, and the avoidance of excess and waste. Gradually, however, efficiency evolved into a more complex notion of utility that placed the needs of the orphanages over the dictates of economy and the divisions of religion.

Schneewind, Jerome B., ed. Giving: *Western Ideas of Philanthropy*. Bloomington: Indiana University Press, 1996. A collection of essays on the history of charity and philanthropy, from antiquity to the Victorian era.

Slack, Paul P. *From Reformation to Improvement: Public Welfare in Early Modern England*. Oxford, U.K.: Clarendon Press, 1999. The author analyzes the early welfare state in England, showing that the English came to believe that piecemeal improvement was more likely to be achieved than total social reformation. He examines social policy and institutions such as workhouses and hospitals to illustrate how the English shaped their social and moral environment, and how they defined the notion of welfare.

Stabile, Donald R. *Work and Welfare: The Social Costs of Labor in the History of Economic Thought.* Westport, Conn.: Greenwood Press, 1996. The author shows that classical economists from Adam Smith to Alfred Marshall had sympathy for workers. For example, the theory of the subsistence wage echoed the theological call for a just wage during the Middle Ages. They also demonstrate how these thinkers promoted either a set of social obligations or a form of social insurance to assist workers, which would maintain and improve workers' efficiency and help them to raise healthy families.

Suzumura, Kotaro. *Competition, Commitment, and Welfare.* Oxford: Oxford University Press, 1995. This book examines one of the classical issues in theoretical welfare economics, the effects on social welfare of increasing competition between firms. The author explores whether promoting competition is in fact desirable—an issue that is central to modern debates about the role of markets.

Tocqueville, Alexis de. *Memoir on Pauperism.* Chicago: University of Chicago Press, 1997. After returning from a journey to England in 1833, the author offered this monograph to the Royal Academic Society of Cherbourg (this edition includes an introduction by Gertrude Himmelfarb, a noted scholar of Tocqueville's Victorian era). He argues that poor laws and social welfare policy degrade morals and create a permanently dependent underclass. In his view, public relief tends to depress wages, slow economic growth, worsen unemployment, and raise prices. Tocqueville favors relief for the sick, the disabled, and the aged; otherwise he holds to the use of private charity, supplemented by temporary public relief only in times of unforeseen social and economic troubles.

## ARTICLES

Cody, Lisa Forman. "The Politics of Illegitimacy in an Age of Reform: Women, Reproduction, and Political Economy in England's New Poor Law of 1834." *Journal of Women's History* 11, no. 4 (2000): 131–157. An article describing the political and social conventions that shaped the new Poor Law passed in England in 1834. The law made illegitimate children the responsibility of single mothers, reflecting a fundamental shift from paternalism to liberalism in the workings of the public relief system. The law challenged society's traditional notions of protecting its weakest members. Single mothers were blamed for overpopulation and the rise of illegitimacy.

Faherty, Vincent. "Social Welfare Before the Elizabethan Poor Laws: The Early Christian Tradition, AD 33 to 313." *Journal of Sociology & Social Welfare* 33 (2006). The author provides an overview of the organization, roles, and services provided by the social welfare system in early Christian communities in Europe, North Africa, and the Middle East.

Lindert, Peter H. "Poor Relief Before the Welfare State: Britain Versus the Continent, 1780–1880." *European Review of Economic History* 2, no. 2 (2006): 101–140. The author gives a wide array of statistics to compare public and private poor relief in the century before 1880 and compares the relief systems between Britain and Europe.

Platt, Anthony M., and Jenifer L. Cooreman. "A Multicultural Chronology of Welfare Policy and Social Work in the United States." *Social Justice* 28, no. 1 (spring 2001): 91–137. An extensive guide (with bibliography) to significant events in the history of social work; welfare policy; and issues concerning ethnic, class, and gender conflict and discrimination.

Quigley, William P. "Five Hundred Years of English Poor Laws, 1349–1834: Regulating the Working and Nonworking Poor." *Akron Law Review* 30, no. 1 (fall 1996): 73–128. The author reviews five centuries of English poor laws, describing how they were affected by popular notions about the role of the church and Christian doctrine and how they affected social welfare policy, labor law, and workplace regulation in the United States.

Sherwin, David. "The Institutionalization of Benevolence in the Eighteenth-Century Social Welfare State: The Great Charity Debate in Samuel Richardson's *Clarissa.*" *Journal of Church and State* 42, no. 3 (2000): 539–562. The author takes Richardson's novel as an example of the poor opinion many held of public relief institutions. In Sherwin's view, Richardson was purposefully setting forth an alternative approach—an imitation of early Christian communities and their systems of mutual aid.

## WEB DOCUMENTS

Brodman, James William. "Charity and Welfare: Hospitals and the Poor in Medieval Catalonia." The Library of Iberian Resources Online. Available online. URL: http://libro.uca.edu/charity/charity.htm. Accessed on October 5, 2007. An online book describing the nature of poverty in medieval Catalonia and the system of hospitals, hospices, and almshouses that emerged in response—a system that developed from the shelters that originally took in religious pilgrims.

"Charity and Charities." The Catholic Encyclopedia. Available online. URL: http://www.newadvent.org/cathen/03592a.htm. Accessed on October 5, 2007. An extensive article describing the biblical basis of charity and its outward expression. It characterizes the nature of charity during the age of the apostles and the early Christian Church and details the work of religious orders and the church in relieving the plight of the poor from the Middle Ages through the present time.

Hale, Sir Matthew. "A Discourse Touching Provision for the Poor." Available online. URL: http://socserv.mcmaster.ca/econ/ugcm/3ll3/hale/poor. Accessed on March 17, 2008. In this document, dating to 1683, a lord chief justice of England discusses the moral obligation to provide for the poor, rather than simply punish them, and describes the kingdom's various mechanisms for doing so, which he finds largely inadequate to the task.

Kahl, Sigrun. "Religion as a Cultural Force: The Case of Poverty Policy." Max Planck Institute, Cologne, Germany. 2006. Available online. URL: http://www.mpi-fg-koeln.mpg.de/people/pm/pdf/religion%20workshop%202006%20Sigrun%20Kahl%205-1-06.pdf. Accessed on October 5, 2007. An examination of the historical role of religion and culture in shaping the attitudes of public officials in charge of passing poor laws and creating systems of public welfare.

Lev, Yaacov. "The Ethics and Practice of Islamic Medieval Charity." History Compass. Available online. URL: http://www.blackwell-compass.com/subject/history/article_view?article_id=hico_articles_bpl396. Accessed on October 5, 2007. This article describes the religious basis of almsgiving in the Islamic faith. It tracks the institutional forms of charity that developed in the Islamic world, including the pious endowment system known as *waqf*, and the social and political ramifications of charity in the medieval Muslim world.

Townsend, Joseph. *A Dissertation on the Poor Laws*. Available online. URL: http://socserv.mcmaster.ca/~econ/ugcm/3ll3/townsend/poorlaw.html. Accessed on March 17, 2008. The author, writing in 1786, finds the poor laws in England working against the interests of the poor and worsening the problems they were meant to correct.

# PRIVATE CHARITY AND PUBLIC RELIEF

## BOOKS

Andrews, Janice, and Michael Reisch. *The Road Not Taken: A History of Radical Social Work in the United States*. London: Routledge, 2002. The authors describe the history of social work as driven by radical and marginalized groups, and how the profession has responded to changes in the social and political climate.

Axinn, June, and Herman Levin. *Social Welfare: A History of the American Response to Need.* New York: Harper & Row, 1982. Reprinted by Allyn & Bacon, 2004. The author gives a well-documented history of American welfare from the colonial period through the George W. Bush administration. The book describes economic and political forces that have shaped social welfare programs through American history.

Barry, Norman P. *Welfare.* 2nd edition. Minneapolis: University of Minnesota Press, 1999. In this historical study, the author traces the origins of the modern welfare system to Enlightenment-era philosophies and describes how welfare has been affected by various social, political, and economic concepts since that time.

Boyer, George R. *An Economic History of the English Poor Law, 1750–1850.* Cambridge: Cambridge University Press, 2006. A study of "outdoor relief" policies in the rural south of England. These policies, which originated in the late 18th century, assisted able-bodied workers unable to find work. ("Indoor relief" refers to such institutions as orphanages, shelters for the destitute and homeless, and workhouses.) The vagaries of an agricultural economy, even in a relatively affluent and powerful nation such as England, placed many laborers at the mercy of market forces. The widely held view was that providing some form of direct relief, without forcing residence in institutions, was a cost-effective and rational policy that benefited society as a whole.

Bremner, Robert. *The Public Good: Philanthropy and Welfare in the Civil War Era.* New York: Knopf, 1980. The author examines private and public charity before, during, and after the American Civil War. The book describes relief programs for soldiers; the postwar Reconstruction programs in the South; the Freedmen's Bureau, created to assist former slaves; and the creation of asylums, libraries, and schools for the handicapped. In this era, voluntary relief on the part of dedicated individuals was considered sufficient to meet social ills, while all those who were classified as the "undeserving" poor were written off as a lost cause.

Broder, Sherri. *Tramps, Unfit Mothers, and Neglected Children: Negotiating the Family in Nineteenth-Century Philadelphia.* Philadelphia: University of Pennsylvania Press, 2002. The author describes the social reform movement concerned uppermost with the repair and maintenance of the traditional family.

Brundage, Anthony. *The English Poor Laws, 1700–1930.* Social History in Perspective series. London: Palgrave Macmillan, 2001. The author describes the evolution of poor laws and the welfare state in England, covering the workhouse, "assisted emigration," child and family welfare programs, and public medicine and housing.

Clement, Priscilla F. *Welfare and the Poor in the Nineteenth-Century City: Philadelphia, 1800–1854.* Rutherford, N.J.: Fairleigh Dickinson University Press, 1985. The author examines the city's outdoor and indoor relief programs, private charity, child welfare, and the changing approach to issues of poverty and joblessness.

Cowherd, Raymond S. *Political Economists and the English Poor Laws: A Historical Study of the Influence of Classical Economics on the Formation of Social Welfare Policy*. Athens: Ohio University Press, 1978. The author examines the public outcry over poverty in late 18th- and early 19th-century England and explores how it brought about the Poor Law Amendment Act of 1834. Prominent social reformers of the time offered radical programs for relief and improvement of the poor; humanitarian idealism was later countered by laissez-faire economists, who believed that poor relief simply led to more dependence and poverty.

Edwards, Richard L., et al., eds. *Encyclopedia of Social Work*. 19th edition. New York: National Association of Social Workers, 1995. 3 volumes plus 1997 and 2003 supplements. A three-volume set with 290 articles on topics relevant to social work and social welfare policy, including extensive historical background and perspective. A biography section in the final volume includes entries on about 150 individuals prominent in the field of social work, welfare policy, and Social Security.

Ehrenreich, John. *The Altruistic Imagination: History of Social Work and Social Policy in the United States*. Ithaca, N.Y.: Cornell University Press, 1985. A scholarly history of the social work profession, tracing its origins in the 19th-century view of poverty that emphasized environmental causes over character defects. The author describes the crisis in social work during the Great Depression and the effect on social work of the Great Society programs of the 1960s.

Englander, David. *Poverty and Poor Law Reform in Britain: From Chadwick to Booth, 1834–1914*. Boston: Addison-Wesley, 1998. An authoritative account of England's Poor Law Amendment Act of 1834, which overthrew the poor law system in effect since the Elizabethan Age. The author covers the social and economic setting, the political debate surrounding the new laws, and the establishment of the English industrial workhouse, which was meant to shelter the destitute but destined to become a symbol of degradation and exploitation of the poor. The book includes glossaries, short biographies, contemporary commission and government studies, and valuable primary source documents.

Fissell, Mary E. *Patients, Power, and the Poor in Eighteenth-Century Bristol*. New York: Cambridge University Press, 1991. A book detailing changes in medical care and the medical establishment in this city in England during the 18th century, as English doctors laid the foundations for a modern system of public health. The book asserts that poor patients lost control of their health care as the medical professions became increasingly knowledgeable and specialized. In the process, doctors marginalized traditional and home remedies and gradually assumed control of the government's public health system.

Friedman, Lawrence J., and Mark D. MacGarvie, eds. *Charity, Philanthropy, and Civility in American History*. Cambridge: Cambridge University Press, 2003. A collection of essays on philanthropy, charity, and the development of civil society in the United States. The essays are organized into three major sections broadly representing the cultural, national, and international activities of philanthropy, historically ranging from the early formative years of American civil society to contemporary industrial society.

Gordon, Linda. *Pitied But Not Entitled: Single Mothers and the History of Welfare 1890–1935*. New York: The Free Press, 1994. A historical view of the social and economic circumstances of single mothers from the late 19th century to the passage of the Social Security Act and the AFDC program. The author describes how social welfare policy came to distinguish between "entitlements" paid to the deserving from "welfare" paid to single mothers.

Green, Elna C. *This Business of Relief: Confronting Poverty in a Southern City, 1740–1940*. Athens: University of Georgia Press, 2003. A study of relief policies and politics in Richmond, Virginia, over two centuries, in which the author places the city's experience in the context of the public policy throughout the South. The author covers unique southern institutions, such as the Freedmen's Bureau, as well as the effects of race policies, the New Deal of the 1930s, and the industrialization of the region in the 20th century.

Herndon, Ruth Wallis. *Unwelcome Americans: Living on the Margin in Early New England*. Philadelphia: University of Pennsylvania Press, 2001. This book recounts the story of 40 individuals forced from unwelcoming communities in 18th-century Rhode Island. There was no public welfare system in existence, and towns relied on the traditional English "warning-out" system.

Himmelfarb, Gertrude. *Poverty and Compassion: The Moral Imagination of the Late Victorians*. New York: Knopf, 1991. The author reveals that Victorian thought on the issue of poverty was not separate from moral positions, whether radical or conservative. She describes the Victorians' attempt to reach an effective scientific method of attacking poverty and covers the Salvation Army, the Fabians, and the reformers Charles Booth and Beatrice Webb.

Horne, Thomas A. *Property Rights and Poverty: Political Argument in Britain, 1605–1834*. Chapel Hill: The University of North Carolina Press, 1990. A book on the developing doctrine of property rights in Britain and how this concept shaped welfare policies and the early poor law.

Humphreys, Robert. *Poor Relief and Charity, 1869–1945: The London Charity Organization Society*. New York: Palgrave Macmillan, 2002. The author offers a negative view of the charity organization society, finding it an ineffective and divisive institution that foundered due to poor administration, overblown expectations, and the opposition of entrenched public and private institutions.

Jensen, Laura. *Patriots, Settlers and the Origins of American Social Policy*. Cambridge: Cambridge University Press, 2003. A history of social policy from colonial times, describing the historical roots of modern "entitlement" programs, which began not with the New Deal or the Great Society but with the country's founding in 1776.

Keyssar, Alexander. *Out of Work: The First Century of Unemployment in Massachusetts*. Cambridge: Cambridge University Press, 1986. A study of unemployment from the early 19th century through the Great Depression. The writer uses Massachusetts as an anchor for general study of unemployment throughout the country, which he finds to have been a pervasive condition from the post–Civil War era through the "Roaring '20s." The book describes the coping strategies of the jobless in the era before unemployment benefits, as well as the effect of unemployment on individual families, neighborhoods, and working-class society as a whole.

Lees, Lynn Hollen. *The Solidarities of Strangers: The English Poor Laws and the People, 1700–1948*. Cambridge: Cambridge University Press, 1998. A study of English policies toward the poor from the 17th century to the present, showing that public relief went through cycles of greater and lesser generosity. The author shows how the poor laws and entitlement to welfare was affected by a constantly changing public attitude toward poverty.

Leonard, Ellen. *Early History of English Poor Relief*. London: Routledge, 1965. In this comprehensive and detailed work, the author traces the medieval history of poor relief in England, the condition of the poor in the Middle Ages, the use of almshouses and orphanages, and how relief was distributed by the church and the civil authorities.

Lowe, Gary R., and Nelson Reid, eds. *The Professionalization of Poverty: Social Work and the Poor in the Twentieth Century*. Hawthorne, N.Y.: Aldine de Gruyter, 1999. A collection of essays on social work and a consideration of the changes to be wrought in the antipoverty system, both public and private, by the federal and state reforms being passed in the 1990s.

Mangum, Garth, and Bruce Blumell. *The Mormons' War on Poverty: A History of LDS Welfare, 1830–1990*. Salt Lake City: University of Utah Press, 1993. The authors trace the history of the Mormon Church from its founding in upstate New York in the 1830s, concentrating on how the church met the needs of its poor and unemployed members. The book focuses on the Church Welfare Program, which was first implemented in

1936 and has since grown into a worldwide institution along with the church.

Mink, Gwendolyn. *The Wages of Motherhood: Inequality in the Welfare State, 1917–1942*. Ithaca, N.Y.: Cornell University Press, 1995. This book examines the racial and cultural regulation of women in welfare policy and politics between the two world wars. The author starts from a now-familiar observation: that female Anglo-American policy activists cleared a place for women in the state and fought for antipoverty policies specifically aimed at women. The book describes how female Anglo-American reformers interwove their own racial and cultural perspectives with their genuine concern for poor women.

Noble, Charles. *Welfare as We Knew It: A Political History of the American Welfare State*. New York: Oxford University Press, 1997. The author compares the United States and other Western welfare states in their welfare policies and in their success in helping the poor. Since the Wilson administration, political factors and racial divisions have risen to become prime factors in the creation of the American welfare state, which the author views as a relative failure. The author makes suggestions for overcoming the institutionalized problems in delivering a minimum standard of living to all citizens.

Pashley, Robert. *Pauperism and Poor Laws*. Boston: Adamant Media Corporation, 2002. A facsimile reprint of an 1852 study of the English system of poor law administration. The author traces the origin of the poor law from Elizabethan times, through the Stuart dynasty, up to and including his own Victorian age. He highlights the shortcomings of what he views as a faulty system and suggests improvements in administration, financing, and taxation.

Porritt, Edward. *The Englishman at Home: His Responsibilities and Privileges*. New York: Thomas Y. Crowell, 1893. A journalist reports to an American audience on the public institutions of England, including the poor laws and the system of relief established in the middle of the 19th century.

———. *Poverty and the Poor Law: A Palgrave Macmillan Archive Collection*. Six volumes. New York: Palgrave Macmillan, 2005. An immense collection of contemporary articles and commentaries on the English poor laws written by philanthropists, workers, business leaders, government officials, writers, journalists, and historians.

Safley, Thomas. *The Reformation of Charity: The Secular and the Religious in Early Modern Poor Relief*. Boston: Brill Academic Publishers, 2003. The author investigates public and private poor relief from the medieval era, showing that the methods of poor relief reflected a community's unique history, culture, politics, social mores, and religious ideals. He refutes the generalization that public and private relief were at odds over economic or political ideology.

———. *Sin, Organized Charity, and the Poor Law in Victorian England*. New York: St. Martin's Press, 1995. An important study of the charity organization society phenomenon in 19th-century England. The movement, which founded bureaus for selecting and aiding the "deserving" and "undeserving" poor, directed the needy either to private charity or to the workhouse, depending on the society's evaluation of their character. Charity organization societies were formed throughout England and imitated in the United States. However, they were hard-pressed for employees and short of funds and public support. They inspired opposition from private charity, from taxpayers, from government officials, and from the poor themselves, who resisted their judgment and attempted rehabilitation by self-appointed poverty agents.

Slack, Paul. *The English Poor Law, 1531–1782*. Cambridge: Cambridge University Press, 1995. This comprehensive scholarly study covers the origins and development of England's poor law policy through the late 18th century. The poor laws had an important effect on English society at the dawn of the Industrial Revolution, and they also provided a model for the English colonies in North America. The author includes a comprehensive bibliography and a helpful checklist of poor law statutes.

Smith, Billy Gordon, ed. *Down and Out in Early America*. University Park: University of Pennsylvania Press, 2004. Smith presents essays on the condition of the poor in historical America; several articles cover the subject of poor relief in various states and the attempts to relieve poverty through public and private initiatives.

Sumner, William Graham. *What the Social Classes Owe Each Other*. Caldwell, Idaho: Caxton, 1963. Writing in 1883, this Yale professor promotes voluntary, private charity and derides the socialist premise that the relief of poverty is the legal and moral obligation of the wealthy.

Traverso, Susan. *Welfare Politics in Boston, 1910–1940*. Amherst: University of Massachusetts Press, 2003. A study of the significant impact of ethnic, religious, and gender conflicts on welfare politics in Boston. The book describes the clash between immigrant communities (including Irish and recent Jewish arrivals) and political leaders over public assistance programs. The debate contested which would be more effective at assisting the needy: private or public welfare systems. The author contends that support for welfare programs often depended on gender; for example, widows' pensions won widespread support, while unemployment benefits, which largely assisted males, did not. As the city population grew to accept men's dependence on welfare, public welfare was expanded through the 1920s and 1930s.

Wagner, David. *The Poorhouse: America's Forgotten Institution*. Lanham, Md.: Rowman & Littlefield, 2005. The author explores the New England poorhouse, covering the original purpose of these common public institutions, their physical conditions, the lives of long-term and short-term inmates as well as overseers, the political issues surrounding the poorhouse, and the demise and resurrection of the poorhouse in the 20th century.

Watson, Frank Dekker. *The Charity Organization Movement in the United States: A Study in American Philanthropy*. New York: Macmillan, 1922. A historical study of the charity organization movement, describing antecedents in foreign countries and the rise and decline of the movement in the United States in the early 20th century.

## ARTICLES

Blaug, Mark. "The Myth of the Old Poor Law and the Making of the New." *Journal of Economic History* 23, no. 2 (June 1963): 151–181. The author forcefully defends the English Poor Law against its many detractors, making the point that guaranteeing a minimum standard of living was beneficial to a national economy in the early Industrial Age. Much of the criticism arises from an influential 1834 report on the law and the tendency of historians to repeat each other.

Clark, Anna. "The New Poor Law and the Breadwinner Wage: Contrasting Assumptions." *Journal of Social History* 34, no. 2 (winter 2000): 261–281. This article analyzes the concept of the "breadwinner wage" in England's new poor law of 1834. As the Victorian age unfolded and attitudes toward the poor and laborers evolved, the breadwinner wage came to represent different things to different people: among some, a rare privilege and responsibility; for others, a reward for respectability; and for the rest, a legal right.

Cook, Jeanne F. "A History of Placing-Out: The Orphan Trains." *Child Welfare* 74, no. 1 (January/February 1995): 181–197. An article describing the "orphan trains," which brought more than 150,000 children west from the streets of various eastern U.S. cities, a forerunner of the modern foster home system.

Feldman, David. "Migrants, Immigrants, and Welfare from the Old Poor Law to the Welfare State." *Transactions of the Royal Historical Society*, 6th series, 13 (February 2003): 79–104. An article describing migration of the poor and an outsider's entitlement to welfare under Britain's old and new poor laws.

Goodlad, Graham. "From Old to New Poor Law." *History Review* 38 (December 1, 2000): 15–20. The author traces the social upheavals that transformed the old poor law of England. The amendments of 1834, which found poverty to be the outcome of individual moral failings, brought about a radical restructuring of the public charity system. The author finds that "New Poor Law" also established a new system of government administration, an information-gathering service that was unmatched in Europe at the time. As attitudes changed in the 20th century, it proved impossible to graft the modern welfare state onto the structures created in the 19th.

Hirschmann, Nancy J. "Liberal Conservatism, Once and Again: Locke's 'Essay on the Poor Law' and Contemporary US Welfare Reform." *Constellations* 9, no. 3 (September 2002): 335–355. The author grounds the modern welfare reform movement in the ideas of John Locke: In an essay written in 1697, when England was under the Elizabethan-era poor law regime, Locke proposed new methods of employment for the poor.

Somers, Margaret, and Fred Block. "From Poverty to Perversity: Ideas, Markets, and Institutions Over 200 Years of Welfare Debate." *American Sociological Review* 70, no. 2 (April 2005): 260–287. The authors compare the U.S. 1996 Personal Responsibility and Work Opportunities Reconciliation Act and the English 1834 New Poor Law—two episodes in which existing welfare regimes were overturned by market-driven ones. Despite dramatic differences across the cases, both laws were based on "the perversity thesis"—a public discourse that reassigned blame for the condition of the poor from "poverty to perversity."

Stokes, Peter M. "Bentham, Dickens, and the Uses of the Workhouse." *Studies in English Literature* 41, no. 2 (spring 2001): 711–728. The article describes the two fundamental views of the Victorian-era workhouse, which was made an integral part of the system of public charity by the Poor Law Amendment Act of 1834. The workhouse was seen as evil as well as necessary; the differing positions were embodied in the works of Jeremy Bentham and Charles Dickens.

Williamson, John B. "Old Age Relief Policy Prior to 1900." *American Journal of Economics and Sociology* 43, no. 3 (July 1984): 369–384. The author reviews the old-age relief policy before the 20th century. Although private charity gave way to publicly funded programs and institutions, his discussion reveals, relief grew more restrictive even as the country grew more prosperous.

Wright, David. "Learning Disability and the New Poor Law in England, 1834–1867." *Disability and Society* 15, no. 5 (August 2000): 731–745. An investigation of the treatment of pauper "idiots" in Victorian England, who fell under two jurisdictions: the Poor Law Board and the Lunacy Commission. The author describes the negotiations that resulted in the congregation of "idiots" and "imbeciles" in Poor Law Union workhouses and explores the 19th-century ideology of "moral treatment," which devalued the learning disabled as "incurable" and thus unworthy of expensive, specialized state provision.

## WEB DOCUMENTS

Boyer, George R. "Politics and Welfare: The Political Economy of the English Poor Law." The Library of Economics and Liberty. Available online. URL: http://www.econlib.org/library/Columns/Boyerpoorlaws. html. Accessed on September 7, 2007. The author explores the English system of public relief, which greatly expanded in the early 19th century to become the most extensive in Europe and which in his opinion was motivated by farmers. Then a powerful political lobby, farmers seeking to lower wage costs through public relief spending had a significant influence on policy. The expansion of public relief alarmed influential economists such as Thomas Malthus and led to the reform of 1834.

Historic Herefordshire On Line. *The Poor Law in Hereford*. Available online. URL: http://www.smr.herefordshire.gov.uk/post-medieval/workhouses /workhouses_poorlaw.htm. Accessed on March 17, 2008. An informal article on the history of poor relief in this English county. It describes the origins of the Elizabethan Poor Law, the Act of Settlement under King James II, the establishment of poorhouses, and public poverty in England as its society transformed from a nation of rural farmers to a largely urban and industrial power.

Quigley, William P. *Five Hundred Years of English Poor Laws, 1349–1834: Regulating the Working and the Nonworking Poor*. Available online. URL: http://www.uakron.edu/law/docs/quigley.pdf. Accessed on June 1, 2007. The author reviews the English poor law legislation over five centuries, beginning with the Statute of Laborers of 1349–50. The poor laws, which were a method of regulating the poor, had a major influence on social welfare legislation in the United States.

Senior, Nassau. *Poor Law Commissioner's Report of 1834: Copy of the Report Made in 1834 by the Commissioners for Inquiring into the Administration and Practical Operation of the Poor Laws*. Available online. URL: http://www. econlib.org/library/YPDBooks/Reports/rptPLC.html. Accessed on March 17, 2008. Part of The Library of Economics and Liberty. A government report dating from 1834 that describes the administration of the English poor law in exhaustive detail, offering a rich source of information on the experience of the poor in England and their interactions with the community and with officialdom.

# THE NEW DEAL AND THE SOCIAL SECURITY LAW

## BOOKS

Achenbaum, W. Andrew. *Social Security: Visions and Revisions*. New York: Cambridge University Press, 1986. This book covers the history of the Social

Security system through 1983, giving a detailed account of the original law and its amendments. In the second half of the book, the author gives policy recommendations that have been largely superseded by later events.

Altmeyer, Arthur J. *The Formative Years of Social Security*. Madison: University of Wisconsin Press, 1966. An account of the origins and implementation of the Social Security system, by one of the authors of the original legislation.

Amenta, Edwin. *Bold Relief: Institutional Politics and the Origins of Modern American Social Policy*. Princeton, N.J.: Princeton University Press, 1998. The author reveals the somewhat surprising fact that the United States was a world leader in social welfare spending during the 1930s. The welfare state was originally expanded by northern Democrats and then contracted by politicians from states where welfare beneficiaries had no vote or influence. The book explains welfare policy as a product of political debate and dynamics.

Bussiere, Elizabeth. *(Dis)Entitling the Poor: The Warren Court, Welfare Rights, and the American Political Tradition*. University Park: Pennsylvania State University Press, 1997. Analyzing the 1989 Supreme Court decision in the case of *DeShaney v. Winnebago County Department of Social Services*, the author covers the constitutional "right to life" as it was first dealt with by the Warren Court, 20 years before the Court presided over by Chief Justice William Rehnquist. Although the Warren Court ruled in many cases that the poor were entitled to constitutional protections, this did not extend to welfare benefits.

Coll, Blanche D. *Safety Net: Welfare and Social Security, 1929–1979*. New Brunswick, N.J.: Rutgers University Press, 1995. A history of federal welfare programs from the 1930s to the present. The author describes the expanding entitlement program; the increasing cost of AFDC and other programs; and the influence of the national economy, changing population trends, and politics on the system.

Edsforth, Ronald. *The New Deal: America's Response to the Great Depression*. Malden, Mass.: Blackwell Publishing, 2000. This book describes the remaking of the American economy through the New Deal legislation passed during Franklin D. Roosevelt's presidency, while describing the economic history of the Great Depression and the social effects of mass unemployment.

Green, Elna C., ed. *Before the New Deal: Social Welfare in the South, 1830–1930*. Atlanta: University of Georgia Press, 1999. Essays on the social welfare politics and institutions of the South before, during, and after the Civil War. The authors cover the impact of the war and Reconstruction, the effects of racism, and unique aspects of the southern economy. The book incorporates interesting local case studies, including essays on a poor farm in Jefferson County, Alabama, and on a home for needy Confederate widows in Richmond, Virginia.

————. *The New Deal and Beyond: Social Welfare in the South Since 1930*. Atlanta: University of Georgia Press, 2003. A collection of 10 studies of the social welfare system in southern states since the New Deal programs of the 1930s. The author points out that in some ways, the region served as a model for modern welfare programs and reform legislation; in other ways endemic racism thwarted efforts at delivering public benefits to the needy.

Lieberman, Robert C. *Shifting the Color Line: Race and the American Welfare State*. Cambridge, Mass.: Harvard University Press, 2001. An exploration of New Deal policies as they affected race relations, in which the author argues that Social Security benefited white workers, while the public assistance programs such as AFDC left minorities to fend for themselves as second-class citizens. The author finds that the modern urban underclass, disproportionately poor and African American, is a direct result of this divided system.

Polenberg, Richard D. *The Era of Franklin D. Roosevelt, 1933–1945: A Brief History with Documents*. New York: Palgrave, 2000. A comprehensive and useful collection of primary source material on the Roosevelt administration, with an important focus on the sweeping legal, economic, and social changes wrought by the New Deal policies. This volume includes articles by Harry Hopkins and Frances Perkins, both key figures in the passage of the Social Security Act.

Schlesinger, Arthur. *The Coming of the New Deal*. Boston: Houghton Mifflin Books, 2003. The second volume of the authoritative "Age of Roosevelt" series, this book profiles Roosevelt and his advisers and describes the political and social scene behind the passage of New Deal legislation, including the Social Security Act.

Singleton, Jeff. *The American Dole Unemployment Relief and the Welfare State in the Great Depression*. Westport, Conn.: Greenwood Press, 2000. A national study of depression-era relief prior to the New Deal that applies its conclusions to the 1990s-era welfare reforms. The author shows how the rapid expansion of unemployment in the early 1930s generated the pressures that led to the first federal welfare programs in the United States.

Venn, Fiona. *The New Deal*. Edinburgh: Edinburgh University Press, 1998. A textbook on the passage and implementation of New Deal policies, and the public reaction to them, during the Great Depression and afterward. The author usefully contrasts the reactions of the U.S. government and European states to the depression and demonstrates how American traditions were reflected in the New Deal.

## ARTICLES

Allard, Scott W. "Competitive Pressures and the Emergence of Mothers' Aid Programs in the United States." *Policy Studies Journal* 32, no. 4

(2004): 521–544. The author analyzes the history of welfare and documents states' tendency to compete in minimizing benefits, both for the sake of lower tax rates and to lessen their reputation as "welfare magnets." He observes that the mothers' aid programs that were the precursor to the Social Security Act and the AFDC program did not inspire this competitive tendency, and he attempts to answer the question of why.

Bartlett, Bruce. "Social Security Then and Now." *Commentary* 119, no. 3 (March, 2005): 52–56. This article discusses the political backdrop to the writing and passage of the Social Security Act of 1935, describing the economic controversies that have surrounded the program since it was first conceived.

Bethell, Thomas N. "Roosevelt Redux: Robert M. Ball and the Battle for Social Security." *American Scholar* 74 (spring (part 1)/summer (part 2) 2005). A general overview of the Social Security system's history, giving statistics to show how it has effectively reduced poverty among the elderly since the 1930s. The article discusses the changing attitudes toward the Social Security system among contemporary economists and politicians.

Davies, Gareth, and Martha Derthick. "Race and Social Welfare Policy: The Social Security Act of 1935." *Political Science Quarterly* 112, 2 (summer 1997): 217–235. A scholarly article dealing with the original Social Security law. The authors explain how the law resulted from racial attitudes and place current attitudes toward the welfare system in this historical racial context.

Grundmann, Herman F. "Adult Assistance Programs Under the Social Security Act." *Social Security Bulletin* 48, no. 10 (October 1985): 10–21. Reviewing the historical and economic background to the Social Security act, the author describes the "two-track" approach of the act in providing assistance to the elderly. One program would be a means-tested effort not dependent on contributions by its beneficiaries—meant to immediately assist the elderly who were unable to work or support themselves. A second program, a contributory annuity, would allow younger workers to prepare for retirement. The Social Security and welfare systems as they are presently constituted are a legacy of this approach.

Peterson, Carol Dawn, and Janice L. Peterson. "Single Mother Families and the Dual Welfare State." *Review of Social Economy* 52, no. 3 (1994): 314. The authors examine the evolution of the welfare state, tracing it to the passage of the Social Security Act and its various amendments. They argue that income support programs were shaped by "the combined interactions of the work ethic, racial politics, and traditional gender ideology" at the time of the act's passage in 1935. The second half of the article compares and contrasts the two major income-support programs, AFDC and Survivors' Insurance (SI), and describes their effect on single mothers.

Quadagno, Jill S. "Welfare Capitalism and the Social Security Act of 1935." *American Sociological Review* 49, no. 5 (October 1984): 632–647. The author maintains that the Social Security Act was a "conservative measure that tied social insurance benefits to labor force participation and left administration of its public assistance programs to the states." She characterizes the law as a mediation between the priorities of different interest groups and class factions and analyzes it as part of the ongoing competition between labor and capital.

## WEB DOCUMENTS

Bortz, Abe. "The Historical Development of the Social Security Act." Social Security Online. Available online. URL: http://www.ssa.gov/history /bortz.html. Accessed on September 6, 2007. Bortz was the first historian of the Social Security Administration. In this lecture, developed as part of the Social Security Administration's training program, he presents a history of the Social Security Act, giving historical background dating to prehistoric times and developments in public welfare policy that finally brought about the modern Social Security system.

Bresiger, Gregory. "The Revolution of 1935." Ludwig von Mises Institute. Available online. URL: http://www.mises.org/journals/essays/bresiger .pdf. Accessed on September 8, 2007. In this essay, the author sees, in the passage of the Social Security Act, a major paradigm shift. According to Bresiger, this revolution in economic thinking enshrined the idea that government spending could, and should, influence economic cycles in order to smooth out the peaks and valleys of the capitalist business cycle and that were contributing to economic insecurity.

Ross, Mary. "Why Social Security?" Social Security Online. Available online. URL: http://www.ssa.gov/history/whybook.html. Accessed on September 6, 2007. This 32-page Social Security Board booklet was published in 1937 as part of the board's efforts to educate the American public about the rationale underlying the new Social Security program. It was illustrated by Hendrik Willem Van Loon.

Social Security Online. The Social Security Act. Available online. URL: http://www.ssa.gov/OP_Home/ssact-toc.htm. Accessed on September 6, 2007. This page, part of the Social Security Administration's web site, is the table of contents to the complete text of the Social Security Act as amended through January 1, 2007. This includes Title IV, the section of the law that established Aid to Dependent Children. The home page of the Social Security Administration (http://www.ssa.gov/) contains a search function that allows the user to further explore the law and its origins.

# POVERTY AND THE GREAT SOCIETY

## BOOKS

Aaron, Henry Joseph. *Politics and the Professors: The Great Society in Perspective*. Washington, D.C.: Brookings Institution Press, 1978. An investigation of the Great Society programs undertaken in the 1960s to relieve poverty, racial discrimination, and unemployment. By the 1970s, the broad consensus supporting these programs had unraveled, and the nation was taking a new political direction hostile to the Great Society. The author describes how scholarly and popular writers changed their views and concludes that the eclipse of the Great Society came about not through its failure as policy but through external social and political factors.

Albeda, Randy, and Chris Tilly. *Glass Ceilings and Bottomless Pits: Women's Work, Women's Poverty*. Boston: South End Press, 1997. The authors describe the effect of poverty and the welfare system on women and mothers. The book advocates adoption of European-style social welfare and employment policies as well as reforms in the workplace to achieve gender equality in pay and benefits.

Andrew, John A. *Lyndon Johnson and the Great Society*. Chicago: Ivan R. Dee, 1999. An account of the origins of Johnson's Great Society programs: the War on Poverty, the Model Cities program, the Civil Rights Act, the Voting Rights Act, and Head Start. The author evaluates how these programs succeeded or failed. He maintains that the sheer complexity of the social problems they attempted to solve eventually turned the voters against them.

Auletta, Ken. *The Underclass*. Woodstock, N.Y.: Overlook Press, 1999. This is a reprint edition of an important work on American poverty originally published in 1982. The author, a *New Yorker* journalist, reports from New York City, the Appalachian Mountains, and Mississippi on the conditions and prospects for the poor. The book discusses crime, race, and labor as the author probes the roots of poverty and the effect it has on cities and the general social environment of the United States. He supports the efforts of nonprofits such as New York's Manpower Demonstration Research Corporation, which educates the poor in work and survival skills. The author added new material on welfare reform for the updated edition.

Bane, Mary Jo, and David T. Ellwood. *Welfare Realities: From Rhetoric to Reform*. Cambridge, Mass.: Harvard University Press, 1996. The authors analyze the AFDC program, describing conditions for recipients, the reasons for "welfare dependency," and prospects for streamlining and reforming the system.

# Welfare and Welfare Reform

Bane, Mary Jo, and Lawrence M. Mead. *Lifting Up the Poor: A Dialogue on Religion, Poverty, and Welfare Reform*. Washington, D.C.: Brookings Institution Press, 2003. Two authors, one from a Catholic and one a Protestant background, explore the impact of religious belief and doctrine on efforts at relieving poverty. While Bane emphasizes the general obligations of Catholic beliefs toward the poor, Mead proposes virtue and responsibility on the part of the individual to improve one's economic station.

Beito, David T. *From Mutual Aid to the Welfare State: Fraternal Societies and Social Services, 1890–1967*. Chapel Hill: University of North Carolina Press, 2000. A history of the fraternal societies, such as the Elks, Moose, and Knights of Tabor, and how they organized and acted collectively for mutual help and benefit. Important social services and benefits were available outside of the government, and such benefits were rights and not handouts, tied to a moral code and given on a reciprocal basis. Women, blacks, and immigrants were especially involved in this phenomenon.

Berkowitz, Edward D., and Kim McQuaid. *Creating the Welfare State: The Political Economy of Twentieth-Century Reform*. New York: Praeger, 1980. The authors describe how business executives cooperated with the federal government to shape welfare policy. The book covers welfare policy from the Progressive era to the years of the New Deal and the Social Security Act. The book counters the prevailing view that the modern welfare state came about despite strong determined opposition from the business community.

Berrick, Jill Duerr. *Faces of Poverty: Portraits of Women and Children on Welfare*. New York: Oxford University Press, 1995. A study of five welfare families, intended to combat the common image of welfare mothers as lazy and/or irresponsible. The author employs statistics to illustrate the limitations of welfare and shows how the system encourages its beneficiaries to cheat in order to survive.

Biddle, Bruce J., ed. *Social Class, Poverty, and Education: Policy and Practice*. London: Routledge, 2001. A series of articles dealing with poverty as it affects education and student performance in the classroom. The book covers the allocation of resources in poor districts, emphasizing the roles that ethnicity and economic class play in access to and quality of public education.

Bremner, Robert. *From the Depths: The Discovery of Poverty in the United States*. New York: New York University Press, 1956. A study of a transformation in public attitudes toward poverty in the late 19th and early 20th century, when poverty was newly seen as a problem to be solved, not simply a permanent condition to be deplored. The author reveals how these attitudes ushered in the modern era of social welfare, Progressive reforms, the New Deal, and, ultimately, the postwar welfare state.

# *Annotated Bibliography*

Brown, Michael K. *Race, Money, and the American Welfare State*. Ithaca, N.Y.: Cornell University Press, 1999. The author faults the welfare system for its systematic discrimination against African Americans. He traces this phenomenon to the provisions of the original Social Security Act. Reliant on privately provided health care and pensions, and simply dispensing cash benefits to the poor, the system results in a permanent black underclass that is at the mercy of the white majority—a majority that controls government and private business and has a constant drive to cut taxes and spending.

Burton, C. Emory. *The Poverty Debate: Politics and the Poor in America*. Westport, Conn.: Praeger/Greenwood, 1992. A review of poverty politics, this book refutes the conservative argument that poverty results from laziness and the existence of a social safety net. The author covers measurements of poverty, homelessness, welfare dependency, and the concept of "workfare," and he makes suggestions for changes in the welfare system that might earn the support of both sides of the political debate. Appendices present basic poverty data from 1990, the last census year before the welfare reform of 1996.

Cheal, David. *New Poverty: Families in Postmodern Society*. Westport, Conn.: Praeger, 1999. The author describes the phenomenon of "new poverty," in which the formerly affluent are subject to downsizing, layoffs, a reduction in work hours, and other events that reduce or end their income. He concludes that the demands of new poverty are overwhelming millions of families who are unprepared for it, and who find systems for improving their lot and reintegrating themselves into the economy sorely lacking. As a result, the poor are actually worse off than they were, and ineffective antipoverty programs are creating social conflict that worsens the situation.

Cook, Fay Lomax, and Edith J. Barrett. *Support for the American Welfare State: The Views of Congress and the Public*. New York: Columbia University Press, 1992. Relying on surveys taken among the public and members of Congress, the authors see support for social welfare programs among politicians and the general public, despite the conventional view of the welfare system as dysfunctional and unpopular.

Davies, Gareth. *From Opportunity to Entitlement: The Transformation and Decline of Great Society Liberalism*. Lawrence: University of Kansas Press, 1996. The author recounts the early promises of the Great Society welfare state and how it rapidly fell from public favor in the 1970s, bringing down with it the post–World War II generation's liberal ideals and social welfare laws and policies.

Davis, Martha. *Brutal Need: Lawyers and the Welfare Rights Movement, 1960–1973*. New Haven, Conn.: Yale University Press, 1995. An account of the "welfare rights" movement of the 1960s. The author describes the movement as driven by lawyers and welfare rights groups seeking to enshrine a constitutional right to public assistance. Although it ultimately failed, the welfare rights movement prompted important changes in the interpretation of constitutional rights as well as the public welfare system.

Edin, Kathryn. *There's a Lot of Month Left at the End of the Money: How Welfare Recipients Make Ends Meet in Chicago*. New York & London: Garland Publishing, 1993. The author describes the complex problems faced by families on welfare as they struggle to maintain a minimum standard of living.

Edin, Kathryn, and Laura Lein. *Making Ends Meet: How Single Mothers Survive Welfare and Low-Wage Work*. New York: Russell Sage Foundation, 1997. The authors interviewed 379 women to draw a comparison between the experiences of two contrasted groups: those drawing benefits from AFDC and those working in low-wage jobs. The study concludes that the Hobson's choice between welfare benefits and poorly paid employment leaves nearly all of their subjects hard-pressed to achieve even a minimal standard of living.

Engel, Jonathan. *Poor People's Medicine: Medicaid and American Charity Care Since 1965*. Durham, N.C: Duke University Press, 2006. A history of Medicaid since it was established in 1965. The author covers the history of charity medical care, the debate over the new law in the 1960s, how Medicare has been implemented differently in each state, and the law's sometimes drastic effects on hospitals, doctors, and the public health system.

Epstein, William M. *Welfare in America: How Social Science Fails the Poor*. Madison: University of Wisconsin Press, 1996. The author faults politicians and policy makers for poorly implemented welfare programs that do more harm than good for those they are supposed to help. The poor and unemployed, he says, wind up as political footballs in the endless rhetorical contest between liberals and conservatives. The book covers AFDC, Medicaid, food stamps, and welfare reform, and it concludes that welfare policy would benefit from a more scientific approach to the problem and the use of more complete data and research.

Esping-Andersen, Gosta. *The Three Worlds of Welfare Capitalism*. Princeton, N.J.: Princeton University Press, 1990. The author studies the effect of political ideology on the public welfare state, distinguishing three different types of modern welfare state arising from the historical forces and movements of the past.

Freedman, Jonathan. *From Cradle to Grave: The Human Face of Poverty in America*. Boston: Athenaeum, 1993. The author presents case histories of those in poverty to demonstrate the shortcomings of public welfare policy in the United States. He recommends a more comprehensive system, a "stair railing" rather than a safety net, that would allow the poor a stable and reliable source of assistance throughout their lives and save the nation the considerable cost of emergency benefits and remedies.

Funiciello, Theresa. *Tyranny of Kindness: Dismantling the Welfare System to End Poverty in America.* Boston: Atlantic Monthly Press, 1994. The author, who speaks from the experience of living as a welfare mother in New York, condemns the welfare bureaucracy as ineffective and capricious. She contrasts the public's view of welfare with that of the Social Security retirement program, criticizes the inefficiency of private charities that depend on public grants, and argues for scrapping welfare and replacing it with a federally guaranteed minimum income.

Galbraith, John Kenneth. *The Affluent Society.* 1958. Reprint, Boston: Mariner Books, 1998. In this famous study of consumer culture and economic inequalities, a renowned economist proposes public investment, and permanent unemployment benefits as a remedy for poverty, joblessness, and the disparities between rich and poor.

Gans, Herbert J. *The War Against the Poor: The Underclass and Antipoverty Policy.* New York: Basic Books, 1996. A Columbia University sociologist examines the public's distorted attitudes toward the poor and the welfare system. The labels and generalizations, in his view, serve to relegate a complex phenomenon to a series of code words and clichéd thinking. The author suggests replacing the welfare system with comprehensive job training, a guaranteed income program, and new methods for media coverage of poverty issues.

Gensler, Howard, ed. *The American Welfare System: Origins, Structure, and Effects.* Westport, Conn.: Praeger Publishers, 1996. This book provides a comprehensive overview and analysis of the American welfare system, covering the historical origins of the American welfare system, the constitutional development of welfare law and entitlements, and the economic structure and effects of welfare based on a large national data set covering the period 1979 through 1990. The book includes policy analyses and recommendations for reform.

Gilder, George. *Wealth and Poverty.* New York: Bantam Doubleday Dell, 1981. The author acclaims free-market capitalism as the most virtuous and successful of economic systems and decries welfare programs as a damaging disincentive to free enterprises and economic security. Taken up enthusiastically by President Reagan and the conservative movement of the 1980s, Gilder's work had wide-ranging influence in the welfare debate of that era.

Ginsberg, Leon. *Conservative Social Welfare Policy.* Belmont, Calif.: Wadsworth Publishing, 1998. The author covers the politically conservative approach to poverty and joblessness, which in his opinion will come to dominate welfare policy. The foundation of this approach in religious doctrine is discussed along with the ideas of conservative thinkers such as Edmund Burke, Charles Murray, Newt Gingrich, and George Gilder.

Goodin, Robert. *Reasons for Welfare: The Political Theory of the Welfare State.* Princeton, N.J.: Princeton University Press, 1988. The author advocates a minimal welfare state free of moralistic attacks from conservatives and utopian idealism of liberals. He supports the idea of welfare as a protection of the neediest members of society from exploitation, an essential role of modern democratic governments in an industrial age.

Gordon, Margaret. *Poverty in America.* San Francisco: Chandler Books, 1965. A collection of essays on antipoverty programs, income distribution, education, the labor market, urban renewal, rural poverty, and related topics, published at the dawn of the Great Society welfare innovations.

Hancock, Ange-Marie. *The Politics of Disgust: The Public Identity of the Welfare Queen.* New York: New York University Press, 2004. A Yale University professor of political science and African-American studies explains the stereotype of the welfare queen and argues that classic public misconceptions about African-American mothers have led to wrongheaded laws and public policy. The argument is supported by analysis of news stories, floor debates in the U.S. Congress, interviews with welfare recipients, and historical evidence.

Harrington, Michael. *The Other America: Poverty in the United States.* New York: Penguin Books, 1962. This classic study of the poor in mid-20th-century America served as a key impetus to the Great Society programs taking shape in the mid-1960s. The author critiques ineffective and poorly thought-out government antipoverty policy, finding that political grandstanding largely prevented cooperative and effective action.

Holloway, Susan D. *Through My Own Eyes: Single Mothers and the Cultures of Poverty.* Cambridge, Mass.: Harvard University Press, 1997. Over a period of three years, the author and several colleagues interviewed poor, single mothers of various racial backgrounds in Boston. The book reports these women's attitudes toward work and family and describes how they cope with the education and support of their children.

Howard, Christopher. *The Hidden Welfare State: Tax Expenditures and Social Policy in the United States.* Princeton, N.J.: Princeton University Press, 1997. The author analyzes tax incentives and loopholes, such as deductions for home mortgage interest, retirement pension funding, the Earned Income Tax Credit, and the Targeted Jobs Tax Credit. This "hidden welfare state," in his view, came about through the actions of the supporting coalitions, vote-seeking politicians, and narrowly focused interest groups that still sustain it. The author believes this system of incentives and benefits distorts the economy in important ways and has damaging effects on the system of welfare benefits for the truly needy.

Jansson, Bruce S. *The Reluctant Welfare State*. Belmont, Calif.: Wadsworth, 1988. A book intended for an academic audience, analyzing the evolution of the welfare state through U.S. history and giving social, economic, and political context for changes in welfare policy and programs. The book focuses on the role of private charity and social workers in historical eras, and it demonstrates how the modern welfare state has allowed minority groups to achieve progressive reforms through their policy advocacy.

Jencks, Christopher. *Rethinking Social Policy: Race, Poverty, and the Underclass*. New York: HarperPerennial, 1993. The author suggests that political leaders and the general public need to develop new critical thinking skills when dealing with the issues of race, poverty, welfare, joblessness, urban crime, and heredity. The 1980 elections, which ushered in the Reagan administration, were an important turning point in the public policy arena. In the author's view, they represent an opportunity to put an end to outdated approaches to social welfare that only perpetuated the problems they were meant to solve.

Katz, Michael B. *Improving Poor People: The Welfare State, the "Underclass," and Urban Schools as History*. Princeton, N.J.: Princeton University Press, 1997. The author reviews 25 years of writing on social policy and welfare programs. The book describes historical answers to poverty and how the political debate shaped the modern welfare state.

Katz, Michael B., ed. *The "Underclass" Debate: Views from History*. Princeton, N.J.: Princeton University Press, 1992. This collection of essays examines historical views of poverty and the "underclass." An important theme is the effect of industrialization and the migration into cities, which has created a permanent stratum of the poor and unemployed inhabiting desolate urban ghettoes. The contributors discuss the influence of African traditions on the family patterns of African Americans; the origins of institutions that serve the urban poor; the reasons for the crisis in urban education; the achievements and limits of the War on Poverty; and the role of income transfers, earnings, and the contributions of family members in overcoming poverty.

Kingfisher, Catherine Pelissier. *Women in the American Welfare Trap*. Philadelphia: University of Pennsylvania Press, 1996. An ethnographic study of a welfare office and two welfare rights groups. The book deals with welfare policy as it is implemented by women, as both caseworkers and beneficiaries, at the local level, and how women in this system achieve a sense of common purpose and identity.

Marmor, Theodore R., Jerry L. Mashaw, and Philip L. Harvey. *America's Misunderstood Welfare State: Persistent Myths, Enduring Realities*. New York: Basic Books, 1990. The authors contend that the Great Society welfare programs have been unjustifiably maligned as exacerbating the problems they were meant to address. Instead, in their view, the programs were popular and effective, up to a point. They advance some ideas for reform of the welfare system, claiming that adjustments to the structure of welfare benefits would work better than simply trashing the entire system and starting from scratch.

Matusow, Allen J. *The Unraveling of America: A History of Liberalism in the 1960s*. New York: Perennial, 1985. The author finds a transformation of liberalism from President Kennedy's laissez-faire economics to the Great Society welfare state initiated by President Johnson, and he goes on to describe the radicalization of leftist politics in the 1970s. In his view, the expanding welfare bureaucracy is key to the division of American politics into two hostile and mutually exclusive viewpoints.

Mead, Lawrence. *The New Politics of Poverty: The Nonworking Poor in America*. New York: Basic Books, 1993. The author, a onetime research director for the Republican National Committee, argues that a growing class of nonworking poor, deliberately relying on public welfare benefits, poses a serious social and economic problem for the United States. He favorably contrasts conservative with liberal responses to poverty, and supports a permanent work requirement for welfare beneficiaries, a policy that would become an integral part of the welfare reform law passed a few years after this book was published.

Mink, Gwendolyn. *Welfare's End*. Ithaca, N.Y.: Cornell University Press, 1998. The author views welfare not as a benefit or entitlement but as a mandated income to women working at home. The book's solution to welfare dependency and the cycle of poverty is an income guarantee, without which women will be unable to achieve equality in the home or in the economy.

———. *Whose Welfare?* Ithaca, N.Y.: Cornell University Press, 1999. Feminist scholars treat welfare reform and its effects on employment; on immigrants; and on issues such as domestic violence, caregiving, and reproductive rights. The book concludes with a history of activism among poor and working-class women.

Moynihan, Daniel Patrick. *Miles to Go: A Personal History of Social Policy*. Cambridge, Mass.: Harvard University Press, 1996. The leading Democratic senator on welfare and social policy issues offers a critique of his party's policy initiatives since the Social Security Act of 1935 and offers a prescription to improve the faltering public image of the Democrats and the Great Society–era welfare state.

Murray, Charles. *Losing Ground: American Social Policy, 1950–1980*. 1984. Reprint, New York: Basic Books, 1994. The author traces the history of federal welfare policy in the post–World War II era and collects data in a variety of forms to demonstrate that the expansion of welfare during the 1960s worsened the plight of the poor. This book emerged as the definitive antiwelfare study during the reform movement of the 1990s.

Nadasen, Premilla. *Welfare Warriors: The Welfare Rights Movement in the United States*. New York: Routledge, 2004. A study of the welfare rights movement, in which the author describes the origins of the movement during the 1960s among African-American single mothers and their demands for a more just and humane system. The author explores the effect of race, gender, class, and feminist attitudes on the welfare rights movement as well as the rising public opposition to it. The book includes firsthand accounts, primary source material, and numerous interviews.

O'Connor, Brendan. *A Political History of the American Welfare System: When Ideas Have Consequences*. Lanham, Md.: Rowman & Littlefield, 2003. The author describes the changes in public attitudes toward welfare, from the idealistic Great Society era of expansion to the 1996 welfare reform–era policies of cutbacks, work requirements, and five-year time limits. The book examines how an increasingly conservative society shaped the debate and how election-year pressures for reform in the system brought about the new law.

Peterson, Paul E., and Mark C. Rom. *Welfare Magnets: A New Case for a National Standard*. Washington, D.C.: Brookings Institution, 1990. In this book, published before the 1996 welfare reform, the authors deal with the diversity in state welfare policies and benefit levels. These differences created "welfare magnets"—states with comparatively high benefits that attract or retain the poor. As a result of the patchwork system of benefits, many states substantially reduced benefit levels; poor families were inhibited in their residential choices; and the employment opportunities of the poor were unnecessarily restricted. The authors recommend that the federal government establish a minimum national welfare standard to reduce the interstate variation in welfare benefits and reverse their overall decline.

Pierson, Paul. *Dismantling the Welfare State? Reagan, Thatcher, and the Politics of Retrenchment*. Cambridge: Cambridge University Press, 1995. A comparative analysis of the policies of Ronald Reagan in the United States and Margaret Thatcher in Britain, both conservative politicians committed to trimming the entrenched welfare institutions of their respective governments. The author concludes that "retrenchment" proved much more difficult than these leaders expected, that the welfare state had the general support of the public, and that welfare institutions usually outlast any efforts to eliminate them.

Pierson, Paul, ed. *The New Politics of the Welfare State*. New York: Oxford University Press, 2001. In this collection, several academics cover the subject of the modern welfare states of the West. These writers describe the gradual transformation of Western welfare systems under the pressures of economic liberalization, "globalization," and calls for budget austerity.

Polakow, Valerie. *Lives on the Edge: Single Mothers and Their Children in the Other America*. Chicago: University of Chicago Press, 1994. Reviewing several case histories of welfare families, the author charges society with marginalizing and demonizing single mothers. She finds the roots of failed public welfare policy in historical attitudes about motherhood, children, child-raising, and the normal nuclear family. The book concludes that mandatory entitlements to health care, housing, and child care would help to correct the system's many failures.

Quadagno, Jill S. *The Color of Welfare: How Racism Undermined the War on Poverty*. New York: Oxford University Press, 1996. The author finds that racial attitudes and conflict, from Reconstruction to her own time, weakened and destroyed antipoverty programs throughout U.S. history. She points out race conflict present in the Social Security law and contends that the Civil Rights movement and a white, middle-class backlash weakened the Great Society initiative, a well-intentioned effort to erase poverty and joblessness. She highlights the Great Society programs that were thus undermined.

Ritz, Joseph P. *The Despised Poor: Newburgh's War on Welfare*. Boston: Beacon Press, 1966. A book discussing the controversy over welfare ordinances passed in 1961 in the city of Newburgh, New York.

Rosanvallon, Pierre. *The New Social Question: Rethinking the Welfare State*. Princeton, N.J.: Princeton University Press, 2000. The author shows that social and intellectual change has shaken a fundamental justification for traditional welfare policies—that all citizens share equal risks. He begins by tracing the history of the welfare state and how it eventually attempted to eliminate economic and social risks, and he points out that some individuals will face much greater risks than others because of their jobs and lifestyle choices. Rosanvallon argues for contracts between providers and receivers of benefits, which he believes would equip welfare programs to better meet individual needs.

Schein, Virginia E. *Working from the Margins: Voices of Mothers in Poverty*. Ithaca, N.Y.: ILR Press, 1995. The author interviews a geographical and social cross-section of poor single mothers and evaluates their needs. She suggests that full-time employment would simply leave them with a new set of problems, and remaining at the edge of survival.

Schram, Sanford F. *Words of Welfare: The Poverty of Social Science and the Social Science of Poverty*. Minneapolis: University of Minnesota Press, 1995. The author maintains that poverty research has to share some of the blame for the failures of the welfare system. The fault, Schram says, lies in the way social scientists examine and ultimately blame the behavior of the poor while disregarding the incentives and disincentives to work built into the prevailing economic system.

Sidel, Ruth. *Keeping Women and Children Last: America's War on the Poor*. New York: Penguin Books, 1996. The sequel to the author's 1986 work, *Women and Children Last*, this book profiles the poor with statistical analysis and anecdotes. Challenging the misperceptions among politicians and the general public about poverty and families on welfare, the author shows that many such families were once hardworking members of the middle class, and that emotional, irrational thinking has demonized them.

Swenson, Peter A. *Capitalists Against Markets: The Making of Labor Markets and Welfare States in the United States and Sweden*. New York: Oxford University Press, 2002. The author traces the influence of businesses and capital markets on the development of the modern welfare state.

Tanner, Michael. *The End of Welfare: Fighting Poverty in the Civil Society*. Washington, D.C.: Cato Institute, 1996. The author suggests that the most humane and effective solution to the problems of poverty is to bring an end to the welfare program entirely. Neither liberal nor conservative approaches to welfare reform will work, in his view, and the wiser path is to end welfare dependence and bring about more economic opportunity through private and public institutions.

West, Guida. *The National Welfare Rights Movement: The Social Protest of Poor Women*. New York: Praeger, 1981. The author offers an insider's account of the welfare rights movement, which brought together different ethnic and socioeconomic groups in its advocacy for a more efficient and effective welfare system. In the author's view, it was the varying outlook and goals of these different groups that caused the dissension and infighting that eventually brought the movement to a standstill.

Wilson, William Julius. *The Truly Disadvantaged: The Inner City, The Underclass, and Public Policy*. Chicago: University of Chicago Press, 1990. A prominent sociologist argues that current urban poverty has been caused primarily by economic factors, such as a decline in the manufacturing sector, and is not due to racism or the breakup of the family.

———. *When Work Disappears: The World of the New Urban Poor*. New York: Vintage, 1997. From studies of the poor in Chicago, the author concludes that the loss of well-paid inner-city jobs in manufacturing industries is the most important factor in contemporary urban poverty. He proposes, among other remedies, a time limit on welfare payments coupled with a public jobs program to train welfare recipients for the general work force.

Zundel, Alan F. *The Politics of Poverty: The Civic Republican Tradition in U.S. Poverty Policy*. Albany: State University of New York Press, 2000. A study that contrasts American political traditions of an earlier era with the demands of a modern industrial state, in which the author sees these now-outdated traditions as distorting the debate over antipoverty programs. After reviewing 19th-century "civic republicanism," he compares and contrasts government policy in homesteading, cash assistance, and the ownership of capital assets.

## ARTICLES

Acs, Gregory, and Pamela Loprest. "The Effect of Disabilities on Exits from AFDC." *Journal of Policy Analysis & Management* 18, no. 1 (winter 1999): 28–49. An analysis of disability and the AFDC program, based on a 1990 survey showing that nearly 30 percent of families receiving AFDC benefits have a disabled mother or child. The article predicts some effects of welfare reform and the TANF program on families with disabilities.

Bauer, Gary. "The Man Who Gave Us Welfare Reform: Robert B. Carleson, 1931–2006." *The Weekly Standard* 11, no. 32, May 8, 2006. A eulogy for the architect of California's welfare reform law, as it was adopted under Governor Ronald Reagan. The success of the program helped to launch Reagan's bid for the presidency.

Brown-Collier, Elba K. "Johnson's Great Society: Its Legacy in the 1990s." *Review of Social Economy* 56, no. 3 (1998): 259. The author reviews the passage of Great Society legislation in the early months of the Johnson administration and traces the remains of the new laws in the contemporary government of the 1990s. The article focuses on five different areas of legislation: civil rights, income assistance, education and training, health care, and housing.

Burnham, Margaret. "Legacy of the 1960s: The Great Society Didn't Fail." *The Nation* 249, no. 4, July 24, 1989, pp. 122–124. The author maintains that the Great Society was a success, as far as it went, and that its abandonment by the Reagan administration—along with an economy that failed to provide employment to many of those willing to work—ultimately doomed the Great Society programs to failure or irrelevance.

Butler, Stuart. "A Conservative War on Poverty." *National Review* 41, no. 21, November 10, 1989, pp. 27–29. The author suggests that conservative leaders, in addition to simply repudiating the Great Society of the Johnson administration, should be capable of creating their own programs for eliminating poverty. Such programs would embrace free-market principles and the empowerment of the individual outside of the regulation of the state.

Hofferth, Sandra L., Julia Smith, Vonnie C. McLoyd, and Jonathan Finkelstein. "Achievement and Behavior Among Children of Welfare Recipients, Welfare Leavers, and Low-Income Single Mothers." *Journal of Social Issues* 56, no. 4 (winter 2000): 747–774. The authors examine fatherless families that either currently draw welfare benefits or have left the system. The study finds that the period of transition out of welfare has a negative emotional effect, although children in these families generally score better on cognitive tests.

Lemann, Nicholas. "The Origins of the Underclass." *Atlantic Monthly* 257, nos. 6–7, June/July 1986. The author traces the origins of the modern urban underclass to an earlier generation of southern farmers and share-croppers. He finds that once-vibrant poor neighborhoods have become desolate, depressing, and dangerous poor neighborhoods, and that the African-American populations of the cities have fallen victim to adverse economic and social trends. These circumstances have contributed to increasing poverty even as the rest of the nation enjoys relative prosperity.

May, Christopher. "Withdrawal of Public Welfare: The Right to a Prior Hearing." *Yale Law Journal* 76, no. 6 (May 1967): 1,234–1,246. This article by a second-year law student analyzes the legal right to a hearing for those denied welfare benefits; it had repercussions in the important case of *Goldberg v. Kelly*.

Mead, Lawrence. "The New Politics of the New Poverty." *The Public Interest* 103 (spring 1991): 3–20. The author reviews current opinions on the source of poverty and its solutions, contrasting the notions of the Progressive era with the "dependency politics" of contemporary society. In his view, the political divide over poverty is hindering the implementation of effective policies, for the most part in the name of avoiding state paternalism.

Niskanen, William A. "Welfare and the Culture of Poverty." *Cato Journal* 16, no. 1 (spring/summer 1996): 1–15. The author characterizes welfare as "both a consequence and a cause of several conditions best described as social pathologies. These conditions include dependency, poverty, out-of-wedlock births, nonemployment, abortion, and violent crime." Using difference in levels of these pathologies among the states as a basis, the study estimates the specific effects of welfare benefits and the extent to which the pathologies result from a common set of root causes.

Reich, Charles. "The New Property." *Yale Law Journal* 73, (April 1964): 733–787. In this seminal law review article, the author argues that a new form of wealth and property in the form of government benefits gives rise to new rights, in which individuals can reasonably expect to have legal entitlement. Such rights, such as the right to welfare benefits, cannot be taken away without due process.

## WEB DOCUMENTS

Austin, Michael J. "Understanding Poverty from Multiple Social Science Perspectives." Available online. URL: http://cssr.berkeley.edu/bassc/public/CompletePovertyReport082306.pdf. Accessed on September 7, 2007. This paper presents a variety of viewpoints—anthropological, political, socio-logical, and economic—on the origins and causes of modern poverty.

Briefs, Goetz. "The Janus Head of the Welfare State." Intercollegiate Stud-ies Institute. Available online. URL: http://www.mmisi.org/ir/07_03 /briefs.pdf. Accessed on September 8, 2007. The author, a Georgetown University economics professor, finds a foreboding vision of modern welfare state "vassalage" in the writings of Alexis de Tocqueville. He de-clares that the welfare system is a danger to capitalist economies and to personal liberty.

Califano, Joseph A. "What Was Really Great About the Great Society?" *The Washington Monthly.* Available online. URL: http://www.washington monthly.com/features/1999/9910.califano.html. Accessed on September 8, 2007. The author maintains that, contrary to widely held conservative opinion, the programs of the Great Society were a resounding success, helping to improve education, employment, and living conditions and greatly reducing the number of Americans living below the poverty line.

Dorn, James A. "The Transfer Society." *Cato Journal.* Available online. URL: http://www.cato.org/pubs/journal/cj6n1/cj6n1-1.pdf. Accessed on September 8, 2007. The author analyzes the growth of "transfers," or payments mandated by government in the form of benefits and made on behalf of certain groups—including the poor, the rich, manufacturers, and farmers—and examines the deleterious effects such transfers have on the economy and society.

PBS.org. "John Gardner: Engineer of the Great Society." Available online. URL: http://www.pbs.org/johngardner/chapters/4.html. Accessed on October 5, 2007. A profile of John Gardner, President Johnson's secretary of Health, Education, and Welfare. Gardner was responsible for imple-menting the dozens of programs originating in Johnson's Great Society.

# THE 1996 WELFARE REFORM LAW

## BOOKS

Blank, Rebecca M., and Ron Haskins. *The New World of Welfare.* Washing-ton, D.C.: Brookings Institution Press, 2001. A collection of essays deal-ing with the effects of the 1996 welfare reform bill, with both supporting and opposing views, from academic and nonacademic sources. The book includes a useful overview of the new law as its first chapter.

Cammisa, Anne Marie. *From Rhetoric to Reform?: Welfare Policy in American Politics.* Boulder, Colo.: Westview Press, 1998. The author traces recent history of the welfare system and shows how reform of welfare became a leading conservative cause in the early 1990s. A chapter is devoted to the 1996 reform law passed just before the book was published.

# Annotated Bibliography

Davis, Dana-ain. *Battered Black Women and Welfare Reform: Between a Rock and a Hard Place*. Albany: State University of New York Press, 2006. The author studies 22 residents of a battered women's shelter to study the effect of the welfare reform law on victims of domestic violence. A central thesis of this study is the difference in public opinion and treatment of white and black women by local welfare systems.

DeParle, Jason. *American Dream: Three Women, Ten Kids, and a Nation's Drive to End Welfare*. New York: Viking Adult, 2004. The author, a reporter for the *New York Times*, analyzes the 1996 welfare reform law through the experience of three families in Milwaukee. The book contrasts the acts and motivations of lawmakers with those of people directly affected by the law, and it concludes that welfare reform was successful in cutting welfare rolls but also responsible for creating a large underclass of working poor.

Duncan, Greg J., and P. Lindsay Chase-Lansdale, eds. *For Better and for Worse: Welfare Reform and the Well-Being of Children and Families*. New York: Russell-Sage Foundation Publications, 2004. A series of articles covering welfare reform in the years after its passage. The authors trace the political debate surrounding the law and how that debate shaped the outcome. Successful aspects of the law are highlighted and analyzed.

Gilbert, Neil, and Antoine Parent. *Welfare Reform: A Comparative Assessment of the French and U.S. Experiences*. New Brunswick, N.J.: Transaction Publishers, 2004. An analysis of the development and structure of modern welfare programs in the United States and France and how they function. The dynamics of welfare reform are covered in the Revenu Minimum d'Insertion in France and Temporary Assistance for Needy Families.

Goldberg, Gertrude Schaffner, and Sheila D. Collins. *Washington's New Poor Law: Welfare "Reform" and the Roads Not Taken, 1935 to the Present*. New York: Apex Press, 2001. A study of the effects of the 1996 welfare reform, tracing the new law's history and describing its consequences. The authors find the new system no improvement on the old, believing that it perpetuates poverty and lacks an important provision that would require work to be provided to all those receiving welfare benefits.

Golden, Olivia. *Poor Children and Welfare Reform*. Westport, Conn.: Auburn House, 1992. Drawing on the approaches of seven successful programs from across the country, the author suggests that under the right circumstances, welfare agencies can become catalysts for change on behalf of children. They can fulfill this potential, she says, both by expanding their own services and by reaching out to other agencies in the community. The book includes recommendations for making the welfare system a source of support and early attention to children and families.

Hage, Dave. *Reforming Welfare by Rewarding Work: One State's Successful Experiment.* Minneapolis: University of Minnesota Press, 2004. A study of the Minnesota Family Investment Program, enacted in 1997 on the recommendations of a "citizens' panel." The program is designed to reward job seekers and provide basic assistance toward living expenses, day care, and transportation. The author follows the experiences of three welfare families, providing real-life illustrations of the effect of policy decisions; he also describes the aftermath of the federal reform program and its effects on the Minnesota effort.

Handler, Joel F. *The Poverty of Welfare Reform.* New Haven, Conn.: Yale University Press, 1995. A UCLA professor debunks several clichés regarding welfare recipients and criticizes welfare reform proposals that were current just before the welfare reform law of 1996. He believes that merely modifying the current system will doom reform efforts to failure. He suggests more effective remedies in expanding health care coverage; providing enhanced tax credits for the working poor; and putting policies in place that will enhance job opportunity, wages, and benefits.

Hansan, John E., and Robert Morris, eds. *Welfare Reform, 1996–2000: Is There a Safety Net?* Westport, Conn.: Auburn House, 1999. In this collection of essays, leading experts on welfare policy examine major issues in the light of the 1996 welfare reform law: personal responsibility versus dependence; child development; and federal versus state, local, and private responsibility.

Haskins, Ron. *Work over Welfare: The Inside Story of the 1996 Welfare Reform Law.* Washington, D.C.: Brookings Institution Press, 2006. A staffer on the Ways and Means Committee of the House of Representatives, Haskins took a leading role in writing the 1996 welfare reform legislation. In this book, he provides a background on the history of the welfare system, continues with the Republican Party's "Contract with America" and early attempts at welfare reform legislation, and then gives three full chapters to the process of hearings, markups, and floor debate in the House of Representatives.

Hershkoff, Helen, and Stephen Loffredo. *The Rights of the Poor: The Authoritative ACLU Guide to Poor People's Rights.* Carbondale: Southern Illinois University Press, 1997. A handbook covering the legal rights of beneficiaries in welfare, food stamps, disability insurance, health care, housing, and education programs, which was published just after the passage of the welfare reform act of 1996.

Imig, Douglas R. *Poverty and Power: The Political Representation of Poor Americans.* Lincoln: University of Nebraska Press, 1996. A history of public policy concerning the poor in the 1980s and 1990s. The author investigates the political activity of various antipoverty groups, who were facing widespread public opposition to antipoverty programs during the

"Reagan revolution." Then he focuses on the passage of the 1987 McKinney Homeless Assistance Act, the first social legislation to pass since the start of the Reagan administration.

Kilty, Keith Michael, and Elizabeth A. Segal, eds. *The Promise of Welfare Reform: Political Rhetoric and the Reality of Poverty in the Twenty-First Century*. Binghamton, N.Y.: Haworth Press, 2006. The authors collect a series of essays illustrating the failings of the 1996 welfare reform law. The articles gathered here illustrate the view that the new law simply forced mothers poorly equipped for the workplace off the rolls and into poorly paid jobs. While a statistical success in reducing the welfare rolls, the authors conclude, welfare reform put an end to the social safety net and had a deleterious effect on families.

Kretsedemas, Philip, Ana Aparicio, Ronald Walters, and Kalyani Rai. *Immigrants, Welfare Reform, and the Poverty of Policy*. Westport, Conn.: Praeger, 2004. This book treats the impact of the 1996 welfare reform act on a wide range of immigrant groups in North America. The articles generally conclude that the law did nothing to improve the lot of working immigrants, and that federal and local laws should take into account labor market conditions and the attitudes of newcomers toward government agencies.

National Research Council. *Studies of Welfare Participation: Data Collection and Research Issues*. Washington, D.C.: National Academies Press, 2002. A collection of papers on various data collection issues for those researchers surveying the welfare system and low-income populations.

Peck, Jamie. *Workfare States*. New York: Guilford Press, 2001. The author covers workfare programs as they were developed in the 1990s during the Clinton presidency. Workfare requires beneficiaries to take jobs as a condition of receiving welfare money; its success or failure is affected by labor markets, political conditions, and economic conditions, both national and global. The book concludes with coverage of workfare programs implemented in Canada and the United Kingdom.

Rector, Robert, and William F. Lauber. *America's Failed $5.4 Trillion War on Poverty*. Washington, D.C.: Heritage Foundation, 1995. This important study contrasts stubbornly persistent social ills with the efforts made through the Great Society programs of the 1960s to address them, finding the federal war on poverty to be a losing effort. Republican lawmakers relied on Rector and Lauber's statistics to support their case against federal welfare programs.

Rodgers, Harrell R. *American Poverty in a New Era of Reform*. Armonk, N. Y.: M. E. Sharpe, 2005. The author examines the effects of the 1996 welfare reform law, presenting economic data broken down by age, sex, educational level, marital status, and other categories. His conclusion is that welfare reform has been a qualified success, although one not completely understood by economists.

Sawhill, Elizabeth. *Welfare Reform and Beyond: The Future of the Safety Net.* Washington, D.C.: Brookings Institution Press, 2002. A collection of 20 essays published between January 2001 and February 2002 that assess the results of welfare reform and attempt to condense and summarize the hundreds of research reports that were issued in the wake of the new law. The essays cover welfare-to-work programs, child care, health insurance, marriage, block grants, welfare for noncitizens, food stamps, and other relevant topics.

Sawicky, Max. *The End of Welfare? Consequences of Federal Devolution for the Nation.* Armonk, N.Y.: M. E. Sharpe, 1999. A collection of essays by economists dealing with the question of federal devolution of welfare oversight to the states. The essays examine the shifting of health care funding to state budgets, the effect of forcing welfare recipients into the labor market, and trends in federal funding.

Weaver, R. Kent. *Ending Welfare as We Know It.* Washington, D.C.: Brookings Institution, 2000. The author, a senior fellow of the Brookings Institution, describes the political debate and legislative compromises that went into the welfare reform law of 1996. The process responded to public pressure and produced a final version of the law closer to proposals from the Republican, conservative side. The author also recounts how institutional research, opinion polls, electioneering, and the work of interest groups all contributed to the outcome.

### ARTICLES

Aaronson, S., and H. Hartmann. "Reform, Not Rhetoric: A Critique of Welfare Policy and Charting of New Directions." *American Journal of Orthopsychiatry* 66, 4, (October 1996): 583–598. The authors give a critique of the plan to reduce or eliminate welfare benefits and argue that mental health and drug abuse programs should be integrated into the welfare benefits system. They suggest a caseworker system in which each family is guided through the system by an individual social worker, thus maximizing benefit to the family and minimizing misuse of the welfare system.

Accordino, John. "The Consequences of Welfare Reform for Central City Economies." *Journal of the American Planning Association* 64, no. 1 (January 1998): 11–15. The author predicts failure by the welfare reform law in improving the economies of the central city or the lives of welfare-dependent families. He favors a full-employment policy and more comprehensive urban development programs, both public and private.

Anderson, Steven G., Anthony P. Halter, and George Julnes. "Job Stability and Wage Progression Patterns Among Early TANF Leavers." *Journal of*

---

*Sociology and Social Welfare* 27, no. 4 (winter 2000): 39–59. A survey of TANF-leavers in Illinois reveals that only about one fourth of them held the same job after 10 months off the welfare rolls. This resulted from the fact that jobs were marginal or temporary; workers also struggled with a lack of health benefits and child care, as well as low wages that were often insufficient to bring them out of poverty.

Bernstein, Jared, and Mark Greenberg. "Reforming Welfare Reform." *American Prospect* 12, no. 1 (January 2001): 10–16. A review of welfare reform, noting that the new law has reduced the number of beneficiaries but has done little to improve the lives of those at the bottom of the economic ladder. The authors believe the reform policy can be salvaged and improved, and they make suggestions for changes in the required reauthorization of the law.

Brooks, M. G., and J. C. Bruckner. "Work and Welfare: Job Histories, Barriers to Employment, and Predictors of Work Among Low-Income Single Mothers." *American Journal of Orthopsychiatry* 66, no. 4 (October 1996): 526–537. The authors review the cases of 436 homeless and low-income women. They make the point that job training, child care, and education are essential to any prospect these women have of entering the full-time workforce and getting off welfare permanently.

Cancian, Maria, Robert H. Haveman, Daniel R. Meyer, and Barbara Wolfe. "Before and After TANF: The Economic Well-Being of Women Leaving Welfare." *Social Service Review* 76, no. 4 (2002): 603–641. The authors compare employment, earnings, and income outcomes for welfare leavers in Wisconsin under early reforms and under the later, more stringent Temporary Assistance for Needy Families (TANF) program. There were substantially higher rates of exit under TANF; while these leavers were somewhat more likely to work, their earnings were lower.

Casse, Daniel. "Why Welfare Reform Is Working." *Commentary* 104, no. 3 (September 1997). The author describes last-minute changes made by Congress and the White House that diluted important provisions of the welfare reform law. Nevertheless, he concludes that the law is the most far reaching and successful policy initiative of the Clinton presidency.

Coe, N. D., et al. "Does Work Pay? A Summary of the Work Incentives Under TANF." The Urban Institute, Series A, No. A-28. Available online. URL: http://www.urban.org/url.cfm?ID/308019.html. Posted on December 1, 1998. Accessed on October 5, 2007. A report on how welfare programs, the Earned Income Tax Credit, and the tax system affect work incentives in 12 different states. In general, TANF payments decline as earned income rises. But states have various ways of making their payment calculations, and income subsidies and the availability of child care have a significant impact.

Gainsbrough, Julie. "To Devolve or Not To Devolve? Welfare Reform in the States." *Policy Studies Journal* 31, no. 4 (November 2003): 603–623. The author analyzes the states' response to the devolution of welfare policy from the federal to state levels.

Goldstein, Andrew. "It Took Three Dead Babies." *Time* 156, no. 2 July 10, 2000, p. 80. A report on problems in the welfare reform experience of Tennessee, where child-care subsidies led to an explosion in day care centers lacking accountability and oversight.

Handler, Joel F. "On Welfare Reform's Hollow Victory." *Daedalus* 135, no. 3 (2006): 114. The author believes that welfare reform has brought a hollow victory: "While caseloads have declined and work participation has increased, most families are still living in poverty and enduring significant hardship." He observes that welfare leavers have entered low-wage jobs, and most who are still eligible for benefit programs do not enroll. Meanwhile, new costs such as child care have left former welfare recipients no better off than they were before the law was passed.

Hartung, William D., and Jennifer Washburn. "Lockheed Martin: From Warfare to Welfare." *The Nation*, March 2, 1998, p. 11. A report on an effort by a large private company to take over the administration of welfare benefits, including food stamps, job placement, and Medicaid. The privatization effort was meant to replace inefficient public bureaucracies, and streamline the delivery of benefits, but the profit motive brings about its own set of problems.

Kalil, A., and S. K. Danziger. "How Teen Mothers Are Faring Under Welfare Reform." *Journal of Social Issues* 56, no. 4 (2000): 775–798. An account of low-income minority mothers and their experience with the welfare system and its mandates on school attendance, work, and residency.

Mead, Lawrence M. "Telling the Poor What to Do." *Public Interest* 132 (summer 1998): 97–112. The author explores paternalistic social policies and the 1996 welfare reform law, which, in his view, turns the government into a supervisor. The article advocates less government supervision with more help from the private sector.

Morgen, Sandra. "The Agency of Welfare Workers: Negotiating Devolution, Privatization, and the Meaning of Self-Sufficiency." *American Anthropologist* 103, no. 3 (September 2001): 747–761. Using a study of welfare reform in Oregon, the author explores how welfare workers deal with the politics of welfare reform and the conflicts of privatization and devolution of welfare policy to the states. The article finds that high caseloads, unrealistic agency expectations, and conflicting mandates bear down hard on workers, creating disenchantment with agency policy and undermining workers' ability to meet their clients' needs.

Offner, Paul. "Welfare Reform and Teenage Girls." *Social Science Quarterly* 86, no. 2 (June 2005): 306–322. Relying on the Census Bureau's March

Current Population Survey for the years 1989–2001, the author explores the effects of the welfare reform law on teenage girls. He finds that the legislation increased school attendance and reduced the rate of teenage childbearing.

## WEB DOCUMENTS

Acs, Gregory, and Pamela Loprest. "Final Synthesis Report from ASPE's 'Leavers' Grants." Washington, D.C.: Urban Institute, 2001. Available online. URL: http://www.urban.org/UploadedPDF/410809_welfare_leavers_synthesis.pdf. Accessed on June 29, 2007. This synthesis of 15 welfare-leaver studies includes information on leavers' employment and earnings, participation in public assistance programs, income and poverty status, material hardships, and the well-being of their children. The individual studies show many differences in specific measures of families' post-TANF experiences, reflecting in part the differences in context across these areas, such as welfare policies, economic conditions, and the characteristics of leavers.

Besharov, Douglas J., and Peter Germanis. "Welfare Reform—Four Years Later." *The Public Interest*, 140 (summer 2000): 17–35. Available online. URL: http://aei.org/publications/pubID.11700,filter.all/pub_detail.asp. Accessed on June 30, 2007. The authors point out the tentative success of welfare reform, noting that welfare rolls within three years had fallen an amazing 49 percent from their historic high of 5 million families in March 1994. They claim, however, that much of the decline was due to a strong economy, aid to the working poor, and support of welfare leavers from friends and family and from government programs other than TANF. Observing that the depiction of welfare reform as a resounding success is politically useful for liberals and conservatives, for different reasons, the authors emphasize the importance of understanding the real consequences of the law for the sake of effective future policy.

Blank, Susan W., and Barbara B. Blum. "A Brief History of Work Expectations for Welfare Mothers." *The Future of Children* 7, no. 1 (spring 1997): 28–38. Available online. URL: http://www.futureofchildren.org/usr_doc/vol7no1ART3.pdf. Accessed on September 6, 2007. In light of the recent passage of the welfare reform law, the authors review the history of the AFDC program and describe how new policies encouraged employment of parents who receive benefits. The significant programs include the Work Incentive Program (WIN), launched in 1967, and the Family Support Act of 1988. The authors contend that these programs were not fully implemented and thus cannot be fairly judged as either successes or failures.

# Welfare and Welfare Reform

Bloom, Dan. "Welfare Time Limits: An Interim Report Card." Manpower Demonstration Research Program. Available online. URL: http://www.mdrc.org/publications/57/full.pdf. Posted April 1999. Accessed on June 29, 2007. This report summarizes the results from studies of several of the earliest state welfare reform initiatives to include time limits. The reforms were initiated under waivers of federal welfare rules between mid-1994 and early 1996, prior to passage of the 1996 federal welfare law; thus, these states' experiences provided some of the first reliable evidence on the operation and impacts of welfare time limits.

Guyer, Jocelyn. "Health Care After Welfare: An Update of Findings from State-Level Leaver Studies." Center on Budget and Policy Priorities. Available online. URL: http://www.cbpp.org/8-16-00wel2.pdf. Posted on August 16, 2000. Accessed on June 29, 2007. A study of welfare leavers from surveys in the late 1990s on health insurance, specifically the federal Medicare program. The study concludes that welfare reform has brought about a rising population of uninsured poor families.

Johns Hopkins University. "Welfare, Children & Families: A Three-City Study." Available online. URL: http://web.jhu.edu/threecitystudy. Accessed on April 1, 2007. A study of Boston, Chicago, and San Antonio to assess the well-being of low-income children and families in the post–welfare reform era. The study began in 1999 and comprises longitudinal surveys, embedded developmental studies, and ethnographic studies.

Payne, James L. "Absence of Judgment: What Social Workers Believe About the Poor Will Hamper Welfare Reform." The Hoover Institution. Available online. URL: http://www.hoover.org/publications/policyreview/3928051.html. Posted November 1996. Accessed on September 7, 2007. The author maintains that professional social workers have a vested interest in the survival of an extensive and complex system of welfare benefits, and that they have a number of ways of undermining the system in order to serve their own interests. Welfare professionals, for example, can seek out exemptions to keep beneficiaries dependent and can also work for political campaigns that pledge to resist any further reform of the system.

W. E. Upjohn Institute for Employment Research. "Welfare-to-Work." Available online. URL: http://www.upjohninstitute.org/welfhub.html. Accessed on September 6, 2007. The Upjohn Institute's "Welfare-to-Work" site provides links to working papers, technical reports, books, articles, and reprints, all examining the relationship between welfare policy and the labor market.

Zeigler, Jenifer. "Implementing Welfare Reform: A State Report Card." *Policy Analysis*, no. 529, Available online. URL: http://www.cato.org/pubs/pas/pa529.pdf. Accessed on March 1, 2007. This Cato Institute paper examines the implementation of the welfare reform law at the state level and offers a state-by-state report card. The author finds that those states with strict time limits, sanctions, and narrower definitions of "work" generally did better at reducing their welfare rolls, which remains the ultimate goal of the entire effort.

# INTERNATIONAL PERSPECTIVES ON SOCIAL WELFARE POLICY

## BOOKS

Alesina, Alberto, and Edward L. Glaeser. *Fighting Poverty in the US and Europe: A World of Difference*. Oxford: Oxford University Press, 2004. The authors examine the question of why redistribution of income by the government is politically popular in Europe, and not in the United States, and why the American welfare state is smaller than those in Europe. The nature and philosophy behind the American welfare system is explained in cultural and political terms that highlight historical differences.

Andersen, Torben M., and Per Molander, eds. *Alternatives for Welfare Policy: Coping with Internationalism and Demographic Change*. Cambridge: Cambridge University Press, 2003. A survey of welfare policy issues using case studies and statistical data. The book describes how and why traditional public welfare has come under attack and explores the alternatives to the system in developed nations.

Boje, Thomas P., and Arnlaug Leira, eds. *Gender, Welfare State, and the Market: Towards a New Division of Labour*. London: Routledge, 2000. This volume represents the present state of the art in theoretical debate in welfare state scholarship, drawing on research from western Europe, North America, and Japan. It gives a broad international overview as well as comparisons between specific welfare states and national case studies.

Burrows, Roger, and Brian Loader, eds. *Towards a Post-Fordist Welfare State?* New York: Routledge, 1994. This article analyzes how traditional British "Fordism," a bureaucratic, hierarchical model of industrial development, has gradually changed and evolved into "Post-Fordism," which emphasizes individual freedom of choice. Authors in a variety of disciplines apply Post-Fordism to the changes taking place in the British welfare state.

Bussemaker, Jet, ed. *Citizenship and Welfare State Reform in Europe*. London: Routledge, 1999. A book describing European welfare states, the concept of citizenship, and the changes in individual legal rights as the welfare system struggles to address unemployment, poverty, and social inequality.

Crane, John A. *Directions for Social Welfare in Canada: The Public's View*. Vancouver: University of British Columbia Press, 1994. A survey of public opinion on social welfare in Canada, including interviews, focus groups, and analysis of media, dating from 1991 and 1992. As the impetus for welfare reform gained strength in the United States, public opinion in Canada showed concern about the erosion of social services and the haste with which public officials were offloading welfare responsibilities.

Crew, David F. *Germans on Welfare: From Weimar to Hitler*. New York: Oxford University Press, 1998. A book about the Weimar Republic, which followed the fall of the German monarchy after World War I. The republic was a welfare state that offered German citizens basic material security after the lost war and the revolution that nearly brought Germany into the communist camp. But the economic burdens of the Great Depression and unemployment undermined the Weimar regime and paved the way for its destruction by the Nazi party in 1933.

Dieterlan, Paulette. *Poverty: A Philosophical Approach*. New York: Rodopi, 2005. The author used a sabbatical year working in Mexico for PROGRESA (Program for Education, Health and Food) as a way to investigate the concept of poverty, as it is applied in public social welfare policies. The book investigates the various methods of determining who should be eligible for welfare benefits and evaluates how these methods fail or succeed in their stated goal of alleviating poverty.

Dixon, John, and Robert P. Scheurell, eds. *The State of Social Welfare: The Twentieth Century in Cross-National Review*. Westport, Conn.: Praeger, 2002. Articles comparing and contrasting the social welfare systems of Brazil, Canada, Australia, France, Sweden, Zimbabwe, and the United States. The editors conclude with an essay comparing social welfare policies in 1900 and 2000.

Dutton, Paul V. *Origins of the French Welfare State: The Struggle for Social Reform in France, 1914–1947*. Cambridge: Cambridge University Press, 2002. The author analyzes the French welfare state, describing its basic features and how influences from Alsace-Lorraine and Great Britain shaped it.

Ebbinghaus, Bernhard, and Philip Manow. *Comparing Welfare Capitalism: Social Policy and Political Economy in Europe, Japan and the USA*. London: Routledge, 2001. Comparing and contrasting the experiences of several nations, the authors conclude that welfare systems are compatible with free enterprise and capitalist economies.

Esping-Andersen, Gosta, with Duncan Gallie, Anton Hemerijck, and John Myles. *Why We Need a New Welfare State*. Oxford: Oxford University Press, 2002. Several scholars of social welfare policy in Europe study retirement systems, child welfare, gender equality, and changes in the labor force. They suggest changes in the welfare state to provide optimal fairness and inclusion for workers as well as the unemployed.

Ferrera, Maurizio, and Martin Rhodes, eds. *Recasting European Welfare States*. London: Routledge, 2000. Essays on European social welfare policy, taken from a colloquium held at the University of Edinburgh in 1999. The topics include health care; unemployment compensation; the "Third Way" in Britain; and the welfare state in France, Germany, Italy, the Netherlands, Belgium, and Scandinavia.

George, Victor, and Paul Wilding. *Ideology and Social Welfare*. Radical Social Policy series. London: Routledge, 1990. A standard British textbook on social welfare issues, defining the modern capitalist welfare state and dividing welfare advocates and opponents into four groups: Marxists, Fabians, "reluctant collectivists," and "anti-collectivists." This is a substantial revision of an earlier textbook.

Haney, Lynne. *Inventing the Needy: Gender and the Politics of Welfare in Hungary*. Berkeley: University of California Press, 2002. The author analyzes welfare policies in Hungary from the post–World War II period to the end of the 20th century, describing three different welfare systems that met different social and economic needs, with varying degrees of success.

Jenson, Jane, and Mariette Sineau. *Who Cares? Women's Work, Childcare, and Welfare State Redesign*. Toronto: University of Toronto Press, 2001. A comparative study of changes in child-care policy in Belgium, France, Italy, and Sweden over the preceding three decades. In the face of globalization, the new European Union, and the "neoliberal" push for cuts in public spending, the four nations have followed a converging path in devising reform and "retrenchment" in public child-care and other social welfare programs.

Kautto, Mikko. *Nordic Welfare States in the European Context*. London: Routledge, 2001. A study of welfare states in Scandinavia over 20 years. The author covers income distribution, health inequalities, and gender equality; gender policies, health and social care services, and policy reaction to family changes; social security and employment policies; and financing of welfare states. The book concludes that the Nordic welfare states are having a strong effect on social welfare policy in European countries to the south.

Kautto, Mikko, et al., eds. *Nordic Social Policy: Changing Welfare States*. London: Routledge, 1999. A collection of articles by more than 20 contributors on the development of welfare policy in Sweden, Finland, Norway, and Denmark during the 1990s. This work examines the changed preconditions of welfare policies, analyzes changes in welfare measures, investigates developments in the welfare of the people, and looks at developments in public support for the welfare states.

Kuhnle, Stein, ed. *Survival of the European Welfare State*. London: Routledge, 2000. The authors review welfare reform in Spain, Denmark, the United Kingdom, Germany, and the European Union (EU) as a whole, giving an optimistic assessment of welfare policies adopted in Europe and of the future of the continent's more generous and comprehensive systems of public aid.

Leibfried, Stephen, and Giuliano Bonoli. *Welfare State Futures*. Cambridge: Cambridge University Press, 2001. The authors examine the rise of the post–World War II welfare state in Europe and its current changes in the face of demographic and economic pressures. The book covers the key challenge to welfare state economics—the pension and retirement system—and suggests possible transformations of welfare policies in the 21st century.

Levine, Daniel. *Poverty and Society: The Growth of the American Welfare State in International Comparison*. New Brunswick, N.J.: Rutgers University Press, 1989. Comparing the welfare systems over a century of their history in Germany, Great Britain, Denmark, and the United States, the author examines public attitudes toward poverty and public assistance programs in all four countries. He concludes that the United States, as a result of its unique socioeconomic outlook, lagged behind the European nations in applying national solutions to the problems of poverty and joblessness.

Lewis, Jane, and Rebecca Surender, eds. *Welfare State Change: Towards a Third Way*. Oxford: Oxford University Press, 2004. This book provides a comprehensive and critical analysis of "Third Way" social policy in the welfare systems of industrialized economies and examines the extent to which "Third Way" ideology and institutional structures converge or vary in different national settings.

Piven, Frances Fox, and Richard A. Cloward. *The Breaking of the American Social Compact*. New York: The New Press, 1998. A series of 21 essays on poverty and welfare issues, covering globalization and the labor market, the role of unions, the general failure of welfare programs, and a comparison of the United States and other Western democracies in their public welfare policies.

Ridge, Tess. *Childhood Poverty and Social Exclusion: From a Child's Perspective*. Bristol, U.K.: The Policy Press, 2002. The author describes historical representations of children and families in poverty. She investigates the contemporary effect of poverty in the United Kingdom on the young, describing social integration of children from poor families and the early formation of their characters. Later chapters cover family life and school experiences.

Sainsbury, Diane, ed. *Gender and Welfare State Regimes*. Oxford: Oxford University Press, 1999. The author treats the relationship of welfare policy, the labor market, and gender politics. The book examines how welfare policies reinforce or lessen inequalities in gender, analyzing how different social and political conditions in various countries have their effect.

Schmidtz, David, and Robert E. Goodin. *Social Welfare and Individual Responsibility (For and Against)*. Cambridge: Cambridge University Press,

2004. The authors debate the merits of public welfare policy, and the question of its proper function: to train the individual for gainful work, or to allow collective public responsibility for the poor. Schmidtz presents the argument for welfare as a temporary measure while an individual's circumstances prevent employment; Goodin supports a more generous and inclusive policy.

Sykes, Robert, Bruno Palier, Pauline M. Prior, and Jo Campling. *Globalization and European Welfare States: Challenges and Change.* New York: Palgrave Macmillan, 2001. Scholarly essays concerning the effect of globalization and free-trade policies on government welfare spending. The articles compare and contrast welfare states in northern, western, southern, and eastern Europe.

Taylor-Gooby, Peter, ed. *New Risks, New Welfare: The Transformation of the European Welfare State.* Oxford: Oxford University Press, 2004. This book identifies "social risks," which include changes in the labor market, the new role of male breadwinners, and the effect of a globalizing economy, and explains how they have affected welfare policy in various European countries.

Wong, Linda. *Marginalization and Social Welfare in China.* London: Routledge, 1998. The author explains the social welfare system in China, how it is applied in urban and rural environments, and how the Chinese tradition of mutual aid within the family affects public attitudes and support of welfare policies.

Wood, Geoff, et al. *Insecurity and Welfare Regimes in Asia, Africa and Latin America: Social Policy in Development Contexts.* Cambridge: Cambridge University Press, 2004. Moving the scholarly focus from North America and Europe, a team of experts describes how welfare policy operates in developing nations, giving background and current conditions in Asia, South America, and Africa.

## ARTICLES

Alesina, Alberto, Edward Glaeser, and Bruce Sacerdote. "Why Doesn't the United States Have a European-Style Welfare System?" NBER Working Paper series, no. 8524. Washington, D.C.: National Bureau of Economic Research, 2001. The authors examine the basic difference between Europe and the United States in the distribution of benefits through the government to citizens. The paper examines European tax systems, regulations designed to protect the poor, and social programs that reach a larger percentage of citizens.

Birdsall, Nancy. "Life Is Unfair: Inequality in the World." *Foreign Policy* 111 (summer 1998): 76–93. The author traces the roots and causes of economic inequality and describes both flawed solutions and effective strategies to deal with it. Welfare and other forms of income transfers are effective on paper but ineffective in practice. Rather than a circumstance that responds to "top-down" solutions, the author argues, inequality is an inevitable condition in a developing industrial economy that eventually leads to the establishment of a stable and prosperous middle class.

Bordas, Maria. "Social Welfare Reform: Comparative Perspectives on Europe and the United States." *International Journal of Public Administration* 24, no. 2 (2001): 225. The author examines the question of whether the American model of "non-interventionist" welfare policy can be applied to European states, which are home to a widely held belief that the free market alone cannot adequately provide for the poor.

Haveman, R., and B. Wolfe. "Welfare to Work in the U.S.: A Model for Other Developed Nations?" *International Tax and Public Finance* 7, no. 1 (February 2000): 95–114. The authors describe the problems inherent in U.S. social welfare policy prior to TANF, emphasizing its serious labor supply disincentives. They catalog the wide variety of economic changes implicit in TANF and describe the policies undertaken by the state of Wisconsin, a leader in implementing the new federal policy.

Hira, Anil. "Time for a Global Welfare System?" *The Futurist* 41, no. 3 (May/June 2007): 27. The author contends that the increasing globalization of the world economy has brought pressing international social issues, such as terrorism, environmental problems, and immigration, that call for an internationally coordinated response. The Western model of nationalism and independence is outdated, the author concludes; the rising economy of Asia will force the world to consider the establishment of a global regulatory system that will set up global social welfare goals and standards.

Jorgensen, Andreas. "Efficiency and Welfare Under Capitalism: Denmark vs. the United States: A Short Comparison." *Monthly Review* 48, no. 9 February 1997, p. 34. The author defends the Danish economic model. He points out that the Danes support a strong system of pensions, welfare, and unemployment benefits and that the U.S. model, which supposedly ensures higher economic growth, has instead resulted in stagnant wages and a declining standard of living for most workers in the United States.

Lloyd, John. "Bruised, Battered, and Out of Power: The European Left Is in Retreat. It Stole the Right's Economic Clothes; Now the Right Threatens to Steal the Left's Social Clothes, by Supporting the Welfare State." *The New Statesman*, November 11, 2002, pp. 26–30. Right-wing parties in Europe have pursued a nationalist political agenda; this approach repudiates the euro, Europe's common currency, and defends the traditional welfare state against the forces of globalization. As a result, the author says, the traditional voting blocs have been turned upside down, and leftist parties are threatened with permanent minority status.

Norberg, Johan. "Swedish Models: The Welfare State and Its Competitors." *The National Interest* 84 (summer 2006): 85–87. The author contends that the Swedish system of generous social welfare spending is contributing to economic stagnation, stating that fundamental change is necessary if the country is to avoid an economic and social crisis.

Osborne, Thomas. "Civility on Trial: Welfare in the Western World." *USA Today*, vol. 127, no. 2640, September 1998, p. 24. A report on attitudes among Europeans toward the American economic, welfare, and health care structures. The author meditates on the differences between the European and American welfare systems, concluding that welfare reform leaves too many beneficiaries in the United States vulnerable.

Singer, Daniel. "Europe: Is There a Fourth Way? If Western Europe Is to Be Truly Independent It Must Defend Its Welfare State." *The Nation*, November 6, 2000, pp. 20–22. The author calls on European nations to seize on their tradition of social welfare, rather than repudiating it, in order to defend against the encroaching commercialization of their societies and cultures.

## WEB DOCUMENTS

Andersen, Toben M. "European Integration and the Welfare State." *Journal of Population Economics* 16 (2003): 1–16. Available online. URL: http://www.popecon.org/download/andersen_01162003.pdf. Accessed on September 10, 2007. The author examines the question of economic integration of the European nations and how this will affect their welfare expenditures. While some believe welfare benefits will have to be rolled back, others believe integration will bring a greater need for antipoverty programs and social insurance.

Cooray, Mark. "The Reality of Welfare and Welfare Rights." Topics Concerning the Australian Community. Available online. URL: http://www.ourcivilisation.com/cooray/btof/index24.htm. Accessed on September 8, 2007. A critique of the welfare system as it exists in Australia, divided into short and readable chapters on welfare history, the origins of the welfare state, and various opinions under the headings of "Welfare as Disincentive to Work," "Soak the Rich," and "Welfare and Increasing Government Keep the Poor, Poor."

Heinisch, Reinhard. "European Welfare States." University of Pittsburgh. Available online. URL: www.pitt.edu/~heinisch/eusocial.html. Accessed on September 10, 2007. Commentary and resources on the subject of European welfare states, for the nonspecialist and casual researcher. The site provides a wealth of links to scholarly papers, relevant compilations of data, and sample graduate and undergraduate courses on the topics of European welfare states and social policy in Europe. There is an annotated bibliography as well as annotated links to other resources and brief analyses of recent developments in European/EU social policy. A useful page gives a country-by-country account of how the various welfare state models developed in Europe and a comparison with the same history in the United States.

Kuhnle, Stein. "Survival of the European Welfare State." Arena Working Papers. Available online. URL: www.arena.uio.no/publications/wp99_19.htm. Accessed on September 10, 2007. An essay by a professor at the University of Bergen, Norway, on the European welfare model. Although there is a general opinion in both Europe and North America that the generous social welfare benefits provided in Europe are unsustainable, the author makes the case that the classic welfare state will and should continue.

Offe, Claus. "The European Welfare State." Eurozine. Available online. URL: http://www.eurozine.com/articles/2002–02–08-offe-en.html. Accessed on September 10, 2007. The author considers the nature of the European Community and the efforts at economic integration of its various members, in light of the tradition of generous social welfare provisions.

Robert Gordon University. "An Introduction to Social Policy: The Welfare State." Public Policy at the Robert Gordon University. Available online. URL: www2.rgu.ac.uk/publicpolicy/introduction/wstate.htm. Accessed on September 10, 2007. This site, hosted at the Robert Gordon University of Aberdeen, Scotland, provides a comprehensive overview of welfare states as they are constituted in Europe, comparing them to the model in place in the United States. A wealth of links and resources are given for the researcher.

VoxEU.org. "Welfare State and Social Europe." Available online. URL: http://www.voxeu.org/index.php?q=node/34. Accessed on September 10, 2007. A research guide with links to papers on the topics of European welfare benefits, pension reforms, immigration, and a comparison of U.S. versus European social policy models.

Warin, Thierry, and Peter Hennessy. "One Welfare State for Europe: A Costly Utopia?" Middlebury College Working Paper series, no. 03-25. Available online. URL: http://www.middlebury.edu/services/econ/repec/mdl/ancoec/0325.pdf. Posted October 2003. Accessed on September 10, 2007. The authors discuss the issues of monetary union, GDP growth, policy "convergence," and social expenditures in the European Union countries. They argue that welfare expenditures in Europe are proving a costly hindrance to economic growth.

# CURRENT ISSUES AND DEBATE

## BOOKS

Besharov, Douglas J., ed. *Family and Child Well-Being After Welfare Reform.* New Brunswick, N.J.: Transaction Publishers, 2003. The essays in this book cover the state of the welfare system and low-income families in the wake of welfare reform. It includes articles on welfare reform, family issues, child care, crime, working mothers, and "food security."

Besharov, Douglas J., and Peter Germanis. *Rethinking WIC: An Evaluation of the Women, Infants, and Children Program.* Washington, D.C.: AEI Press, 2001. The authors analyze the research on the effectiveness of the Special Supplemental Nutrition Program for Women, Infants, and Children. They challenge claims for the program's success, arguing that policy makers should undertake a sustained effort to make the WIC more effective.

Bommes, Michael, and Andrew Geddes, eds. *Immigration and Welfare: Challenging the Borders of the Welfare State.* London: Routledge, 2000. Fourteen essays on the problems of immigration, asylum, and cross-border labor migration within Europe's modern welfare states.

Castles, Francis G. *The Future of the Welfare State: Crisis Myths and Crisis Realities.* Oxford: Oxford University Press, 2004. The author examines the issues of globalization and changing demographics (aging of the population and a declining birth rate) and assesses the problems they will pose for Western welfare states. The book uses data for 21 nations to show that welfare spending has been increasing and converging among these countries. The author concludes that popular notions of a crisis in the welfare state are more myth than reality.

Davis, Derek, and Barry Hankins, eds. *Welfare Reform & Faith-Based Organizations.* Waco, Tex.: J. M. Dawson Institute of Church-State Studies, 1999. A collection of essays from a symposium, held in April 1998, entitled "Welfare Reform and the Churches." The articles reveal an effort to balance the symposium program between those who support the "Charitable Choice" provision of the 1996 welfare reform law and those who oppose it.

DiNitto, Diana, and Linda K. Cummins. *Social Welfare: Politics and Public Policy.* 6th ed. Boston: Allyn & Bacon, 2003. A popular academic textbook that serves as a general introduction to welfare policy and practice, as well as the current and historical debates surrounding the welfare system. The authors include in this edition new coverage of health care, including HMOs and managed care, vocational training, child support, and recent court decisions.

Ehrenreich, Barbara. *Nickel and Dimed: On (Not) Getting By in America.* New York: Owl Books, 2002. The author explores low-wage employment in

193

various locales, describing working and living conditions for those hold-ing entry-level jobs in the modern service sector.

Gilbert, Neil. *Transformation of the Welfare State: The Silent Surrender of Public Responsibility*. New York: Oxford University Press, 2004. A survey of global welfare policies and the effects of the movement for welfare reform in the United States. The author observes that U.S. welfare re-form has been imitated in many countries seeking to limit welfare depen-dence and force beneficiaries to return to the private-sector workforce.

Gilens, Martin. *Why Americans Hate Welfare: Race, Media, and the Politics of Antipoverty Policy*. Studies in Communication, Media, and Public Opinion series. Chicago: University of Chicago Press, 2000. An analysis of public opinion surveys and media reports over four decades. The author reaches the conclusion that opposition to welfare programs is based on racist misperceptions among the general public.

Goldson, Barry, Michael Lavalette, and Jim McKechnie, eds. *Children, Wel-fare, and the State*. London: Sage Publications, 2003. A collection of essays that study the welfare state as it affects children, from a historical and contemporary perspective. Essays cover class, education, labor, crime, child abuse and child protection, and psychology.

Grogger, Jeffrey, and Lynn A. Karoly. *Welfare Reform: Effects of a Decade of Change*. Cambridge, Mass.: Harvard University Press, 2005. The authors evaluate more than 30 academic studies to assess the effects of the welfare reform laws of the 1990s.

Hacker, Jacob S. *The Divided Welfare State: The Battle over Public and Private Social Benefits in the United States*. Cambridge: Cambridge University Press, 2002. The author gives a comprehensive survey of past welfare legislation, the Great Society programs of the 1960s, and welfare reform of the 1990s, to study the longstanding conflict between public welfare programs such as AFDC and "private" welfare initiatives, such as em-ployer-sponsored pensions and health insurance.

Handler, J. F. *Reforming the Poor: Welfare Policy, Federalism, and Morality*. New York: Basic Books, 1972. The author investigates the attempt to regulate private behavior and morality through strictures built into welfare law, particularly the AFDC program. From the earliest qualifications for AFDC beneficiaries to much later work requirements, measures intended to regu-late behavior lie at the heart of efforts to reform the welfare system.

Hage, Dave. *Reforming Welfare by Rewarding Work: One State's Successful Experiment*. Minneapolis: University of Minnesota Press, 2004. A study of the Minnesota Family Investment Program, enacted in 1997 to reward job-seekers and provide basic assistance toward day-care and transporta-tion expenses.

Harrington, Michael. *The Other America: Poverty in the United States*. New York: Penguin Books, 1962. A widely studied book on the conditions endured by America's poor, who in the author's opinion are largely hidden from view and have little reason to hope their lives will ever change for the better. The author believes government assistance programs do little to help the needy; nevertheless, the book was a key impetus for the Great Society programs that followed soon after its publication.

Haveman, Robert. *Starting Even: An Equal Opportunity Program to Combat the Nation's New Poverty*. New York: Simon & Schuster, 1988. This book represents an answer to Charles Murray's *Losing Ground*. The author asserts that the welfare system made important strides in lessening poverty during the 1960s and only began to fail under the Reagan-era cutbacks of the 1980s.

Hays, Sharon. *Flat Broke with Children: Women in the Age of Welfare Reform*. New York: Oxford University Press, 2003. The author researches the effects of welfare reform in two towns and finds that it has brought little improvement in the lives of many single mothers. The law gives welfare recipients strong incentives to work and marry, but does it in such a rigid and bureaucratized manner that the unintended consequences often include broken families, poor health, homelessness, and further dependence on public institutions.

Herrick, John M., and Paul H. Stuart. *Encyclopedia of Social Welfare History in North America*. London: Sage Publications, 2004. In 180 entries, contributors to this reference book give a comprehensive account of private and public welfare systems in Canada, the United States, and Mexico. This reference title includes useful bibliographies and chronologies.

Himmelfarb, Gertrude. *The Idea of Poverty: England in the Early Industrial Age*. New York: Knopf, 1984. The author gives an overview of the writings of economists, philosophers, and politicians dealing with England's rising tide of urban poverty while the nation was industrializing, from 1750 to 1850. The book covers works of Adam Smith, Thomas Carlyle, Thomas Paine, Edmund Burke, Charles Dickens, Benjamin Disraeli, and Friedrich Engels.

Howard, Christopher. *The Hidden Welfare State: Tax Expenditures and Social Policy in the United States*. Princeton, N.J.: Princeton University Press, 1997. This book discusses "tax expenditures" or loopholes that are created to subsidize social welfare programs or encourage certain kinds of behavior on the part of individuals or corporations. Describing the system as a "hidden welfare state," the author gives detailed histories of four of these expenditures, including the Earned Income Tax Credit, and shows how tax policy is created in order to enhance the authority of Congress and help the two main political parties.

Jansson, Bruce S. *The Reluctant Welfare State*. Belmont, Calif.: Wadsworth, 1988. A well-researched textbook on the American welfare system, from the colonies to the 21st century, and how it has affected designated segments of the population, including African Americans, Latinos, women, gays and lesbians, Asian Americans, Native Americans, the elderly, and the poor.

Katz, Michael B. *In the Shadow of the Poorhouse: A Social History of Welfare in America*. New York: Basic Books, 1996. The author reviews the history of welfare in the United States and concludes that full employment, and a living wage guaranteed to those unable to work, may provide an answer to flaws in the current system.

————. *The Price of Citizenship: Redefining the American Welfare State*. New York: Owl Books, 2002. The author blames market-based thinking, and America's individualistic mythologies, for the failure of 20th-century welfare programs and modern efforts at welfare reform. He derides the shift of responsibility for welfare from the federal government to the states and foresees a further unraveling of the social fabric as the poor become increasingly marginalized and estranged.

Langan, Mary, ed. *Welfare: Needs, Rights and Risks*. New York: Routledge, 1998. The author examines the rationing of welfare benefits and services in an age of budget cutting and general hostility to public support systems for the needy.

Mink, Gwendolyn, and Alice O'Connor. *Poverty in the United States: An Encyclopedia of History, Politics and Policy*. Santa Barbara, Calif.: ABC-CLIO, 2004. A comprehensive reference work of more than 300 entries on the history of poverty in America, private and public charity and welfare programs, Social Security, academic studies on poverty and welfare, and various ideological debates surrounding the welfare system. The book offers important historical documents, speeches, and useful bibliographies.

Murray, Charles. *In Our Hands: A Plan to Replace the Welfare State*. Washington, D.C.: American Enterprise Institute, 2006. The author believes current welfare programs have failed in their task and that the end of welfare at all levels of government will force individuals to rely on their own initiative to overcome poverty. He advances a plan to completely eliminate current welfare programs, including Social Security and Medicare, and replace them with a $10,000 cash grant to every person over the age of 21.

Neubeck, Kenneth J., and Noel A. Cazenave. *Welfare Racism: Playing the Race Card against America's Poor*. New York: Routledge, 2001. This book describes the "racialization" of welfare, in which politicians exploit racial animus to promote their political ambitions through use of the word *welfare*. The authors decry the effects of what they believe are punitive welfare reform and welfare policy on beneficiaries.

O'Connor, Alice. *Poverty Knowledge: Social Science, Social Policy, and the Poor in Twentieth-Century U.S. History*. Princeton, N.J.: Princeton University

Press, 2002. The author describes Progressive-era "poverty warriors" who cast poverty as a problem of unemployment, low wages, labor exploitation, and political disfranchisement, and compares this outlook with that of the 1990s, when policy specialists made "dependency" the issue and crafted incentives to get people off welfare. The book inquires into the politics, institutions, ideologies, and social science that shaped poverty research and policy in the United States over the last century.

Olasky, Marvin. *The Tragedy of American Compassion*. Memphis, Tenn.: Crossway Books, 1995. A University of Texas journalism professor critically analyzes the growth of historic public relief systems and finds they never met the true needs of the needy: the development of work and survival skills. The author faults social workers of earlier times who systemized relief through government agencies and required nothing in return from welfare recipients. He favors religious and private charity for addressing the spiritual needs of the poor.

Patterson, James T. *America's Struggle Against Poverty in the Twentieth Century*. Cambridge, Mass.: Harvard University Press, 2000. A survey of welfare history from the Progressive age of the early 1900s through the economic boom times of the 1990s.

Rank, Mark Robert. *One Nation, Underprivileged: Why American Poverty Affects Us All*. New York: Oxford University Press, 2005. The author argues that widespread poverty and a permanent underclass are built into the American economic system, which he likens to a game of musical chairs. He urges individuals enjoying economic security to take increased action to alleviate this inequality.

Schwartz, Joel. *Fighting Poverty with Virtue: Moral Reform and America's Urban Poor, 1825–2000*. Bloomington: Indiana University Press, 2000. A study of historical efforts at alleviating poverty through moral instruction. The practice fell out of favor in the 20th century, to be replaced by direct transfers of money and benefits to the poor through the public treasury. The author believes that society is currently returning to such moral instruction through "self-help" welfare programs and "faith-based" initiatives.

Shipler, David K. *The Working Poor: Invisible in America*. New York: Knopf, 2004. The author interviews people working hard but living at the edge of poverty, making low wages without benefits, having little opportunity for advancement, and surviving poor conditions in their homes. Citing extensive statistics covering the low-wage economy, he suggests improvements in the health care, vocational training, and welfare systems to improve the lives of the working poor.

Spicker, Paul. *The Idea of Poverty*. Bristol, U.K.: Policy Press, 2007. The author attempts to define poverty by examining different views of what it is and how it should be handled. The book challenges common perceptions and understandings of the nature of poverty. The author makes the

**197**

case for an inclusive definition of poverty, which would take into account material deprivation, lack of money, dependency on benefits, social exclusion, and inequality.

Stoker, Robert Phillip, and Laura Ann Wilson. *When Work Is Not Enough: State and Federal Policies to Support Needy Workers*. Washington, D.C.: Brookings Institution Press, 2006. The authors cover "work-support" systems that aid low-wage workers: the minimum wage, earned income tax credit (EITC) programs, medical assistance programs, food programs, Temporary Assistance for Needy Families (TANF) earned income disregards, child-care grants, and rental assistance. The authors believe these programs are essential for moving people from the welfare rolls permanently but fault them for inequities across state lines and among income groups, and they suggest improvements.

Tanner, Michael D. *The Poverty of Welfare: Helping Others in a Civil Society*. Washington, D.C.: Cato Institute, 2003. The author reviews the effects of the 1996 welfare reform. He argues that the total elimination of the public welfare system is desirable and attainable through private charity and a reduced tax burden on those creating employment.

———. *Social Security and Its Discontents: Perspectives on Choice*. Washington, D.C.: Cato Institute, 2004. This book explores structural problems in the current Social Security system and the effect of proposed reforms on those benefiting from it now and in the future.

Trattner, W. I. *From Poor Law to Welfare State: A History of Social Welfare in America*. 6th ed. New York: The Free Press, 1998. A comprehensive history of social welfare policy in the United States.

## ARTICLES

Acs, Gregory, and Pamela Loprest. "The Effect of Disabilities on Exits from AFDC." *Journal of Policy Analysis & Management* 18, no. 1 (1999): 28–49. The authors review the statistics concerning the experience of disabled persons in the welfare system, and they evaluate how having a disability affects one's chances of achieving the stated goal of the welfare reform law: eventually leaving the AFDC/TANF rolls for employment.

Cancian, M., and D. Meyer. "Work After Welfare: Women's Work Effort, Occupation, and Economic Well-Being." *Social Work Research* 24, no. 2 (June 2000): 69–86. The authors tackle the subject of welfare-to-work programs, which force beneficiaries into job-training or job-placement programs as a condition of receiving welfare benefits. The article gauges the successes and failures of welfare-to-work policies for beneficiaries in the five years after leaving welfare.

Chavkin, Wendy, Diana Romero, and Paul H. Wise. "State Welfare Reform Policies and Declines in Health Insurance." *American Jour-*

*nal of Public Health* 90, no. 6 (2000): 900–908. The authors review the causes of lack of health insurance and the links between welfare cases and the increasingly complex and expensive public health-insurance system. Policies that deter beneficiaries from participating in TANF also lead to declines in Medicaid enrollment and a rise in uninsured families.

Conniff, Ruth. "The Right Welfare Reform." *The Nation* July 22, 2002, p. 5. The author reviews the political debate surrounding the reauthorization of the 1996 welfare reform law, pointing out differences in versions offered by the White House and members of Congress, in particular Senator Hillary Rodham Clinton. The author faults Clinton for compromising on effective welfare programs in order to position herself as a political centrist.

Corcoran, M., S. K. Danziger, A. Kalil, and K. Seefeldt. "How Welfare Reform is Affecting Women's Work." *Annual Review of Sociology* 26 (2000): 241–269. An article describing the implementation of the 1996 welfare reform law in the various states, as it affects working women, using surveys on employment, earnings, and physical and emotional well-being of beneficiaries and leavers.

Cranford, John. "Missed Opportunity.'" *CQ Weekly*, January 9, 2006, p. 77. The author believes welfare reform reauthorization has become an exercise in administrative cost control. The law, he says, is not addressing underlying causes of poverty, the widening gap between the rich and poor, or the need for stable working families.

Culhane, Dennis. "Tax-Saving Tip: House the Homeless." *Esquire* December 2005, p. 219. The author, a professor of social welfare policy at the University of Pennsylvania, has collected statistics on the urban homeless and concludes that the current system of temporary shelters is a massive failure. The solution he favors is long-term or permanent housing that would offer intensive social services.

Dinerman, M., and A. O. Faulkner. "Women and the New American Welfare." *Affilia: Journal of Woman and Social Work* 15, no. 2 (2000): 125–132. The authors give background to the new welfare law and describe how the various states are implementing the program. Through restrictions on education and job training, the new law limits the opportunity women have independence and a stable, well-paying job.

Duncan, G. J., M. K. Harris, and J. Boisjoly. "Time Limits and Welfare Reform: New Estimates of the Number and Characteristics of Affected Families." *Social Service Review* 74, no. 1 (1997): 55–75. A statistical analysis of time limits under welfare reform, finding that the median length of total welfare receipt is about four years. The authors also describe characteristics of long-term welfare recipients, defined as those receiving benefits for 60 months or more.

Ehrenreich, Barbara. "Chamber of Welfare Reform." *The Progressive* 66 (May 2002). The author finds that even after the sweeping changes wrought by the welfare reform law of 1996, welfare remains a class issue. "Racism and misogyny helped blind many to this fact six years ago, when welfare reform was passed," she writes, "but we cannot let that happen again." The required reauthorization of the program offers an opportunity to reform this aspect.

Feuerherd, Joe. "War on Poverty: New Consensus Promotes Work and 'Safety Net' to Help the Nation's Poor." *National Catholic Reporter*, August 12, 2005, p. 4. The author reviews the War on Poverty and the debate surrounding the welfare reform law of 1996. He reports that the Bush administration sees churches and the private sector as the key ingredients in current efforts to alleviate poverty.

Francis, Richard M. "Predictions, Patterns, and Policymaking: A Regional Study of Devolution." *Publius* 28, no. 3 (summer 1998): 143–160. A study of variations in welfare policy in six states since the passage of welfare reform in 1996. The "devolution" of welfare policy from the federal to the state level places decisions in the hands of local administrators, whose actions are generally shaped by the bureaucratic and political character of the state institutions in which they work.

Jencks, Christopher. "Liberal Lessons from Welfare Reform: Why Welfare-to-Work Turned Out Better Than We Expected." *American Prospect*, July 15, 2002, p. 9. The author declares that welfare reform turned out far better than most liberals expected. He concludes that "shifting benefits toward those who work was a good idea," as was turning welfare over to the states and instructing prospective parents in their responsibility for supporting their families.

Jencks, Christopher, Joe Swingle, and Scott Winship. "Welfare Redux: Back in 1996, We Were Pessimistic About Reform. We Were Wrong, But New Rules Just Pushed Through May Confirm Our Worst Fears." *American Prospect*, March 2006, p. 36. The authors study the condition of single mothers after a peak in unemployment in 2003. They find that they were no worse off in 2003 than they were in 1996, before welfare reform. But new rules adopted within welfare reauthorization give incentives for states to simply push welfare beneficiaries off the rolls rather than putting them in work-related activities.

Meyer, D., and M. Cancian. "Ten Years Later: Economic Well-Being Among Those Who Left Welfare." *Journal of Applied Social Sciences* 25, no. 1 (fall/winter 2000/2001): 13–30. A survey of the conditions for single mothers in the 10 years after leaving the welfare rolls. The article relies on the comprehensive "National Longitudinal Survey of Youth" from 1979 through 1996. The conclusion is that some, but not all, of the welfare-leavers enjoyed relative success and family stability once off the welfare rolls.

# *Annotated Bibliography*

Pelton, Leroy H. "Getting What We Deserve." *The Humanist* 66, no. 4 (July/August 2006): 14–17. The author finds delusional the promise of improving behavior through incentives built into the welfare reform law. The concept of the "deserving" and "undeserving" poor, for example, often punishes children for the transgressions of their parents.

Schwartz, Joel. "What the Poor Need Most." *American Enterprise*, March 2001, p. 52. The author describes the recent transformation in welfare policy. Rather than simply paying out benefits, it encourages positive behaviors, such as thrift, diligence, and hard work, on the part of beneficiaries.

Wayne, Alex. "Welfare Overhaul One Step Away." *CQ Weekly*, December 26, 2005, p. 22. In the author's opinion, Congress is missing an opportunity for a "broad rewrite" of the welfare law. He believes that the reauthorization bill will fall short of what lawmakers of both parties had hoped to accomplish in the federal welfare program.

## WEB DOCUMENTS

Albelda, Randy. "Fallacies of Welfare-to-Work Policies." *Annals of the American Academy of Political and Social Science* 577, no. 1 (2001): 66–78. Available online. URL: http://intl-ann.sagepub.com/cgi/content/abstract/577/1/66. Downloaded May 2007. The article addresses the problems of welfare-to-work, including a lack of jobs, low pay, poor training, transportation, and child care. Low-wage jobs generally are inadequate to support families, including single mothers raising children on their own.

Brauner, S., and P. Loprest. "Where Are They Now? What States' Studies of People Who Left Welfare Tell Us." The Urban Institute, series A, no. A-32. Available online. URL: http://www.urban.org/publications/309065 .html. Posted on May 1, 1999. Accessed on October 5, 2007. The authors review current state reviews of welfare programs, noting that employment rates for welfare leavers have reached 65 percent to 80 percent in most states. Welfare leavers generally hold low-wage jobs, and most have lower income after exiting welfare, with the income discrepancy greatest among families with three or more children.

Marshall, Jennifer A., Robert Lerman, Barbara Dafoe Whitehead, Wade Horn, and Robert Rector. "The Collapse of Marriage and the Rise of Welfare Dependence." The Heritage Foundation. Available online. URL: http://www.heritage.org/Research/Welfare/hl959.cfm. Posted on August 15, 2006. Accessed on June 30, 2007. A transcript of a discussion among several experts on the issues of family disintegration and fatherlessness and their impact on the welfare system.

New, Michael J. "Welfare Reform at 10: Analyzing Welfare Caseload Fluctuations, 1996–2006." The Heritage Foundation. Available online. URL: http://www.heritage.org/Research/Welfare/cda06-07.cfm.

Accessed on October 5, 2007. Since the 1960s, observers with political agendas have given varying reasons for the rise and fall in the number of welfare caseloads. The author analyzes changes in welfare caseloads as well as economic and social reasons that might be coming into play, and reaches the conclusion that, in recent years, the state-by-state sanctions on welfare beneficiaries might be the single most important factor.

Office of Human Services Policy. "National Evaluation of Welfare-to-Work Strategies (NEWWS)." United States Department of Health & Human Services. Available online. URL: http://aspe.hhs.gov/hsp/NEWWS. Accessed on September 6, 2007. This collection of reports was initially known as the Job Opportunities and Basic Skills (JOBS) Training Program Evaluation. Originally mandated by the U.S. Congress in 1988, it was jointly produced by the Department of Health and Human Services, the Department of Education, and the Manpower Development Research Corporation. The program's goal was to evaluate the results of different welfare-to-work programs operating in various cities and states. In these programs, adult welfare recipients were required to participate in job search, education, work experience, vocational training, and other job-related assistance or lose part or all of their welfare benefits.

Rector, Robert J. "Amnesty Will Cost U.S. Taxpayers at Least $2.6 Trillion." The Heritage Foundation. Available online. URL: http://www.heritage.org/Research/Immigration/wm1490.cfm. Posted on June 6, 2007. Accessed on June 30, 2007. The author analyzes the possible fiscal costs of passage of proposed immigration legislation, the "Secure Borders, Economic Opportunity and Immigration Reform Act of 2007" (S. 1348). In his research regarding amnestied immigrants who will begin paying a full share of taxes, he finds that benefits from Social Security, Medicare, and most means-tested welfare programs (such as food stamps, public housing, and Temporary Assistance to Needy Families) will be delayed for many years. Although taxes and fines paid by amnestied immigrants will at first provide a net gain to the Treasury, eventually retirement benefits and other costs will rise to the sum of $2.6 trillion. The articles was of prime importance in the defeat of the "comprehensive immigration" legislation proposed in 2007.

———. "Congress Re-Starts Welfare Reform." The Heritage Foundation. Available online. URL: http://www.heritage.org/Research/Welfare/wm991.cfm. Posted on February 7, 2006. Accessed on October 5, 2007. The author reviews the results of the welfare reform law, finding it successful in reducing caseloads and welfare dependence. The article covers the changes in the law that came with the reauthorization of 2005, including the "healthy marriage" incentives provided to the states.

Tanner, Michael. "The Critics Were Wrong: Welfare Reform Turns 10." *San Francisco Chronicle*. Available online. URL: http://www.cato.org/pub_ display.php?pub_id=6629. Posted on August 21, 2006. Accessed on June 30, 2007. The author asserts in strong terms that critics of the original welfare reform bill were wrong. In consequence, he reasons, similar fearful predictions of the result of reform initiatives in Social Security and Medicare are probably also wrong.

Zeigler, Jenifer. "Implementing Welfare Reform: A State Report Card." *Policy Analysis*. Available online. URL: http://www.cato.org/pub_display. php?pub_id=2477. Posted on October 19, 2004. Accessed on June 30, 2007. When this Cato Institute paper was originally published, Congress was debating the reauthorization of PRWORA. The report examines the policy decisions that states made over the preceding seven years and compares the results, giving state-by-state rankings and grades.

# CHAPTER 8

## ORGANIZATIONS AND AGENCIES

This chapter presents an annotated list of private and public organizations that concentrate in the field of welfare. They include prominent think tanks dealing with social policy issues, public agencies of the federal government, and nongovernmental agencies. Where available, online locations are given through URLs (universal resource locaters); in addition, e-mail addresses and phone numbers are provided.

**American Enterprise Institute for Public Policy Research**
URL: http://www.aei.org/
E-mail: VRodman@aei.org
Phone: (202) 862-5800
1150 17th Street NW
Washington, DC 20036
Founded in 1943, this influential nonprofit is dedicated to research on issues of government, politics, economics, and social welfare. The AEI sponsors research and conferences and publishes books, monographs, and periodicals. It places welfare under the research rubric of "Social and Individual Responsibility" and offers papers focusing on welfare and Medicaid reform, private initiatives to alleviate poverty, and the effectiveness of federal programs in the areas of nutrition, rehabilitation, and vocational training.

**The Brookings Institution**
URL: http://www.brook.edu/index.htm
E-mail: webmaster@Brookings.edu
Phone: (202) 797-6000
1775 Massachusetts Avenue NW
Washington, DC 20036
This influential Washington think tank, founded in 1916 as the first private public policy research institution, undertakes research in economic, governmental, and foreign policy issues. The Brookings Institution is generally regarded as politically left of center, and it is generally supportive of public welfare spending and the development of new public welfare initiatives. The Center on Children and Families offers briefing papers and other publications on the topic of welfare.

**CATO Institute**
URL: http://www.cato.org
E-mail: jdettmer@cato.org
Phone: (202) 842-0200
1000 Massachusetts Avenue NW
Washington, DC 20001-5403
The Cato Institute is a nonprofit policy research foundation founded in 1977 by Edward H. Crane. The institute promotes principles of limited government, individual liberty, free markets, and peace. It publishes books, research, and policy papers on welfare under the research area "Welfare and Workforce."

**Center for Law and Social Policy**
URL: http://www.clasp.org
E-mail: sthorngate@clasp.org
Phone: (202) 906-8000
1015 15th Street NW
Suite 400
Washington, DC 20005
The Center for Law and Social Policy (CLASP) is a national nonprofit advocacy group that seeks to improve economic security, educational and workforce prospects, and the family stability of low-income parents and children. The group conducts research and policy analysis related to federal and state welfare law, and it offers information and technical assistance for policy makers, advocates, researchers, and the media.

**Center on Budget and Policy Priorities**
URL: http://www.cbpp.org
E-mail: center@cbpp.org
Phone: (202) 408-1080
820 First Street NE
Suite 510
Washington, DC 20002
The Center on Budget and Policy Priorities (CBPP) was founded in 1981 to analyze the federal budget and its impact on low-income Americans. CBPP now works at both federal and state levels to analyze fiscal policy and public welfare programs. It publishes reports and briefs on budgeting, taxes, and welfare programs, with one area of concentration being the results of welfare reform laws and on government antipoverty policies. Besides collaborating with nonprofit agencies, it has also established the International Budget Project to help developing countries conduct budget analysis and study the impact of their spending policies on the poor.

**Child Welfare League of America**
URL: http://www.cwla.org/
E-mail: This varies by region;
*see* URL: http://www.cwla.org/ members/regionaloffices.asp
Phone: (202) 638-2952
440 First Street NW
Third Floor
Washington, DC 20001-2085
This organization lobbies legislatures and public administrators on child-welfare issues, including federal and state welfare law and regulation. Other areas of interest include child-abuse issues, adoption, health care, the Head Start program, parental visitation and child support, and juvenile justice.

**Economic Opportunity Institute**
URL: http://www.econop.org
E-mail: info@eoionline.org
Phone: (206) 633-6580
1900 North Northlake Way
Suite 237
Seattle, WA 98103
Founded in 1998, the Economic Opportunity Institute is based in Washington State. The group's mission is to promote better policy in the fields of Social Security, minimum/living wages, child-care workers' wages, paid family leave, welfare reform, and health care. The group formulates policy and then promotes it through extensive media campaigns.

**The Finance Project/Economic Success Clearinghouse**
URL: http://www.financeproject.org
E-mail: info@financeproject.org
Phone: (202) 628-4200
1401 New York Avenue
Suite 800
Washington, DC 20005
This site explains policies, programs, and financing strategies to help low-income and working poor families under several general headings: Welfare, Workforce Development, Work Supports, Income Supplements, and Asset Development. The Economic Success Clearinghouse (formerly called the Welfare Information Network) discusses the topics of applicant diversion, earned income disregards, welfare eligibility and benefits, sanctions for noncompliance, time limits, work requirements, engaging hard-to-serve recipients, and promoting healthy marriages.

**Institute for Research on Poverty/ University of Wisconsin–Madison**
URL: http://www.ssc.wisc.edu/irp/
E-mail: irpweb@ssc.wisc.edu
Phone: (608) 262-6358
1180 Observatory Drive
3412 Social Science Building
Madison, WI 53706-1393
A national, university-based center for research into the causes and consequences of poverty and social inequality in the United States, the Institute for Research on Poverty is one of three Area Poverty Research Centers sponsored by the Department of Health and Human Services. The institute was established in 1966 at the University of Wisconsin–Madison by the U.S. Office of Economic Opportunity. The group's affiliates have conducted research on current economic trends among the low-income population, and they have developed and evaluated social policy alternatives.

**Joint Center for Poverty Research**
URL: http://www.jcpr.org
E-mail: jcpr@uchicago.edu; ipr@northwestern.edu
Phone: (773) 702-2028; (847) 491-3395
University of Chicago
Harris Graduate School of Public Policy Studies
1155 East 60th Street
Chicago, IL 60637
This academic research center combines social policy departments of

two Chicago-area universities. The center conducts research on many issues related to poverty. It holds conferences related to the universities' research, and publishes policy briefs, newsletters, and working papers on all topics related to welfare reform.

**National Association for Welfare Research and Statistics**
URL: http://www.nawrs.org
E-mail: webmaster@nawrs.org
Phone: (304) 558-3413
**West Virginia Department of Health and Human Resources**
**Capital Complex**
**Building 3, Room 451**
**Charleston, WV 25305**
This nonprofit educational association exchanges ideas for the advancement of research and statistics in the field of public welfare. NAWRS sponsors an annual workshop for discussion of research, statistics, public policy, and reporting issues. Workshop participants include representatives from state, federal, and local government; from universities; and from for-profit and nonprofit organizations. The NAWRS annual workshop is open to all persons involved in the field of public welfare.

**National Center for Children in Poverty**
URL: http://www.nccp.org
E-mail: info@nccp.org
Phone: (646) 284-9600
**Columbia University/**
**Mailman School of Public Health**
**215 West 125th Street**

**3rd Floor**
**New York, NY 10027**
A national research center at Columbia University that seeks to improve the lives of low-income children and their families by identifying and promoting strategies to prevent child poverty in the United States. The NCCP hosts a useful collection of welfare reform reports at the part of its web site called the Research Forum on Children, Families, and the New Federalism (URL: http://www.researchforum .org).

**National Center for Law and Economic Justice**
URL: http://www.nclej.org
E-mail: info@nclej.org
Phone: (212) 633-6967
**275 Seventh Avenue**
**Suite 1506**
**New York, NY 10001-6708**
Formerly the Welfare Law Center, the NCLEJ is a legal advocacy organization for the poor and disabled. The group combines litigation services, policy advocacy, and training. The group recently worked to help Hurricane Katrina victims with disabilities find temporary housing, challenged a Missouri regulation that ended Medicaid coverage for medical equipment, and sued New York City welfare agencies to demand better procedures and treatment of clients.

**National Center for Policy Analysis**
URL: http://www.ncpa.org
E-mail: media@ncpa.org
Phone: (202) 220-3082

601 Pennsylvania Avenue NW
South Building
Suite 900
Washington, DC 20004

This nonprofit public policy research organization was established at the University of Dallas by founder John C. Goodman in 1983. The NCPA's stated goal is to develop private alternatives to government regulation and control; it promotes entrepreneurial solutions to social issues. Welfare is one of the major topics addressed by its policy papers.

**National Conference of State
  Legislatures**
URL: http://www.ncsl.org/index
  .htm
E-mail: ncslnet-admin@ncsl.org
Phone: (202) 624-5400
444 North Capitol Street NW
Suite 515
Washington, DC 20001

This group was founded in 1975 to assist state legislatures and administrators with research, analysis, technical assistance, and forums on issues facing lawmakers in the passage and administration of laws. The pages of the organization's web site concerning welfare reform (URL: http://www.ncsl.org/statefed/welfare/welfare.htm) offer articles, research reports, and guidelines on welfare law and welfare reauthorization.

**National Welfare Rights Union**
URL: http://www.nationalwru
  .org/
E-mail: nationalwru@hotmail.
  com; bakerm0060@sbcglobal.
  net

Phone: (313) 832-0618
4760 Woodward Avenue
Suite 402
Detroit, MI 48201

This organization succeeded the National Welfare Rights Organization, founded in 1966 in protest of inadequate benefits and services of the federal welfare system. The group now advocates for the poor and against the welfare reform law of 1996.

**Office of Family Assistance
Administration for Children and
  Families
U.S. Department of Health and
  Human Services**
URL: http://www.acf.dhhs.gov/
  programs/ofa
E-mail: varies by program; *see*
  URL: http://www.acf.hhs.gov/
  acf_contact_us.html
Phone: (202) 401-9215
370 L'Enfant Promenade SW
Washington, DC 20447

This government agency oversees the federal Temporary Assistance for Needy Families (TANF) program, which replaced Aid to Families with Dependent Children (AFDC) in 1996. The web site has a large database of tables and charts detailing TANF participation state by state and reports on the characteristics and financial circumstances of TANF recipients and state TANF annual reports. There is also a comprehensive listing of state TANF agencies and contact agencies, the names of state TANF agencies, and a guide to funding services for children and families.

**Urban Institute**
URL: http://www.urban.org
E-mail: web form
Phone: (202) 833-7200
2100 M Street NW
Washington, DC 20037
The Urban Institute is a research center dealing with economic and social policy. The work of this organization is gathered under 10 general divisions, including "Assessing the New Federalism," which analyzes the impact of welfare reform and other laws that are changing the terms of public income-support programs. The section "Income and Benefits Policy Center," which covers the effect of public welfare programs, "informs the public on how well current systems of income support meet the needs of the elderly, the disabled, and the poor." The organization's web site also offers databases, fact sheets, and a handy "Policy Jargon Decoder" (glossary) that defines and interprets various terms in the field of welfare policy.

**United States Department of**
  **Health and Human Services**
URL: http://www.hhs.gov
E-mail: This varies by topic; *see*
  URL: http://www.hhs.gov/
  ContactUs.html
Phone: (202) 619-0257;
  (877) 696-6775
200 Independence Avenue SW
Washington, DC 20201

HHS is the federal agency responsible for oversight of state welfare programs. The agency sets guidelines that determine federal block-grant funding of state Temporary Assistance for Needy Families (TANF) benefits. The agency was created in 1979 when the Department of Health, Education, and Welfare was split into the Department of Education and HHS. The department's web site has complete information on a broad range of federal initiatives and laws (including health and disease, population issues, family services, aging, homelessness, antismoking efforts, and nursing homes) as well as a large statistical database. The Administration for Children and Families is a branch of HHS that oversees welfare; this branch includes the Office of Family Assistance, the Office of Child Support Enforcement, the Head Start Bureau, the Children's Bureau, and the Low-Income Home Energy Assistance Bureau.

**Welfare Reform Academy**
**University of Maryland School**
  **of Public Policy**
URL: http://welfareacademy
  .org/
E-mail: web form
Phone: (202) 862-5941
1150 17th Street NW
Washington, DC 20036
Founded in 1997, this academic organization helps public and private officials to understand and apply the 1996 welfare reform law. The

Welfare Reform Academy provides training in design, implementation, and evaluation of Temporary Assistance to Needy Families (TANF), Head Start, food stamps, Medicaid, job training, child welfare, and child support programs.

# PART III

## APPENDICES

# APPENDIX A

---

# NATIONAL RADIO ADDRESS DELIVERED BY FRANCES PERKINS (1935)

*Secretary of Labor Frances Perkins was an outspoken supporter of President Frank-lin Roosevelt's New Deal programs, which were undertaken to combat the devastat-ing social and economic consequences of the Great Depression. Having served on several public boards in New York State during the 1920s, she had been invited by Roosevelt to join the presidential cabinet shortly after his inauguration. The first female cabinet member in U.S. history, she brought to the federal government a range of policy ideas from New York—on social insurance, unemployment, and child labor—that served as pilot programs for the federal initiatives of the New Deal.*

*To prepare legislation on federal insurance programs, Roosevelt appointed Per-kins the head of the Committee on Economic Security, which in 1934 prepared a report and recommendations for the president. These proposals included unemploy-ment benefits and disability insurance, as well as benefits for low-income mothers with dependent children—the foundation of AFDC and the modern welfare system. On February 25, 1935, a month after Roosevelt presented the committee's report to Congress, Perkins gave the following national radio address to explain the pro-posed new laws.*

I have been asked to speak to you tonight on the administration's program for economic security which is now, as you know, before Congress. It seems to me that few legislative proposals have had as careful study, as thorough and conscientious deliberation as went into the preparation of these mea-sures. The program now under consideration represents, I believe, a most significant step in our National development, a milestone in our progress toward the better-ordered society.

As I look back on the tragic years since 1929, it seems to me that we as a Nation, not unlike some individuals, have been able to pass through a bitter experience to emerge with a newfound insight and maturity. We have had the courage to face our problems and find a way out. The heedless optimism of the boom years is past. We now stand ready to build the future with sanity and wisdom.

The process of recovery is not a simple one. We cannot be satisfied merely with makeshift arrangements which will tide us over the present emergencies. We must devise plans that will not merely alleviate the ills of today, but will prevent, as far as it is humanly possible to do so, their recurrence in the future. The task of recovery is inseparable from the fundamental task of social reconstruction.

Among the objectives of that reconstruction, President Roosevelt in his message of June 8, 1934, to the Congress placed "the security of the men, women and children of the Nation first." He went on to suggest the social insurances with which European countries have had a long and favorable experience as one means of providing safeguards against "misfortunes which cannot be wholly eliminated in this man-made world of ours."

Subsequent to this message he created the Committee on Economic Security, of which I have the honor to be the chairman, to make recommendations to him with regard to these problems. The recommendations of that committee are embodied in the economic security bill, now pending in Congress. The measures we propose do not by any means provide a complete and permanent solution of our difficulties. If put into effect, however, they will provide a greater degree of security for the American citizen and his family than he has heretofore known. The bill is, I believe, a sound beginning on which we can build by degrees to our ultimate goal.

We cannot hope to accomplish all in one bold stroke. To begin too ambitiously in the program of social security might very well result in errors which would entirely discredit this very necessary type of legislation. It is not amiss to note here that social legislation in European countries, begun some 25 years ago, is still in a developmental state and has been subjected to numerous changes as experience and changing conditions dictated.

It may come as a surprise to many of us that we in this country should be so far behind Europe in providing our citizens with those safeguards which assure a decent standard of living in both good times and bad, but the reasons are not far to seek. We are much younger than our European neighbors. Our abundant pioneer days are not very far behind us. With unlimited opportunities, in those days, for the individual who wished to take advantage of them, dependency seemed a reflection on the individual himself, rather than the result of social or economic conditions. There seemed little need for any systematic organized plan, such as has now become necessary.

It has taken the rapid industrialization of the last few decades, with its mass-production methods, to teach us that a man might become a victim of circumstances far beyond his control, and finally it "took a depression to dramatize for us the appalling insecurity of the great mass of the population, and to stimulate interest in social insurance in the United States." We have come to learn that the large majority of our citizens must have protection against the loss of income due to unemployment, old age, death of the breadwinners and disabling accident and illness, not only on humanitarian grounds, but in the interest of our National welfare. If we are to maintain a healthy economy and thriving production, we need to maintain the standard of living of the lower income groups in our population who constitute 90 per cent of our purchasing power.

England, with its earlier industrialization, learned this lesson earlier, as well. The world depression caught up with Great Britain sooner than it did with us. She has known the haunting fear of insecurity as well as we. The foresight of nearly three decades has, however, found her somewhat better prepared with the basic framework of a social insurance system. Social insurance in Great Britain has proceeded progressively since the first decade of the century. Championed by the liberal Lloyd George and beginning with the old age pension act of 1908, it has known many revisions and extensions. Since its inception, however, it has gradually overcome the opposition of its critics, and there has never been any thought of abandoning the system. It is today in a healthy state of growth.

Practically all the other industrial countries of Europe have had similar experiences. In the trial and error procedure of Europe's quarter century of social legislation—in that concrete experience—is contained sound truths as well as mistakes from which we can learn much.

But we cannot build solely on European experience. We, with our particular kind of State-Federal Government, our wide, expansive country, with its varying economic and social standards, have many needs different from those of the more closely knit, homogeneous European countries.

The American program for economic security now before our Congress follows no single pattern. It is broader than social insurance, and does not attempt merely to copy a European model. Where other measures seemed more appropriate to our background or present situation, we have not hesitated to deviate from strict social insurance principles. In doing so we feel that we have recommended the measures which at this time seemed best calculated under our American conditions to protect individuals in the years immediately ahead from the hazards which might otherwise plunge them into destitution and dependency.

Our program deals with safeguards against unemployment, with old-age security, with maternal aid and aid to crippled and dependent children and public health services. Another major subject—health insurance—is dealt with briefly in the report of the Committee on Economic Security, but without any definite recommendations. Fortunate in having secured the cooperation of the medical and other professions directly concerned, the committee is working on a plan for health insurance which will be reported later in the year. Our present program calls for the extension of existing public health services to meet conditions accentuated by the depression. Similarly, the provisions for maternal aid and aid to dependent and crippled children are not new departures, but rather the extension and amplification of safeguards which for a number of years have been a recognized part of public responsibility.

Let me briefly describe the other measures now under consideration which do represent something of a departure from our usual course.

Recognizing unemployment as the greatest of all hazards, the committee gave primary emphasis to provisions for unemployment—employment assurance. This measure is embodied in the $4,800,000,000 public works resolution, which is separate from, but complementary to, the economic security bill itself. Employment assurance, the stimulation of private employment and the provision of public employment for those able-bodied workers whom private industry cannot yet absorb is to be solely a responsibility of the Federal Government and its major contribution in providing safeguards against unemployment. It should be noted that this is the largest employment program ever considered in any country. As outlined by the President, it will furnish employment for able-bodied men now on relief, and enable them to earn their support in a decent and socially useful way. It will uphold morale, as well as purchasing power, and directly provide jobs for many in private industry who would otherwise have none.

For the 80 per cent of our industrial workers who are employed, we propose a system of unemployment compensation, or insurance, as it is usually called. In our concern for the unemployed, we must not overlook this much larger group who also need protection.

No one who is now employed can feel secure while so many of his fellows anxiously seek work. Unemployment compensation, while it has distinct limitations which are not always clearly understood, is particularly valuable for the ordinarily regularly employed industrial worker who is laid off for short periods because of seasonal demands or other minor industrial disturbances. He can, during this period when he has a reasonable expectation of returning to work within a short time, receive compensation for his loss of income for a limited period as a definite, contractual right. His standard of living need not be undermined, he is not forced on relief nor must he accept other work unsuited to his skill and training.

Unemployment insurance, wherever it has been tried, has demonstrated its value in maintaining purchasing power and stabilizing business conditions. It is very valuable at the onset of a depression, and even in the later stages will serve to carry a part of the burden of providing for the unemployed. For those who have exhausted their rights to unemployment benefits and for those who, in any case, must be excluded from its provisions, we suggest that they be given employment opportunities on public work projects. In these two measures, employment assurance and unemployment compensation, we have a first and second line of defense which together should form a better safeguard than either standing alone.

The unemployment compensation system has been designed to remove an obstacle which has long prevented progressive industrial States from enacting unemployment insurance laws—fear of interstate competition with States not having such laws. Having removed that obstacle, the law allows the States full latitude to develop the kind of unemployment compensation systems best suited to their individual needs.

The bill provides for a Federal tax on pay rolls against which credit is allowed the employer for contributions to an approved State unemployment compensation fund. By this Federal tax every employer will be placed on the same competitive basis from a National standpoint, and at the same time, aside from compliance with a few minimum Federal standards, every State will be free to adopt the kind of law it wants.

One of the most important of the Federal requirements is that all unemployment compensation funds shall be deposited with the Federal Treasury in Washington, so as to assure their availability when needed and make it possible to utilize the reserves which will accumulate in conformity with the credit policy of the Nation.

We feel that this is a most fortunate time for the Government to take action on unemployment insurance. There has been a rapidly growing enthusiasm for it in the States for years. Many States have already prepared excellent legislation of this kind or are studying the subject, and they are but waiting word from Washington, so that they may proceed with the plans which have been so long under consideration.

I come now to the other major phase of our program. The plan for providing against need and dependency in old age is divided into three separate and distinct parts. We advocate, first, free Federally-aided pensions for those now old and in need; second, a system of compulsory contributory old-age insurance for workers in the lower income brackets, and third, a voluntary system of low-cost annuities purchasable by those who do not come under the compulsory system.

Enlightened opinion has long since discarded the old poor-house method of caring for the indigent aged, and 28 States already have old-age pension laws. Due to financial difficulties, many of these laws are now far less effective than they were intended to be. Public sentiment in this country is strongly in favor of providing these old people with a decent and dignified subsistence in their declining years. Exploiting that very creditable sentiment, impossible, harebrained schemes for providing for the aged have sprung into existence and attracted misguided supporters. But the administration is confident that its plan for meeting the situation is both humane and practical and will receive the enthusiastic support of the people.

We propose that the Federal Government shall come to the aid of the State pension systems already in existence and stimulate the enactment of similar legislation elsewhere by grants-in-aid equal to one half the State expenditures for such purposes but not exceeding $15 per month. This does not necessarily mean that State pensions would not anywhere exceed $30 per month. Progressive States may find it possible to grant more than $15 per month as their share. The size of the pension would, of course, be proportionate to the need of the applicant and would quite likely vary with conditions in different States. A larger pension would, for example, be necessary in certain industrial States than in communities where living conditions are easier.

For those now young or even middle-aged, a system of compulsory old-age insurance will enable them to build up, with matching contributions from their employers, an annuity from which they can draw as a right upon reaching old age. These workers will be able to care for themselves in their old age, not merely on a subsistence basis, which is all that gratuitous pensions have anywhere provided, but with a modest comfort and security. Such a system will greatly lessen the hazards of old age to the many workers who could not, unaided, provide for themselves and would greatly lessen the enormous burden of caring for the aged of future generations from public funds. The voluntary system of old-age annuities is designed to cover the same income groups as does the compulsory system, but will afford those who for many reasons cannot be included in a compulsory system an opportunity to provide for themselves.

Many of you will be interested to know that the two proposed annuity systems in no way infringe on the commercial annuity markets. Officials of insurance companies have themselves remarked that these measures would touch a strata of our population for whom commercial annuities are prohibitively expensive. These officials feel that the measures we propose will prove advantageous to their companies rather than the reverse, in so far as they promote public interest in the insurance movement.

This, in broad outlines, is the program now before us. We feel that it is a sound and reasonable plan and framed with due regard for the present state of economic recovery. I can do no better than to pass on to you the words with which President Roosevelt closed his letter submitting these recommendations to the Congress now in session:

"The establishment of sound means toward a greater future economic security of the American people is dictated by a prudent consideration of the hazards involved in our national life. No one can guarantee this country against the dangers of future depressions, but we can reduce these dangers. We can eliminate many of the factors that cause economic depressions, and we can provide the means of mitigating their results. This plan for economic security is at once a measure of prevention and a method of alleviation.

"We pay now for the dreadful consequence of economic insecurity—and dearly. This plan presents a more equitable and infinitely less expensive means of meeting these costs. We cannot afford to neglect the plain duty before us. I strongly recommend action to attain the objectives sought in this report."

*Source:* Social Security Online History Pages. Available online. URL: http://www.ssa.gov/history/perkinsradio.html. Accessed on September 11, 2007.

# APPENDIX B

# SPEECH BY PRESIDENT FRANKLIN ROOSEVELT ON SIGNING THE SOCIAL SECURITY ACT OF 1935

*The 1934 midterm elections gave the Democrats solid majorities in both houses of Congress. Buoyed by the victory, Roosevelt pressed forward with the "second act" of his New Deal legislation, which would soon include the Works Progress Administration, the National Labor Relations Act, and the Social Security Act, which established a financial safety net for the disabled and the elderly. The last law, the most important remnant of the New Deal to survive into the 21st century, included a provision for federally funded, state-paid benefits to low-income mothers with dependent children, as well as unemployment relief. At the signing ceremony for the Social Security Act on August 14, 1935, Roosevelt delivered the following remarks on the design and purpose of the legislation.*

Today, a hope of many years' standing is in large part fulfilled.

The civilization of the past hundred years, with its startling industrial changes, had tended more and more to make life insecure.

Young people have come to wonder what will be their lot when they came to old age.

The man with a job has wondered how long the job would last.

This social security measure gives at least some protection to 50 millions of our citizens who will reap direct benefits through unemployment compensation, through old-age pensions, and through increased services for the protection of children and the prevention of ill health.

We can never insure 100 percent of the population against 100 percent of the hazards and vicissitudes of life, but we have tried to frame a law which will give some measure of protection to the average citizen and to his family against the loss of a job and against poverty-stricken old age.

This law, too, represents a cornerstone in a structure which is being built but is by no means complete. It is a structure intended to lessen the force of possible future depressions. It will act as a protection to future administrations against the necessity of going deeply into debt to furnish relief to the needy. The law will flatten out the peaks and valleys of deflation and of inflation. It is, in short, a law that will take care of human needs and at the same time provide the United States an economic structure of vastly greater soundness.

I congratulate all of you ladies and gentlemen, all of you in the Congress, in the executive departments and all of you who come from private life, and I thank you for your splendid efforts in behalf of this sound, needed and patriotic legislation.

It seems to me that if the Senate and the House of Representatives, in this long and arduous session, had done nothing more than pass this security Bill, Social Security Act, the session would be regarded as historic for all time.

*Source:* "Statement on Signing the Social Security Act." The American Presidency Project. Available online. URL: http://www.presidency.ucsb.edu/ws/index.php?pid=14916. Accessed on September 11, 2007.

# APPENDIX C

---

# PRESIDENT LYNDON JOHNSON'S "GREAT SOCIETY" SPEECH (1964)

*Toward the end of his first brief term as president, Lyndon Johnson envisioned a "Great Society" ushered into existence by federal programs intended to alleviate poverty, racial discrimination, and other ills plaguing American inner cities. Inspired by the success of the New Deal in alleviating the Great Depression, Johnson created "Great Society" as a catchall term for new initiatives in education, health care, urban renewal, and transportation. Johnson first introduced the term in the following speech, delivered on May 22, 1964, at the University of Michigan at Ann Arbor.*

President Hatcher, Governor Romney, Senators McNamara and Hart, Congressmen Meader and Staebler, and other members of the fine Michigan delegation, members of the graduating class, my fellow Americans:

It is a great pleasure to be here today. This university has been coeducational since 1870, but I do not believe it was on the basis of your accomplishments that a Detroit high school girl said, "In choosing a college, you first have to decide whether you want a coeducational school or an educational school."

Well, we can find both here at Michigan, although perhaps at different hours.

I came out here today very anxious to meet the Michigan student whose father told a friend of mine that his son's education had been a real value. It stopped his mother from bragging about him.

I have come today from the turmoil of your Capital to the tranquillity of your campus to speak about the future of your country.

The purpose of protecting the life of our Nation and preserving the liberty of our citizens is to pursue the happiness of our people. Our success in that pursuit is the test of our success as a Nation.

# Welfare and Welfare Reform

For a century we labored to settle and to subdue a continent. For half a century we called upon unbounded invention and untiring industry to create an order of plenty for all of our people.

The challenge of the next half century is whether we have the wisdom to use that wealth to enrich and elevate our national life, and to advance the quality of our American civilization.

Your imagination, your initiative, and your indignation will determine whether we build a society where progress is the servant of our needs, or a society where old values and new visions are buried under unbridled growth. For in your time we have the opportunity to move not only toward the rich society and the powerful society, but upward to the Great Society.

The Great Society rests on abundance and liberty for all. It demands an end to poverty and racial injustice, to which we are totally committed in out time. But that is just the beginning.

The Great Society is a place where every child can find knowledge to enrich his mind and to enlarge his talents. It is a place where leisure is a welcome chance to build and reflect, not a feared cause of boredom and restlessness. It is a place where the city of man serves not only the needs of the body and the demands of commerce but the desire for beauty and the hunger for community.

It is a place where man can renew contact with nature. It is a place which honors creation for its own sake and for what it adds to the understanding of the race. It is a place where men are more concerned with the quality of their goals than the quantity of their goods.

But most of all, the Great Society is not a safe harbor, a resting place, a final objective, a finished work. It is a challenge constantly renewed, beckoning us toward a destiny where the meaning of our lives matches the marvelous products of our labor.

So I want to talk to you today about three places where we begin to build the Great Society—in our cities, in our countryside, and in our classrooms.

Many of you will live to see the day, perhaps 50 years from now, when there will be 400 million Americans—four-fifths of them in urban areas. In the remainder of this century urban population will double, city land will double, and we will have to build homes, highways, and facilities equal to all those built since this country was first settled. So in the next 40 years we must re-build the entire urban United States.

Aristotle said: "Men come together in cities in order to live, but they remain together in order to live the good life." It is harder and harder to live the good life in American cities today.

The catalog of ills is long: there is the decay of the centers and the despoiling of the suburbs. There is not enough housing for our people or transportation for our traffic. Open land is vanishing and old landmarks are violated.

226

Worst of all expansion is eroding the precious and time honored values of community with neighbors and communion with nature. The loss of these values breeds loneliness and boredom and indifference.

Our society will never be great until our cities are great. Today the frontier of imagination and innovation is inside those cities and not beyond their borders.

New experiments are already going on. It will be the task of your generation to make the American city a place where future generations will come, not only to live but to live the good life.

I understand that if I stayed here tonight I would see that Michigan students are really doing their best to live the good life.

This is the place where the Peace Corps was started. It is inspiring to see how all of you, while you are in this country, are trying so hard to live at the level of the people.

A second place where we begin to build the Great Society is in our countryside. We have always prided ourselves on being not only America the strong and America the free, but America the beautiful. Today that beauty is in danger. The water we drink, the food we eat, the very air that we breathe, are threatened with pollution. Our parks are overcrowded, our seashores overburdened. Green fields and dense forests are disappearing.

A few years ago we were greatly concerned about the "Ugly American." Today we must act to prevent an ugly America.

For once the battle is lost, once our natural splendor is destroyed, it can never be recaptured. And once man can no longer walk with beauty or wonder at nature his spirit will wither and his sustenance be wasted.

A third place to build the Great Society is in the classrooms of America. There your children's lives will be shaped. Our society will not be great until every young mind is set free to scan the farthest reaches of thought and imagination. We are still far from that goal.

Today, 8 million adult Americans, more than the entire population of Michigan, have not finished 5 years of school. Nearly 20 million have not finished 8 years of school. Nearly 54 million—more than one quarter of all America—have not even finished high school.

Each year more than 100,000 high school graduates, with proved ability, do not enter college because they cannot afford it. And if we cannot educate today's youth, what will we do in 1970 when elementary school enrollment will be 5 million greater than 1960? And high school enrollment will rise by 5 million. College enrollment will increase by more than 3 million.

In many places, classrooms are overcrowded and curricula are outdated. Most of our qualified teachers are underpaid, and many of our paid teachers are unqualified. So we must give every child a place to sit and a teacher to learn from. Poverty must not be a bar to learning, and learning must offer an escape from poverty.

But more classrooms and more teachers are not enough. We must seek an educational system which grows in excellence as it grows in size. This means better training for our teachers. It means preparing youth to enjoy their hours of leisure as well as their hours of labor. It means exploring new techniques of teaching, to find new ways to stimulate the love of learning and the capacity for creation.

These are three of the central issues of the Great Society. While our Government has many programs directed at those issues, I do not pretend that we have the full answer to those problems.

But I do promise this: We are going to assemble the best thought and the broadest knowledge from all over the world to find those answers for America. I intend to establish working groups to prepare a series of White House conferences and meetings—on the cities, on natural beauty, on the quality of education, and on other emerging challenges. And from these meetings and from this inspiration and from these studies we will begin to set our course toward the Great Society.

The solution to these problems does not rest on a massive program in Washington, nor can it rely solely on the strained resources of local authority. They require us to create new concepts of cooperation, a creative federalism, between the National Capital and the leaders of local communities.

Woodrow Wilson once wrote: "Every man sent out from his university should be a man of his Nation as well as a man of his time."

Within your lifetime powerful forces, already loosed, will take us toward a way of life beyond the realm of our experience, almost beyond the bounds of our imagination.

For better or for worse, your generation has been appointed by history to deal with those problems and to lead America toward a new age. You have the chance never before afforded to any people in any age. You can help build a society where the demands of morality, and the needs of the spirit, can be realized in the life of the Nation.

So, will you join in the battle to give every citizen the full equality which God enjoins and the law requires, whatever his belief, or race, or the color of his skin?

Will you join in the battle to give every citizen an escape from the crushing weight of poverty?

Will you join in the battle to make it possible for all nations to live in enduring peace—as neighbors and not as mortal enemies?

Will you join in the battle to build the Great Society, to prove that our material progress is only the foundation on which we will build a richer life of mind and spirit?

There are those timid souls who say this battle cannot be won; that we are condemned to a soulless wealth. I do not agree. We have the power to shape the civilization that we want. But we need your will, your labor, your hearts, if we are to build that kind of society.

Those who came to this land sought to build more than just a new country. They sought a new world. So I have come here today to your campus to say that you can make their vision our reality. So let us from this moment begin our work so that in the future men will look back and say: It was then, after a long and weary way, that man turned the exploits of his genius to the full enrichment of his life.

Thank you. Good-bye.

*Source:* "LBJ's Great Society Speech." CNN Interactive. Available online. URL: http://www.cnn.com/SPECIALS/cold.war/episodes/13/documents/lbj/. Accessed on September 11, 2007.

# APPENDIX D

---

# DANIEL PATRICK MOYNIHAN'S SPEECH OPPOSING WELFARE REFORM (1995)

*An advocate of reforming the welfare system since the 1960s, Senator Daniel Patrick Moynihan of New York vehemently opposed the welfare reform bill that finally emerged in 1996. The bill was a compromise between Republican legislators and President Bill Clinton, and it provided for sweeping changes in the welfare system, notably a five-year lifetime time limit on Temporary Aid to Needy Families (TANF) benefits—the former AFDC. Moynihan, along with many Democrats and liberal critics, believed that welfare reform would leave the poor without an essential safety net and unleash a tide of hunger, homelessness, and desperation when time limits were reached and beneficiaries were left without resources, unable to cope or compete in an economy that could not provide adequate jobs, education, or child care. Moynihan saw the greatest danger in relaxing federal guidelines and allowing the states to formulate their own policies and benefit levels. He expressed this sentiment in the following speech delivered on the Senate floor on September 16, 1995.*

On this, the likely final day of the debate on the welfare reform measure before us, it is worth noting that in the lead story of the *New York Times* this morning, a story by Robin Toner, we read that "the White House, exceedingly eager to support a law that promises to change the welfare system, was sending increasingly friendly signals about the bill."

That is a bill that would repeal Title IV A of the Social Security Act of 1935 that provides aid to dependent children. It will be the first time in the history of the nation that we have repealed a section of the Social Security Act. That the White House should be eager to support such a law is beyond my understanding, and certainly in thirty-four years' service in Washington, beyond my experience.

# Welfare and Welfare Reform

I regret it. I can only wish some who are involved in the White House or those in the Administration would know that they might well resign if they disagree with the proposal that violates every principle they have asserted in their careers, honorable careers in public service.

I will state once again, we yesterday read Mr. Rahm Emanuel, a White House spokesman, saying the measure was coming along "nicely." Today we get the same message in a lead story in the *Times*. If this administration wishes to go down in history as one that abandoned, eagerly abandoned, the national commitment to dependent children, so be it. I would not want to be associated with such an enterprise, and I shall not be.

There being some spare time in our schedule just now, I would like to take the occasion, and exercise the privilege, as I see it, of reading to the Senate the lead editorial in the *Washington Post*. It is entitled "Welfare Theories." This is an editorial page which has been dealing thoughtfully, supportively, with welfare problems for thirty-five years.

"On the opposite page, columnist George Will musters the most powerful argument against the welfare bill now on the Senate floor. The bill purports to be a way of sending strong messages to welfare recipients that it is time for them to mend their ways. But as Mr. Will notes, 'no child is going to be spiritually improved by being collateral damage in a bombardment of severities targeted at adults who may or may not deserve more severe treatment from the welfare system.'

"The bill is reckless because it could endanger the well-being of the poorest children in society in the name of a series of untested theories about how people may respond to some new incentives. Surely a Congress whose majority proudly carries the mantle 'conservative' should be wary of risking human suffering on behalf of some ideologically-driven preconceptions. Isn't that what conservatives always accuse liberals of doing?

"The best thing that can be said of this bill is that it's not as bad as it might have been. Some of the most obviously flawed proposals—mandating that States end welfare assistance to children born to mothers while they are on welfare and that they cut off assistance to teen mothers—have been voted down. There will be at least some requirements that States continue to invest resources in programs for the poor in exchange for their current federal budget allocations. But they are still not strong enough, and are potentially loophole-ridden. Some new money for child care may also be sprinkled onto this confection.

"But the structure of the bill is wrong, and a fundamental untruth lies at its heart. Congress wants to claim that it is (1) doing something about a whole series of social and economic pathologies, while at the same time (2) cutting spending. But a welfare reform that is serious about both promoting work and helping children in single-parent homes will cost more than writing checks, especially given the extremely modest sums now spent by so many states on the poor.

"Going to a block grant formula would destroy one of the few obvious merits of the current system, which is its ability to respond flexibly to regional economic upturns or downturns. On top of this, the bill's provisions on foodstamps and its reductions in assistance to disabled children under the Supplemental Security Income program go beyond what might constitute reasonable reforms. And its provisions cutting aid to legal immigrants would backfire on states with large immigrant populations.

"Many senators will be tempted to vote for this bill anyway, arguing that it has been 'improved' and fearing the political consequences of voting against anything labeled welfare reform. But many of the 'improvements' will disappear once the bill goes to a conference with the House, which has passed an even more objectionable bill. In any event, voting this bill down would be exactly the opposite of a negative act. It would be an affirmation that real welfare reform is both necessary and possible. To get to that point, a dangerous bill posing as the genuine article must be defeated first."

That is the end of the editorial.

What I cannot comprehend is why this is so difficult for the administration to understand. The administration has abandoned us, those of us who oppose this legislation.

Why do we not see the endless parade of petitioners as when health care reform was before us in the last Congress, the lobbyists, the pretend citizen groups, the real citizen groups? None are here. I can recall the extraordinary energy that went into any change in the welfare system thirty years ago, twenty-five years ago. Fifteen years ago, if there was a proposal to take $40 out of some demonstration project here on the Senate floor, there would be forty representatives of various advocacy groups outside.

There are very few advocacy groups outside. You can stand where I stand and look straight out at the Supreme Court—not a person in between that view. Not one of those flaunted, vaunted advocacy groups forever protecting the interests of the children and the helpless and the homeless and the what-you-will. Are they increasingly subsidized and therefore increasingly coopted? Are they silent because the White House is silent? They should be ashamed. History will shame them.

One group was in Washington yesterday and I can speak with some spirit on that. This was a group of Catholic bishops and members from Catholic Charities. They were here. They were in Washington. Nobody else. None of the great marchers, the great chanters, the great nonnegotiable demanders. There is one police officer that has just appeared, but otherwise the lobby by the elevators is as empty this morning as it was when I left the Chamber last night about 10 o'clock.

I read in *The New York Times* this morning, the front page, lead article: "And the White House, exceedingly eager to support a law that promises to change the welfare system, was sending increasingly friendly signals about the bill."

I see my friend from Indiana, Senator Coats, on the floor. I know his view will be different from mine on the bill. But I recall that extraordinary address he gave yesterday on civil society, citing such as Nathan Glazer and James Q. Wilson. In response, I quoted some of their observations to the effect that we know we have to do these things, but we do not know how to do them. We are just at the beginning of recognizing how profound a question it is, as the Senator so brilliantly set forth. But first, do no harm. Do not pretend that you know what you do not know. Look at the beginnings of research and evaluation that say, "Very hard, not clear." Do not hurt children on the basis of an unproven theory and untested hypothesis. That is what the Senator was citing, persons yesterday who said just that.

This morning the *Washington Post* in its lead editorial, speaks of the structure of the bill being wrong, that a fundamental untruth lies at its heart. "Congress wants to claim that it is (1) doing something about a whole series of social and economic pathologies, while at the same time (2) cutting spending."

The nostrums, the unsupported beliefs, the unsupported assertions, are quite astounding. White House spokesman Rahm Emanuel yesterday told us things are going well. I say once again there is such a thing as resigning in government, and there comes a time when, if principle matters at all, you resign. People who resign on principle come back; people whose real views are less important than their temporary position, "their brief authority," as Shakespeare once put it, disappear.

If that brief authority is more important than the enduring principles of protecting children and childhood, then what is to be said of those who prefer the one to the other? What is to be said of a White House that was almost on the edge of excess in its claims of empathy and concern in the last Congress but is now prepared to see things like this happen in the present Congress? All they want, and I quote again from The *Washington Post*, is that "some new money for child care may also be sprinkled onto this confection."

It will shame this Congress. It will spoil the conservative revolution. The *Washington Post* makes this clear. If "conservative" means anything, it means be careful, be thoughtful, and anticipate the unanticipated or understand that things will happen that you do not expect. And be very careful with the lives of children.

I had no idea how profoundly what used to be known as liberalism was shaken by the last election. No president, Republican or Democrat, in history, or sixty years' history, would dream of agreeing to the repeal of

Title IV A of Social Security. Clearly this administration is contemplating just that.

I cannot understand how this could be happening. It has never happened before.

I make no claim to access. Hardly a soul in the White House has talked to me about this subject since it arose. They know what I think and they know what I would say; not about the particulars but the principle—the principle. Does the Federal Government maintain a commitment to State programs providing aid to dependent children?

It is not as if we had just a few. Ten million is a round number, at any moment.

As George Will observes in his column, and the *Washington Post* editorial refers to his column—the numbers are extraordinary: Here are the percentages of children on AFDC at some point during 1993 in five cities: Detroit (67), Philadelphia (57), Chicago (46), New York (39), Los Angeles (38). Then he cites this Senator: "There are . . . not enough social workers, not enough nuns, not enough Salvation Army workers to care for children who would be purged from the welfare rolls were Congress to decree . . . a two-year limit for welfare eligibility."

Mr. Will goes on to cite Nicholas Eberstadt, of Harvard and the American Enterprise Institute. Citing Eberstadt, Mr. Will observes: "Suppose today's welfare policy incentives to illegitimacy were transported back in time to Salem, Mass., in, say, 1660. How many additional illegitimate births would have occurred in Puritan Salem? Few, because the people of Salem in 1660 believed in hell and believed that what are today called 'disorganized lifestyles' led to hell. Congress cannot legislate useful attitudes."

I can say of my friend Mr. Eberstadt, I do not know where his politics would be, save they would be moderate, sensible, based on research. He is a thoughtful man; a demographer. He has studied these things with great care. And he, too, cannot comprehend national policy at this point.

Scholars have been working at these issues for years now, and the more capable they are, the more tentative and incremental their findings. I cited yesterday a research evaluation of a program, now in its fifth year, of very intensive counseling and training with respect to the issue of teen births—with no results. No results. It is a very common encounter, when things as profound in human character and behavior are dealt with. The capacity of external influences to change it is so very small.

And that we should think otherwise? That men and women have stood in this Chamber and talked about a genuine crisis. And I have said, if nothing else comes out of this awful process, at least we shall have addressed the central subject. But if it is that serious, how can we suppose it will be changed by marginal measures? It will not.

Are there no serious persons in the administration who can say, "Stop, stop right now. No. We won't have this. We agree with the *Washington Post* that, 'It would be an affirmation that real welfare reform is both necessary and possible. To get to that point a dangerous bill posing as the genuine article must be defeated first.'" If not, profoundly serious questions are raised about the year to come.

*Source:* "Daniel Patrick Moynihan's Speech on Welfare Reform." Available online. URL: http://econ161.berkeley.edu/Politics/danielpatrickmoynihans spee.html. Accessed on September 11, 2007.

# APPENDIX E

---

# PRESIDENT BILL CLINTON'S REMARKS ON SIGNING THE PERSONAL RESPONSIBILITY AND WORK OPPORTUNITY RECONCILIATION ACT OF 1996

*The AFDC program had reached new lows in popularity among the voters during the 1980s. The benefit program established by the Social Security Act came to represent inefficient federal spending, mandates on the states, and disincentives to work and produce. As a Democratic candidate for president in 1992, Bill Clinton often vowed to end "welfare as we know it." Clinton supported the federal waivers that allowed certain states to modify their welfare programs while meeting certain guidelines. Although the waiver program came under frequent attack by congressional Republicans, it served as the basis for the compromise welfare reform legislation that was introduced and passed in 1996, much to the chagrin of many in Clinton's own party. Clinton introduced the Personal Responsibility and Work Opportunity Reconciliation Act at a formal signing ceremony on August 22, 1996, when he made the following remarks.*

Thank you very much. Thank you very much. Lillie, thank you. Thank you, Mr. Vice President, to the members of the Cabinet. All of the members of Congress who are here, thank you very much.

I'd like to say to Congressman Castle, I'm especially glad to see you here, because eight years ago about this time when you were the Governor of Delaware and Governor Carper was the Congressman from Delaware, you and I were together at a signing like this.

Thank you, Senator Long, for coming here. Thank you, Governors Romer, Carper, Miller and Caperton.

# Welfare and Welfare Reform

I'd also like to thank Penelope Howard and Janet Ferrel for coming here. They, too, have worked their way from welfare to independence and we're honored to have them here. I'd like to thank all of the people who worked on this bill who have been introduced from our staff and Cabinet, but I'd also like to especially thank Bruce Reed, who had a lot to do with working on the final compromises of this bill; I thank him.

Lillie Harden was up there talking, and I want to tell you how she happens to be here today. Ten years ago, Governor Castle and I were asked to cochair a Governors Task Force on Welfare Reform, and we were asked together on it, and when we met at Hilton Head in South Carolina, we had a little panel. And 41 governors showed up to listen to people who were on welfare from several states.

So I asked Carol Rasco to find me somebody from our state who had been in one of our welfare reform programs and had gone to work. She found Lillie Harden and Lillie showed up at the program. And I was conducting this meeting and I committed a mistake that they always tell lawyers never to do: never ask a question you do not know the answer to. (Laughter.)

But she was doing so well talking about it, as you saw how well-spoken she was today— and I said, "Lillie, what's the best thing about being off welfare?" And she looked me straight in the eye and said, "When my boy goes to school and they say what does your mama do for a living, he can give an answer." I have never forgotten that. (Applause.) And when I saw the success of all of her children and the success that she's had in the past 10 years, I can tell you, you've had a bigger impact on me than I've had on you. And I thank you for the power of your example, for your family's. And for all of America, thank you very much. (Applause.)

What we are trying to do today is to overcome the flaws of the welfare system for the people who are trapped on it. We all know that the typical family on welfare today is very different from the one that welfare was designed to deal with 60 years ago. We all know that there are a lot of good people on welfare who just get off of it in the ordinary course of business, but that a significant number of people are trapped on welfare for a very long time, exiling them from the entire community of work that gives structure to our lives.

Nearly 30 years ago, Robert Kennedy said, "Work is the meaning of what this country is all about. We need it as individuals, we need to sense it in our fellow citizens, and we need it as a society and as a people." He was right then, and it's right now.

From now on, our nation's answer to this great social challenge will no longer be a never-ending cycle of welfare, it will be the dignity, the power and the ethic of work. Today, we are taking an historic chance to make welfare what it was meant to be: a second chance, not a way of life.

# *Appendix E*

The bill I'm about to sign, as I have said many times, is far from perfect, but it has come a very long way. Congress sent me two previous bills that I strongly believe failed to protect our children and did too little to move people from welfare to work. I vetoed both of them. This bill had broad bipartisan support and is much, much better on both counts.

The new bill restores America's basic bargain of providing opportunity and demanding in return responsibility. It provides $14 billion for child care, $4 billion more than the present law does. It is good because without the assurance of child care it's all but impossible for a mother with young children to go to work. It requires states to maintain their own spending on welfare reform and gives them powerful performance incentives to place more people on welfare in jobs. It gives states the capacity to create jobs by taking money now used for welfare checks and giving it to employers as subsidies as incentives to hire people. This bill will help people to go to work so they can stop drawing a welfare check and start drawing a paycheck.

It's also better for children. It preserves the national safety net of food stamps and school lunches. It drops the deep cuts and the devastating changes in child protection, adoption, and help for disabled children. It preserves the national guarantee of health care for poor children, the disabled, the elderly, and people on welfare—the most important preservation of all.

It includes the tough child support enforcement measures that, as far as I know, every member of Congress and everybody in the administration and every thinking person in the country has supported for more than two years.

It's the most sweeping crackdown on deadbeat parents in history. We have succeeded in increasing child support collection 40 percent, but over a third of the cases where there's delinquencies involve [people] who cross state lines. For a lot of women and children, the only reason they're on welfare today—the only reason—is that the father up and walked away when he could have made a contribution to the welfare of the children. That is wrong. If every parent paid the child support that he or she owes legally today, we could move 800,000 women and children off welfare immediately.

With this bill we say, if you don't pay the child support you owe we'll garnish your wages, take away your driver's license, track you across state lines; if necessary, make you work off what you pay—what you owe. It is a good thing and it will help dramatically to reduce welfare, increase independence, and reinforce parental responsibility.

As the Vice President said, we strongly disagree with a couple of provisions of this bill. We believe that the nutritional cuts are too deep, especially as they affect low-income working people and children. We should not be punishing people who are working for a living already; we should do everything we can to lift them up and keep them at work and help them to support their children. We also believe that the congressional leadership insisted in cuts in programs for legal immigrants that are far too deep.

These cuts, however, have nothing to do with the fundamental purpose of welfare reform. I signed this bill because this is an historic chance—where Republicans and Democrats got together and said, we're going to take this historic chance to try to recreate the nation's social bargain with the poor. We're going to try to change the parameters of the debate. We're going to make it all new again and see if we can't create a system of incentives which reinforce work and family and independence.

We can change what is wrong. We should not have passed this historic opportunity to do what is right. And so I want to ask all of you, without regard to party, to think through the implications of these other non-welfare issues on the American people and let's work together in good spirits and good faith to remedy what is wrong. We can balance the budget without these cuts, but let's not obscure the fundamental purpose of the welfare provisions of this legislation which are good and solid, and which can give us at least the chance to end the terrible, almost physical isolation of huge numbers of poor people and their children from the rest of mainstream America. We have to do that.

Let me also say that there's something really good about this legislation. When I sign it we all have to start again. And this becomes everybody's responsibility. After I sign my name to this bill, welfare will no longer be a political issue. The two parties cannot attack each other over it. Politicians cannot attack poor people over it. There are no encrusted habits, systems and failures that can be laid at the foot of someone else. We have to begin again. This is not the end of welfare reform, this is the beginning. And we have to all assume responsibility. (Applause.)

Now that we are saying with this bill we expect work, we have to make sure the people have a chance to go to work. If we really value work, everybody in this society—businesses, non-profits, religious institutions, individuals, those in government—all have a responsibility to make sure the jobs are there.

These three women have great stories. Almost everybody on welfare would like to have a story like that. And the rest of us now have a responsibility to give them that story. We cannot blame the system for the jobs they don't have anymore. If it doesn't work now, it's everybody's fault—mine, yours, and everybody else. There is no longer a system in the way.

I've worked hard over the past four years to create jobs and to steer investment into places where there are large numbers of people on welfare because there's been no economic recovery. That's what the empowerment zone program was all about. That's what the community development bank initiative was all about. That's what our urban Brownfield cleanup initiative was all about—trying to give people the means to make a living in areas that had been left behind.

I think we have to do more here in Washington to do that, and I'll have more to say about that later. But let me say again, we have to build a new work and family system. And this is everybody's responsibility now. The people on welfare are people just like these three people we honor here today and their families. They are human beings. And we owe it to all of them to give them a chance to come back.

I talked the other day when the Vice President and I went down to Tennessee and we were working with Congressman Tanner's district, we were working on a church that had burned. And there was a pastor there from a church in North Carolina that brought a group of his people in to work. And he started asking me about welfare reform, and I started telling him about it. And I said, "You know what you ought to do? You ought to go tell Governor Hunt that you would hire somebody on welfare to work in your church if he would give you the welfare check as a wage supplement, you'd double their pay and you'd keep them employed for a year or so and see if you couldn't train them and help their families and see if their kids were all right." I said, "Would you do that?" He said, "In a heartbeat."

I think there are people all over America like that. I think there are people all over America like that. That's what I want all of you to be thinking about today—what are we going to do now? This is not over, this is just beginning. The Congress deserves our thanks for creating a new reality, but we have to fill in the blanks. The governors asked for this responsibility; now they've got to live up to it. There are mayors that have responsibilities, county officials that have responsibilities. Every employer in this country that ever made a disparaging remark about the welfare system needs to think about whether he or she should now hire somebody from welfare and go to work. Go to the state and say, okay, you give me the check, I'll use it as an income supplement, I'll train these people, I'll help them to start their lives and we'll go forward from here.

Every single person needs to be thinking—every person in America tonight who sees a report of this who has ever said a disparaging word about the welfare system should now say, "Okay, that's gone. What is my responsibility to make it better?"

Two days ago we signed a bill increasing the minimum wage here and making it easier for people in small businesses to get and keep pensions. Yesterday we signed the Kassebaum-Kennedy bill which makes health care more available to up to 25 million Americans, many of them in lower-income jobs where they're more vulnerable.

The bill I'm signing today preserves the increases in the earned income tax credit for working families. It is now clearly better to go to work than to stay on welfare—clearly better. Because of actions taken by the Congress in this session, it is clearly better. And what we have to do now is to make that work a reality.

I've said this many times, but, you know, most American families find that the greatest challenge of their lives is how to do a good job raising their kids and do a good job at work. Trying to balance work and family is the challenge that most Americans in the workplace face. Thankfully, that's the challenge Lillie Harden's had to face for the last 10 years. That's just what we want for everybody. We want at least the chance to strike the right balance for everybody.

Today, we are ending welfare as we know it. But I hope this day will be remembered not for what it ended, but for what it began—a new day that offers hope, honors responsibility, rewards work, and changes the terms of the debate so that no one in America ever feels again the need to criticize people who are poor on welfare, but instead feels the responsibility to reach out to men and women and children who are isolated, who need opportunity, and who are willing to assume responsibility, and give them the opportunity and the terms of responsibility.

*Source:* William J. Clinton Foundation. "Speech by President at Welfare Bill Signing." Available online. URL: www.clintonfoundation.org/legacy/082296 -speech-by-president-at-welfare-bill-signing.htm. Accessed on September 11, 2007.

# APPENDIX F

## SELECTION FROM THE PERSONAL RESPONSIBILITY AND WORK OPPORTUNITY RECONCILIATION ACT OF 1996

*The following passage introduces the Personal Responsibility and Work Opportunity Reconciliation Act of 1996, also known as the welfare reform law. The "Findings" text offers statistics supporting the basic philosophy behind the act: that the federal government should encourage and help maintain the traditional nuclear family, through temporary welfare benefits, as a means to end permanent welfare dependency.*

## SEC. 101. FINDINGS.

2. The Congress makes the following findings:
   (1) Marriage is the foundation of a successful society.
   (2) Marriage is an essential institution of a successful society which promotes the interests of children.
   (3) Promotion of responsible fatherhood and motherhood is integral to successful child rearing and the well-being of children.
   (4) In 1992, only 54 percent of single-parent families with children had a child support order established and, of that 54 percent, only about one-half received the full amount due. Of the cases enforced through the public child support enforcement system, only 18 percent of the caseload has a collection.
   (5) The number of individuals receiving aid to families with dependent children (in this section referred to as 'AFDC') has more than tripled since 1965. More than two-thirds of these recipients are children. Eighty-nine percent of children receiving AFDC benefits now live in homes in which no father is present.

    (A) (i)  The average monthly number of children receiving AFDC benefits —
        (I)  was 3,300,000 in 1965;
        (II)  was 6,200,000 in 1970;
        (III)  was 7,400,000 in 1980; and
        (IV)  was 9,300,000 in 1992.
       (ii)  While the number of children receiving AFDC benefits increased nearly threefold between 1965 and 1992, the total number of children in the United States aged 0 to 18 has declined by 5.5 percent.
    (B)  The Department of Health and Human Services has estimated that 12,000,000 children will receive AFDC benefits within 10 years.
    (C)  The increase in the number of children receiving public assistance is closely related to the increase in births to unmarried women. Between 1970 and 1991, the percentage of live births to unmarried women increased nearly threefold, from 10.7 percent to 29.5 percent.
(6)  The increase of out-of-wedlock pregnancies and births is well documented as follows:
    (A)  It is estimated that the rate of nonmarital teen pregnancy rose 23 percent from 54 pregnancies per 1,000 unmarried teenagers in 1976 to 66.7 pregnancies in 1991. The overall rate of nonmarital pregnancy rose 14 percent from 90.8 pregnancies per 1,000 unmarried women in 1980 to 103 in both 1991 and 1992. In contrast, the overall pregnancy rate for married couples decreased 7.3 percent between 1980 and 1991, from 126.9 pregnancies per 1,000 married women in 1980 to 117.6 pregnancies in 1991.
    (B)  The total of all out-of-wedlock births between 1970 and 1991 has risen from 10.7 percent to 29.5 percent and if the current trend continues, 50 percent of all births by the year 2015 will be out-of-wedlock.
(7)  An effective strategy to combat teenage pregnancy must address the issue of male responsibility, including statutory rape culpability and prevention. The increase of teenage pregnancies among the youngest girls is particularly severe and is linked to predatory sexual practices by men who are significantly older.
    (A)  It is estimated that in the late 1980's, the rate for girls age 14 and under giving birth increased 26 percent.
    (B)  Data indicates that at least half of the children born to teenage mothers are fathered by adult men. Available data suggests that almost 70 percent of births to teenage girls are fathered by men over age 20.

(C) Surveys of teen mothers have revealed that a majority of such mothers have histories of sexual and physical abuse, primarily with older adult men.

(8) The negative consequences of an out-of-wedlock birth on the mother, the child, the family, and society are well documented as follows:

(A) Young women 17 and under who give birth outside of marriage are more likely to go on public assistance and to spend more years on welfare once enrolled. These combined effects of 'younger and longer' increase total AFDC costs per household by 25 percent to 30 percent for 17-year-olds.

(B) Children born out-of-wedlock have a substantially higher risk of being born at a very low or moderately low birth weight.

(C) Children born out-of-wedlock are more likely to experience low verbal cognitive attainment, as well as more child abuse, and neglect.

(D) Children born out-of-wedlock were more likely to have lower cognitive scores, lower educational aspirations, and a greater likelihood of becoming teenage parents themselves.

(E) Being born out-of-wedlock significantly reduces the chances of the child growing up to have an intact marriage.

(F) Children born out-of-wedlock are 3 times more likely to be on welfare when they grow up.

(9) Currently 35 percent of children in single-parent homes were born out-of-wedlock, nearly the same percentage as that of children in single-parent homes whose parents are divorced (37 percent). While many parents find themselves, through divorce or tragic circumstances beyond their control, facing the difficult task of raising children alone, nevertheless, the negative consequences of raising children in single-parent homes are well documented as follows:

(A) Only 9 percent of married-couple families with children under 18 years of age have income below the national poverty level. In contrast, 46 percent of female-headed households with children under 18 years of age are below the national poverty level.

## HIGHLIGHTS

**Work requirements.** Under the new law, recipients must work after two years on assistance, with few exceptions. Twenty-five percent of all families in each state must be engaged in work activities or have left the rolls in fiscal year (FY) 1997, rising to 50 percent in FY 2002. Single parents must participate for at least 20 hours per week the first year, increasing to at least 30 hours per week by FY 2000. Two-parent families must work 35 hours per week by July 1, 1997.

**Supports for families transitioning into jobs.** The new welfare law provides $14 billion in child care funding—an increase of $3.5 billion over current law—to help more mothers move into jobs. The new law also guarantees that women on welfare continue to receive health coverage for their families, including at least one year of transitional Medicaid when they leave welfare for work.

**Work Activities.** To count toward state work requirements, recipients will be required to participate in unsubsidized or subsidized employment, on-the-job training, work experience, community service, 12 months of vocational training, or provide child care services to individuals who are participating in community service. Up to 6 weeks of job search (no more than 4 consecutive weeks) would count toward the work requirement. However, no more than 20 percent of each state's caseload may count toward the work requirement solely by participating in vocational training or by being a teen parent in secondary school. Single parents with a child under 6 who cannot find child care cannot be penalized for failure to meet the work requirements. States can exempt from the work requirement single parents with children under age one and disregard these individuals in the calculation of participation rates for up to 12 months.

**A five-year time limit.** Families who have received assistance for five cumulative years (or less at state option) will be ineligible for cash aid under the new welfare law. States will be permitted to exempt up to 20 percent of their caseload from the time limit, and states will have the option to provide non-cash assistance and vouchers to families that reach the time limit using Social Services Block Grant or state funds.

**Personal employability plans.** Under the new plan, states are required to make an initial assessment of recipients' skills. States can also develop personal responsibility plans for recipients identifying the education, training, and job placement services needed to move into the workforce.

**State maintenance of effort requirements.** The new welfare law requires states to maintain their own spending on welfare at least 80 percent of FY 1994 levels. States must also maintain spending at 100 percent of FY 1994 levels to access a $2 billion contingency fund designed to assist states affected by high population growth or economic downturn. In addition, states must maintain 100 percent of FY 1994 or FY 1995 spending on child care (whichever is greater) to access additional child care funds beyond their initial allotment.

**Job subsidies.** The law also allows states to create jobs by taking money now used for welfare checks and using it to create community service jobs or to provide income subsidies or hiring incentives for potential employers.

# *Appendix F*

**Performance bonus to reward work.** $1 billion will be available through FY 2003 for performance bonuses to reward states for moving welfare recipients into jobs. The Secretary of HHS, in consultation with the National Governors' Association (NGA) and American Public Welfare Association (APWA), will develop criteria for measuring state performance.

**State flexibility.** Under the new law, states which receive approval for welfare reform waivers before July 1, 1997 have the option to operate their cash assistance program under some or all of these waivers. For states electing this option, some provisions of the new law which are inconsistent with the waivers would not take effect until the expiration of the applicable waivers in the geographical areas covered by the waivers.

### *Comprehensive Child Support Enforcement*

The new law includes the child support enforcement measures President Clinton proposed in 1994—the most sweeping crackdown on non-paying parents in history. These measures could increase child support collections by $24 billion and reduce federal welfare costs by $4 billion over 10 years. Under the new law, each state must operate a child support enforcement program meeting federal requirements in order to be eligible for Temporary Assistance to Needy Families (TANF) block grants. Provisions include:

**National new hire reporting system.** The law establishes a Federal Case Registry and National Directory of New Hires to track delinquent parents across state lines. It also requires that employers report all new hires to state agencies for transmittal of new hire information to the National Directory of New Hires. This builds on President Clinton's June 1996 executive action to track delinquent parents across state lines. The law also expands and streamlines procedures for direct withholding of child support from wages.

**Streamlined paternity establishment.** The new law streamlines the legal process for paternity establishment, making it easier and faster to establish paternities. It also expands the voluntary in-hospital paternity establishment program, started by the Clinton Administration in 1993, and requires a state form for voluntary paternity acknowledgement. In addition, the law mandates that states publicize the availability and encourage the use of voluntary paternity establishment processes. Individuals who fail to cooperate with paternity establishment will have their monthly cash assistance reduced by at least 25 percent.

**Uniform interstate child support laws.** The new law provides for uniform rules, procedures, and forms for interstate cases.

**Computerized state-wide collections.** The new law requires states to establish central registries of child support orders and centralized collection and disbursement units. It also requires expedited state procedures for child support enforcement.

**Tough new penalties.** Under the new law, states can implement tough child support enforcement techniques. The new law will expand wage garnishment, allow states to seize assets, allow states to require community service in some cases, and enable states to revoke drivers and professional licenses for parents who owe delinquent child support.

**"Families First."** Under a new "Family First" policy, families no longer receiving assistance will have priority in the distribution of child support arrears. This new policy will bring families who have left welfare for work about $1 billion in support over the first six years.

**Access and visitation programs.** In an effort to increase noncustodial parents' involvement in their children's lives, the new law includes grants to help states establish programs that support and facilitate noncustodial parents' visitation with and access to their children.

### Teen Parent Provisions

**Live at home and stay in school requirements.** Under the new law, unmarried minor parents will be required to live with a responsible adult or in an adult-supervised setting and participate in educational and training activities in order to receive assistance. States will be responsible for locating or assisting in locating adult-supervised settings for teens.

**Teen Pregnancy Prevention.** Starting in FY 1998, $50 million a year in mandatory funds would be added to the appropriations of the Maternal and Child Health (MCH) Block Grant for abstinence education. In addition, the Secretary of HHS will establish and implement a strategy to (1) prevent nonmarital teen births, and (2) assure that at least 25 percent of communities have teen pregnancy prevention programs. No later than January 1, 1997, the Attorney General will establish a program that studies the linkage between statutory rape and teen pregnancy, and that educates law enforcement officials on the prevention and prosecution of statutory rape.

*Source:* U.S. Department of Health and Human Services, Administration for Children and Families. Available online. UR: http://www.acf.dhhs.gov/ programs/ofa/prwora96.htm. Accessed on September 11, 2007.

# APPENDIX G

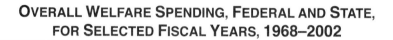

# OVERALL WELFARE SPENDING, FEDERAL AND STATE, 1968–2002

*The following graph, assembled from data prepared by the Congressional Research Service, shows total overall spending at the federal and state levels for 1968 through 2002. The figures include spending for more than 80 benefit programs that provide cash and noncash aid for eligible low-income individuals and families, presented in constant dollars (adjusted for inflation and changes in purchasing power).*

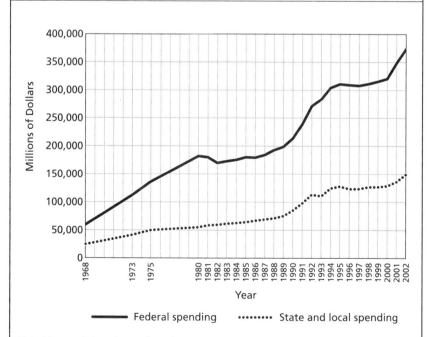

## OVERALL WELFARE SPENDING, FEDERAL AND STATE, FOR SELECTED FISCAL YEARS, 1968–2002

——— Federal spending ⋯⋯⋯⋯ State and local spending

*Note:* All amounts have been adjusted to the value of fiscal year 2002 dollars. Total aid includes the following categories: medical benefits, cash aid, food benefits, housing benefits, education benefits, jobs/training, services, and energy aid.

*Source:* Data from Vee Burke, *Cash and Noncash Benefits for Persons with Limited Income: Eligibility Rules, Recipient and Expenditure Data, FY2000–FY2002*. Washington, D.C.: Congressional Research Service, 2003.

© Infobase Publishing

# APPENDIX H

---

# HIGHLIGHTS OF WELFARE PROVISIONS WITHIN THE DEFICIT REDUCTION ACT OF 2005

*Congress passed, and President Bush signed into law, legislation that reauthorized the Temporary Assistance for Needy Families (TANF) program of 1996. The Deficit Reduction Act of 2005 requires states to engage more TANF cases in productive work activities leading to self-sufficiency. Following are highlights of the new TANF provisions as passed by the House and Senate.*

## S.1932 DEFICIT REDUCTION ACT OF 2005 SUBTITLE A—TANF

### SEC. 7101. TEMPORARY ASSISTANCE FOR NEEDY FAMILIES AND RELATED PROGRAMS FUNDING THROUGH SEPTEMBER 30, 2010.

(a) In General—Activities authorized by part A of title IV and section 1108(b) of the Social Security Act (adjusted, as applicable, by or under this subtitle, the amendments made by this subtitle, and the TANF Emergency Response and Recovery Act of 2005) shall continue through September 30, 2010, in the manner authorized for fiscal year 2004, and out of any money in the Treasury of the United States not otherwise appropriated, there are hereby appropriated such sums as may be necessary for such purpose. Grants and payments may be made pursuant to this authority on a quarterly basis through fiscal year 2010 at the level provided for such activities for the corresponding quarter of fiscal year 2004 (or, as applicable, at such greater level as may result from the application of this subtitle, the amendments made by this subtitle, and the TANF Emergency Response and Recovery Act of 2005), except that in the case of section 403(a)(3) of the Social Security Act, grants and payments may be made pursuant to this authority only through fiscal year 2008 and in the case of section 403(a)(4) of the Social Security Act, no grants shall be made for any fiscal year occurring after fiscal year 2005.

\* \* \*

(c) Extension of the National Random Sample Study of Child Welfare Through September 30, 2010—Activities authorized by section 429A of the Social Security Act shall continue through September 30, 2010, in the manner authorized for fiscal year 2004, and out of any money in the Treasury of the United States not otherwise appropriated, there are hereby appropriated such sums as may be necessary for such purpose. Grants and payments may be made pursuant to this authority on a quarterly basis through fiscal year 2010 at the level provided for such activities for the corresponding quarter of fiscal year 2004.

## SEC. 7102. IMPROVED CALCULATION OF WORK PARTICIPATION RATES AND PROGRAM INTEGRITY.

\* \* \*

(c) Improved Verification and Oversight of Work Participation —
  (1) IN GENERAL—Section 409(i)(U.S.C. 607(i)) is amended to read as follows:

\* \* \*

(i) In General—Not later than June 30, 2006, the Secretary shall promulgate regulations to ensure consistent measurement of work participation rates under State programs funded under this part and State programs funded with qualified State expenditures (as defined in section 409(a)(7)(B)(i)), which shall include information with respect to —
    "(I) determining whether an activity of a recipient of assistance may be treated as a work activity under subsection (d);
    "(II) uniform methods for reporting hours of work by a recipient of assistance;
    "(III) the type of documentation needed to verify reported hours of work by a recipient of assistance; and
    "(IV) the circumstances under which a parent who resides with a child who is a recipient of assistance should be included in the work participation rates.

* * *

"(2) REQUIREMENT FOR STATES TO ESTABLISH AND MAINTAIN WORK PARTICIPATION VERIFICATION PROCE-DURES—Not later than September 30, 2006, a State to which a grant is made under section 403 shall establish procedures for determining, with respect to recipients of assistance under the State program funded under this part or under any State programs funded with qualified State expenditures (as so defined), whether activities may be counted as work activities, how to count and verify reported hours of work, and who is a work-eligible individual, in accordance with the regulations promulgated pursuant to paragraph (1)(A)(i) and shall establish internal controls to ensure compliance with the procedures.

* * *

"(15) PENALTY FOR FAILURE TO ESTABLISH OR COMPLY WITH WORK PARTICIPATION VERIFICATION PROCE-DURES —

"(A) IN GENERAL—If the Secretary determines that a State to which a grant is made under section 403 in a fiscal year has violated section 407(i)(2) during the fiscal year, the Secretary shall reduce the grant payable to the State under section 403(a)(1) for the immediately succeeding fiscal year by an amount equal to not less than 1 percent and not more than 5 percent of the State family assistance grant.

"(B) PENALTY BASED ON SEVERITY OF FAILURE—The Secretary shall impose reductions under subparagraph (A) with respect to a fiscal year based on the degree of noncompliance."

* * *

## SEC. 7103. GRANTS FOR HEALTHY MARRIAGE PROMOTION AND RESPONSIBLE FATHERHOOD.

(a) Healthy Marriage and Family Funds—Section 403(a)(2) (42U.S.C 603(a)(2)) is amended to read as follows:

"(2) HEALTHY MARRIAGE PROMOTION AND RESPONSI-BLE FATHERHOOD

GRANTS —

"(A) IN GENERAL

"(i) USE OF FUNDS—Subject to subparagraphs (B) and (C), the Secretary may use the funds made available under subparagraph (D) for the purpose of conducting and supporting research and demonstration projects by public or private entities, and providing technical assistance to States, Indian tribes and tribal organizations, and such other entities as the Secretary may specify that are receiving a grant under another provision of this part.

"(ii) LIMITATIONS—The Secretary may not award funds made available under this paragraph on a noncompetitive basis, and may not provide any such funds to an entity for the purpose of carrying out healthy marriage promotion activities or for the purpose of carrying out activities promoting responsible fatherhood unless the entity has submitted to the Secretary an application which —

"(I) describes —

"(aa) how the programs or activities proposed in the application will address, as appropriate, issues of domestic violence; and

"(bb) what the applicant will do, to the extent relevant, to ensure that participation in the programs or activities is voluntary, and to inform potential participants that their participation is voluntary; and

"(II) contains a commitment by the entity —

"(aa) to not use the funds for any other purpose; and

"(bb) to consult with experts in domestic violence or relevant community domestic violence coalitions in developing the programs and activities.

"(iii) HEALTHY MARRIAGE PROMOTION ACTIVITIES—In clause (ii), the term 'healthy marriage promotion activities' means the following:

"(I) Public advertising campaigns on the value of marriage and the skills needed to increase marital stability and health.

"(II) Education in high schools on the value of marriage, relationship skills, and budgeting.

"(III) Marriage education, marriage skills, and relationship skills programs, that may include parenting skills, financial management, conflict resolution, and job and career advancement, for non-married pregnant women and non-married expectant fathers.

"(IV) Pre-marital education and marriage skills training for engaged couples and for couples or individuals interested in marriage.

"(V) Marriage enhancement and marriage skills training programs for married couples.

"(VI) Divorce reduction programs that teach relationship skills.

"(VII) Marriage mentoring programs which use married couples as role models and mentors in at-risk communities.

"(VIII) Programs to reduce the disincentives to marriage in means-tested aid programs, if offered in conjunction with any activity described in this subparagraph.

\* \* \*

"(C) LIMITATION ON USE OF FUNDS FOR ACTIVITIES PROMOTING RESPONSIBLE FATHERHOOD —

"(i) IN GENERAL—Of the amounts made available under subparagraph (D) for a fiscal year, the Secretary may not award more than $50,000,000 on a competitive basis to States, territories, Indian tribes and tribal organizations, and public and nonprofit community entities, including religious organizations, for activities promoting responsible fatherhood.

"(ii) ACTIVITIES PROMOTING RESPONSIBLE FATHERHOOD—In this paragraph, the term 'activities promoting responsible fatherhood' means the following:

"(I) Activities to promote marriage or sustain marriage through activities such as counseling, mentoring, disseminating information about the benefits of marriage and 2-parent involvement for children, enhancing relationship skills, education regarding how to control aggressive behavior, disseminating information on the causes of domestic violence and child abuse, marriage preparation programs, premarital counseling, marital inventories, skills-based marriage education, financial planning seminars, including improving a family's ability to effectively manage family business affairs by means such as education, counseling, or mentoring on matters related to family finances, including household management, budgeting, banking, and handling of financial transactions and home maintenance, and divorce education and reduction programs, including mediation and counseling.

"(II) Activities to promote responsible parenting through activities such as counseling, mentoring, and mediation, disseminating information about good parenting practices, skills-based parenting education, encouraging child support payments, and other methods.

"(III) Activities to foster economic stability by helping fathers improve their economic status by providing activities such as work first services, job search, job training, subsidized employment, job retention, job enhancement, and encouraging education, including career-advancing education, dissemination of employment materials, coordination with existing employment services such as welfare-to-work programs, referrals to local employment training initiatives, and other methods.

"(IV) Activities to promote responsible fatherhood that are conducted through a contract with a nationally recognized, nonprofit fatherhood promotion organization, such as the development, promotion, and distribution of a media campaign to encourage the appropriate involvement of parents in the life of any child and specifically the issue of responsible fatherhood, and the development of a national clearinghouse to assist States and communities in efforts to promote and support marriage and responsible fatherhood."

\* \* \*

# SUBTITLE C—CHILD SUPPORT

## SEC. 7301. ASSIGNMENT AND DISTRIBUTION OF CHILD SUPPORT.

(a) Modification of Rule Requiring Assignment of Support Rights as a Condition of Receiving TANF—Section 408(a)(3) (42 U.S.C. 608(a)(3)) is amended to read as follows:

"(3) NO ASSISTANCE FOR FAMILIES NOT ASSIGNING CERTAIN SUPPORT RIGHTS TO THE STATE—A State to which a grant is made under section 403 shall require, as a condition of paying assistance to a family under the State program funded under this part, that a member of the family assign to the State any right the family member may have (on behalf of the family member or of any other person for whom the family member has applied for or is receiving such assistance) to support from any other person, not exceeding the total amount of assistance so paid to the family, which accrues during the period that the family receives assistance under the program."

*Source:* The Library of Congress, THOMAS database. Available online. URL: http://thomas.loc.gov/cgi-bin/query/D?c109:2:./temp/~mdbsMrSE1i::. Accessed on September 11, 2007.

# APPENDIX I

# SEVENTH ANNUAL REPORT OF THE OFFICE OF FAMILY ASSISTANCE/TEMPORARY ASSISTANCE FOR NEEDY FAMILIES (2006)

*The following is the latest in a series of annual reports issued by the Department of Health and Human Services, Office of Family Assistance, on the Temporary Assistance for Needy Families (TANF) program. The reports cover spending, caseload numbers, work participation by beneficiaries, child welfare, the tribal TANF program, and current research by the federal departments responsible for directing and regulating the program.*

## EXECUTIVE SUMMARY

In 1996, Congress created the Temporary Assistance for Needy Families (TANF) program. This $16.5 billion a year block grant was established under the Personal Responsibility and Work Opportunity Reconciliation Act (PRWORA), which replaced Aid to Families with Dependent Children (AFDC) and other related welfare programs. Fostering self-sufficiency through work was the major goal of the 1996 reform, which requires States to meet minimum levels of work participation and offers bonuses for high performance in specific areas. States have been given significant flexibility in designing their own eligibility criteria and benefit rules, which require work in exchange for time-limited assistance.

Since the enactment of TANF, millions of families have avoided dependence on welfare in favor of greater independence through work. Employment among low-income single mothers (incomes below 200 percent of poverty), reported in the U.S. Census Bureau's Current Population Survey (CPS), has increased significantly since 1996. Overall, earnings in female-headed families remain significantly higher than in 1996 despite the brief economic downturn. In addition, child poverty rates have declined substantially since the start of the program. States are using their flexibility to focus an increasing portion of welfare dollars on helping individuals retain jobs and advance in their employment.

This report describes the characteristics and financial circumstances of TANF recipients and presents information regarding TANF caseloads and expenditures, work participation and earnings, State High Performance Bonus awards, child support collections, two-parent family formation and maintenance activities, out-of-wedlock births, and child poverty. In addition, it documents specific provisions of State programs, summarizes current TANF research and evaluation, and provides profiles for each State. Below is a short summary of each chapter in this report.

## CASELOAD

The national TANF caseload continued to decline in Fiscal Year (FY) 2003. Some States have moved TANF recipients who have reached the Federal time limit to Separate State Programs (SSPs), but the combined caseload still continued to decline in FY 2003. This decline has also occurred even though some States have modified their eligibility criteria to include more low-income families.

Child-only cases continue to comprise a large fraction of the total TANF caseload. These are cases where no adult is included in the benefit calculation and only the children are aided. In FY 2003, child-only cases represented 38.6 percent of the total TANF caseload. Of these child-only cases, 53 percent involve children living with a caretaker relative who has sufficient income not to receive assistance, 19 percent are families in which the parent is disabled and receiving Supplemental Security Income, and 18 percent are families in which the parent is ineligible for TANF because of his or her citizenship status.

In FY 2003, 23 percent of TANF adult recipients were employed. Although this is a small decrease from FY 2002, it appears that welfare reform continues to be effective in sustaining TANF clients' connections to the workforce, even when overall unemployment has increased.

FY 2002 was the first year that families in each State could have reached the Federal five-year lifetime limit on assistance. Case closure data for 38 States show that less than one half of one percent of cases had been closed due to the five-year limitation during FY 2003. In addition, although up to 20 percent of the State caseload can be exempted from this limit, only 1.7 percent of families were receiving assistance beyond the 60-month

# Appendix I

limitation. In FY 2003, families receiving TANF had accrued an average of 29 months of assistance countable toward the Federal five-year time limit (over one or more spells of welfare receipt).

## EXPENDITURES AND BALANCES

In fiscal year (FY) 2003, combined Federal and State expenditures for the Temporary Assistance for Needy Families (TANF) program totaled $26.3 billion, an increase of $926 million from FY 2002. States spent $10.1 billion, or 41.8 percent of their total expenditures, on cash assistance. They also spent significant amounts on various non-cash services designed to promote work, stable families, or other TANF objectives, including work activities ($2.6 billion), child care ($3.5 billion), transportation and work supports ($543 million), administrative and systems costs ($2.5 billion), and a wide range of other benefits and services ($6.3 billion). This latter category includes $1.2 billion in expenditures on activities designed to either reduce the incidence of out-of-wedlock pregnancies or encourage paternal involvement in the lives of their children—up $220 million from FY 2002. These expenditure patterns represent a significant shift since the enactment of TANF, when spending on cash assistance amounted to 73.1 percent of total expenditures.

In addition to these expenditures, States also can transfer up to 30 percent of their TANF block grant into the Child Care and Development Fund (CCDF) or the Social Services Block Grant (SSBG). In FY 2003, States transferred $1.8 billion into the CCDF and $927 million into the SSBG (including adjustments made to prior year spending).

At the beginning of FY 2003, States had $5.7 billion in unspent TANF funds—$2.6 billion in unobligated funds and $3.1 billion in unliquidated obligations. By the end of the year, the amount of unspent funds declined to $3.9 billion—$2.3 billion in unobligated funds and $1.6 billion in unliquidated obligations.

## WORK PARTICIPATION RATES

All States (except Nevada) met the overall participation rate standard in FY 2003, as did the District of Columbia, the Virgin Islands, and Puerto Rico. An average of 31.3 percent of non-exempt TANF adults met Federal family work participation standards by averaging monthly participation in qualified work activities for at least 30 hours per week, or 20 hours per week if they had children under age six. This represents a decline from FY 2002, when average participation was 33.4 percent. The FY 2003 rate remains above the 30.7 percent attained in FY 1997, but well below the 38.3 percent peak achieved in FY 1999. All family work rates increased in 26 States and Territories (up from 19 in FY 2002) and declined in 27.

An additional 13.4 percent of non-exempt TANF adults participated in countable work activities for at least one hour per week, but did not attain sufficient hours to qualify toward the work rate. States reported zero hours of participation in qualified activities for the remaining 58.8 percent of non-exempt adults (although some likely participated in non-qualifying activities), which is 0.5 percentage points higher than in FY 2002.

In FY 2003, the all family nominal minimum participation rate was 50 percent for single-parent families, and 90 percent for two-parent families. However, due to tremendous caseload reductions since TANF enactment, the average (weighted) effective minimum work participation requirement in FY 2003 (because of the caseload reduction credit) was only 3.9 percent for all families and 20.2 percent for two-parent families. Nineteen States and one Territory had sufficient caseload reduction credits to reduce their effective required all families rate to zero, and only nineteen States faced an effective minimum greater than ten percent.

## WORK AND EARNINGS

In 2003, 56.4 percent of single mothers with children under 18 that had income below 200 percent of poverty were employed. Although the employment rate of those with children under 18 declined from 59.3 percent in 2002, it is still 5 percentage points higher than in 1996—a remarkable achievement, particularly because of the brief recession in 2001. Among single mothers with children under age six—a group particularly vulnerable to welfare dependency—employment rates are over 9 percentage points higher than in 1996.

Overall, earnings in female-headed families remain significantly higher than in 1996 despite the brief economic downturn. For the one fifth of families with the lowest income, single mother families fell to an average of $1,989 in 2003 but remain above the average of $1,823 in 1996; this reflects the decline in employment of lower income single mothers. For the next 20 percent of families, earnings remained well above their 1996 levels when the average was $5,313; in 2003 the average earnings for the second quintile was $9,800.

In FY 2003, 28.1 percent of adult recipients were working or engaged in work preparation activities, down slightly from 30.1 percent in FY 2002. Seventy-five percent of recipients who were working were doing so in paid employment; the remainder were involved in work experience, community service, and subsidized employment. State-reported data for welfare recipients show that the average monthly earnings of those employed increased in nominal dollars from $466 per month in FY 1996 to $647 in FY 2003, a 39 percent increase. In FY 2003, about 17.9 percent of case closings were reported as closing due to employment. These data likely underestimate the true proportion by a large margin. An additional 23.9 percent of closed cases did so for failure to comply with program requirements, many of whom are clients who left for employment. Characteristics data show that 30 percent of adults in closed cases were employed.

## HIGH PERFORMANCE BONUS

The TANF High Performance Bonus (HPB) program provides cash awards to States for high relative achievement on certain measures related to the goals and purposes of the TANF program. These measures include a job entry rate, a success-in-the-workforce rate (measured by combining a job retention rate and an earnings gain rate), and the change in each of these rates over the prior year.

In 2000, changes were made to the HPB measures and these changes apply to award years 2002 and 2003. First, four new non-work indicators were added: participation of low-income working families in the Food Stamp Program, participation of former TANF recipients in the Medicaid Program and in States' Children's Health Insurance Programs (SCHIP), a child care subsidy measure, and a family formation and stability measure. Second, a major change was made in the source of the employment data used to calculate performance under the work measures. In performance year FY 2003, 50 States and the District of Columbia competed for at least one of the 80 individual awards; 37 States and the District of Columbia received awards.

## CHILD SUPPORT COLLECTIONS

Single parents receiving TANF are required to cooperate with child support enforcement efforts. FY 2003 efforts produced a one percent increase in the percentage of current assistance cases that had orders established, and a two percent increase in the percentage of former assistance cases that had orders established. This means that over 51 percent of current assistance cases had orders established, and about 78 percent of former assistance cases had orders established. In FY 2003, about $21.2 billion was collected for children by the Child Support Enforcement (IV-D) Program, an increase of five percent from FY 2002, and a 33 percent increase since FY 1999. Total collections included almost $1.6 billion in overdue child support intercepted from Federal tax refunds. In addition, the Passport Denial Program collected nearly $12 million in calendar year (CY) 2003, double the $6 million collected in CY 2002. There were also over 1.5 million paternities established in FY 2003.

In FY 2003, over 50 percent of the total child support cases had a collection, significantly more than the 38 percent achieved in FY 1999. About 70 percent of the cases with orders established reported a collection, an increase over the 64 percent achieved in FY 1999. Nationally, about $2,653 was collected per case for those with a collection. In FY 2003, as in FY 1999, States collected about $4 in child support for every $1 spent. Of the 15.9 million child support cases served by IV-D agencies, only 2.8 million are currently receiving public assistance, 5.8 million have never received assistance, and 7.4 million formerly received assistance.

## FORMATION AND MAINTENANCE OF MARRIED TWO-PARENT FAMILIES

State governments have explored many different strategies for helping couples form and sustain healthy marriages as part of an effort to help families achieve self-sufficiency and improve child well-being. These strategies include how States can and are spending TANF dollars and shaping TANF policy to support the formation and maintenance of married two-parent families. The Administration for Children and Families, and specifically the Office of Family Assistance, has provided ongoing support for the Healthy Marriage Initiative, including the creation of the National Healthy Marriage Resource Center. These and other strategies, as well as a summary of State efforts, are described in the chapter.

## OUT-OF-WEDLOCK BIRTHS

The Department of Health and Human Services (HHS) is required to rank States based on a ratio of the total number of out-of-wedlock births in TANF families to the total number of births in TANF families and to show the net changes in the ratios between the current year and the previous year. HHS is also required to award, for FY 1999 and subsequent years, a "Bonus to Reward Decrease in Illegitimacy Ratio" to as many as five States (and three Territories, if eligible) that achieve the largest decrease in out-of-wedlock births without experiencing an increase in their abortion rates above 1995 levels. In FY 2003, the District of Columbia, the Virgin Islands, Colorado, Texas, Maryland, and Wyoming received awards.

## CHILD POVERTY AND TANF

The 2003 child poverty rate stood at 17.6 percent, up from 16.7 percent in the prior year but well below the 1996 level of 20.5 percent and the 1993 peak of 22.7 percent. The reduction in poverty since 1996 is even more marked for specific groups: the African American child poverty rate was 33.6 percent in 2003 compared to 39.9 percent in 1996 and the Hispanic child poverty rate was 29.7 percent in 2003 down from 40.3 percent in 1996.

# Appendix I

There are also significant differences in the child poverty rate by marital status. In married, two parent families, about one child in twelve is poor (8.6 percent), while two in five or 42 percent of the children living in female-headed, single parent families are poor.

If a State experiences an increase in its child poverty rate of five percent or more as a result of the TANF program(s) in the State, it must submit and implement a corrective action plan to reduce the State's child poverty rate. To date, based on child poverty rates for 1996 through 2002, no State was required to submit a corrective action plan or any additional information for these child poverty assessment periods.

## CHARACTERISTICS AND FINANCIAL CIRCUMSTANCES OF TANF RECIPIENTS

The average monthly number of TANF families was 2,027,600 in FY 2003. The estimated average monthly number of TANF recipients was 1,249,000 adults and 3,737,000 children. The average monthly number of TANF families decreased in 24 States and reflects an overall 1.6 percent decrease from 2,060,300 families in FY 2002. During FY 2003, an average of 166,700 TANF families had their assistance terminated each month.

There has been little change in the racial composition of TANF families since FY 2002. African-American families comprised 38 percent of TANF families, white families comprised 32 percent, 25 percent were Hispanic, 2.0 percent were Asian, and 1.5 percent were Native American. Of all closed-case families, 33 percent were African-American, 37 percent were white, and 24 percent were Hispanic.

The racial distribution of TANF recipient children has not significantly changed when compared to FY 2002. African-American children continued to be the largest group of welfare children, comprising about 39 percent of recipient children. About 27 percent of TANF recipient children were white, and 28 percent were Hispanic.

Eighty percent of TANF families received Food Stamp assistance, which is consistent with previous levels. These families received average monthly Food Stamp benefits of $247. Of closed-case families, about 79 percent received Food Stamp benefits in the month of closure. In addition, almost every TANF family was eligible to receive medical assistance under the State plan approved under title XIX of the Social Security Act.

Ninety-eight percent of TANF families received cash and cash equivalent assistance, with an average monthly amount of $354. Monthly cash payments to TANF families averaged $296 for one child, $365 for two children, $437 for three children, and $521 for four or more children. Some TANF families who were not employed received other forms of assistance such as child care, transportation and other supportive services.

263

In FY 2003, one in every five TANF families had non-TANF income. The average monthly amount of non-TANF income was $560 per family. Twelve percent of the TANF families had earned income with an average monthly amount of $655, while eight percent of the TANF families had unearned income with an average monthly amount of $336. Of all closed-case families, 36 percent had non-TANF income with an average monthly amount of $860. Of TANF recipient adults, 20 percent had earned income with an average monthly amount of $647. Seven percent of adult recipients had unearned income averaging about $341 per month. Three percent of recipient children had unearned income with an average monthly amount of $236.

## TRIBAL TANF

By the close of FY 2003, 40 Tribal TANF plans were approved to operate on behalf of 184 Tribes and Alaska Native villages. All together, Tribal TANF programs are funded to serve approximately 29,000 assistance units or families. State TANF programs serve American Indian and Alaska Native families not served by Tribal TANF programs. State governments in FY 2003 also served about 29,000 American Indian families, up from 27,000 in FY 2002. Of the 9,983 Tribal TANF families reported, 6,483, (64.9 percent) were single parent families and 2,291 (22.9 percent) were child-only cases.

FY 2003 funds available to Tribes with approved TANF plans totaled $110,645,560; this was the prorated portion of the approved Tribal TANF grants, which totaled $116,761,376 annually. This prorating occurred because not all Tribal TANF programs were operational for the full fiscal year. The amount of the approved grants is based on American Indian families served under State AFDC programs in FY 1994 in the Tribal grantee's service area. Seventy-nine Indian Tribes, Alaska Native organizations, and Tribal consortia operated Native Employment Works (NEW) programs during Program Year (PY) 2002–2003 (July 1, 2002–June 30, 2003). The most frequently provided NEW program activities were job search, classroom training, and work experience. The most frequently provided supportive and job retention service was transportation.

NEW programs coordinated education, training, work experience, job search, and job referral with other Tribal programs and with local educational institutions and employers. They provided intensive case management, behavioral and health counseling, and life skills training. Many Tribes with NEW programs located training, employment, and social services in "one-stop" centers where staff assessed clients' needs and then provided targeted activities and services to meet those needs. Information/resource centers and learning centers containing resource materials, classrooms, and computer labs provided job preparation services, including individual needs assessments, case management, and classroom instruction.

## SPECIFIC PROVISIONS OF STATE PROGRAMS

The tables in Chapter XII were derived from information from each State's TANF plan and amendments and have been reviewed by each State prior to submission of the report. These tables include State-by-State information on benefit levels, work requirements, waiver rules, eligibility and benefit determination, Individual Development Accounts, sanction policies, cash diversion programs, time limits, domestic violence provisions, and family cap policies. In general, they show little change in State policy from FY 2002.

## TANF RESEARCH AND EVALUATION

HHS undertakes several research and evaluation initiatives each year. Major research reports include a child outcome synthesis report discussing the impact of welfare reform on children in five States and a final synthesis paper on all six States that participated in the TANF caseload study. Final reports were issued on the characteristics of the District of Columbia's, Colorado's, Maryland's and South Carolina's TANF caseload, the profile of families that cycle on and off of welfare, work participation and full engagement strategies, the use of TANF work-oriented sanctions, the effects of fiscal capacity on State spending choices on programs to support low-income populations, the differences among single and married parent families in the TANF and Food Stamp programs, and a literature review on the effectiveness of services to strengthen marriage. Studies continue on devolution and urban change, interventions to increase the well-being of children through provision of voluntary healthy marriage education services, evaluating fragile families demonstrations, gathering more complete marriage and divorce data, the effectiveness of different approaches to promoting healthy marriage, documentation of State policies to promote marriage, and a compendium of existing measures and tools to measure couple relationships across a broad range of categories.

This report also presents information about the progress of ACF's latest major initiative related to increasing employment among welfare recipients, *The Employment Retention and Advancement Evaluation*. Fifteen intervention strategies have been implemented in eight States in this multi-year demonstration and evaluation project. Reports issued in 2004 and early 2005 detailed lessons learned, the relationship of TANF and Workforce Investment Act agencies in the provision of retention and advancement services for low-income workers, and early impact findings of four of the longest operating interventions.

*Source:* Department of Health and Human Services, Office of Family Assistance, Temporary Assistance for Needy Families Seventh Annual Report. Available online. URL: http://www.acf.dhhs.gov/programs/ofa/annualreport7/index.htm. Accessed on September 11, 2007.

# INDEX

Locators in **boldface** indicate main topics. Locators followed by *c* indicate chronology entries. Locators followed by *b* indicate biographical entries. Locators followed by *g* indicate glossary entries.

# Index

# Index

# Index

# *Index*

# Index